GW00601899

· EU-Mediterranean and
Gulf Trade Agreements ·

EU-Mediterranean
· and Gulf Trade ·
Agreements

Fadi S Hakura
BA, LLB
Solicitor

Palladian Law Publishing Ltd

© Fadi S Hakura
1999

Published by
Palladian Law Publishing Ltd
Beach Road
Bembridge
Isle of Wight PO35 5NQ

www.palladianlaw.com

ISBN 1 902558 11 1

Typeset by Heath Lodge Publishing Services
Printed in Great Britain by The Cromwell Press Ltd

· Contents ·

· Preface ·

My primary aim in writing this book is to provide explanation and understanding on the various practical ways in which businessmen and foreign traders may exploit the EU-Mediterranean and EU-Gulf Co-operation Council Agreements to their advantage. In short, how to use these Agreements as a sword and a shield.

Never has there seemed a better moment to consider the important trade issues that link Europe with the different countries that border the Mediterranean and the practical ways in which these operate. While the European Union faces up to the challenge of enlargement, free market reforms sweeping through the Middle East and North Africa have stimulated moves towards co-operation, growth and development.

Much has happened since 1994, when the European Commission proposed the establishment of a Euro-Mediterranean Partnership and the creation of a free trade zone that encompassed the European Union and its Mediterranean neighbours. The adoption of the Barcelona Declaration, the progress of bilateral negotiations between the EU and individual Mediterranean countries, the advancement of free trade talks between the EU and the Gulf Co-operation Council – all have helped bring us to this point.

My own interest in the subject was inspired by my father. It was he who first encouraged me to take an active interest in this unique area of law, combining my enjoyment of European Community Law with a fascination for the Middle East and North Africa and the increasingly important role they play in world trade matters.

Writing first on the subject in 1995, I began by analysing the Euro-Mediterranean Partnership in terms of its legal, political and economic significance. My work was fostered and encouraged then by Professor David O'Keeffe of University College, London and was subsequently published in the *Common Market Law Review*. Since then, I have been able to develop different ideas and themes in other published articles, but - given the importance of the subject in the development of trade relations - it seemed right now to bring all these strands and others together in one definitive study, even though many of them constitute uncharted territory.

In seeking to write a book that is both comprehensive and yet in a form that readers will find easy to understand, I have sought to avoid legal jargon or else explain it. The commercial provisions of the Agreements are discussed in their entirety – ranging from free movement to rules of origin. Key political and administrative matters are also included, together with issues relating to judicial enforcement. The General Agreement on Tariffs and Trade and the World Trade Organisation are also incorporated in the text, where applicable.

Many have helped with the book, but I am especially grateful to Professor O' Keeffe for his encouragement and guidance and to Birgit Ris of Dibb Lupton Alsop in Brussels, who played an important part in promoting the idea for the book. I would also like to thank my publisher, Jane Belford, for her valuable experience and insight on the style and presentation of the text.

Above all, my gratitude extends to God the Almighty and to my family for their support and encouragement.

The law is up to date to September 1999

Fadi S Hakura
London,
September 1999

· Table of Cases & Decisions ·

· Table of Treaties ·

· Table of EU Legislation ·

Regulations

Directives & Decisions

· Table of Abbreviations ·

CEEC	Central and Eastern European Country
CN	Combined Nomenclature
DSB	Dispute Settlement Body
DSS	Department for Social Security (UK)
EC	European Community
ECSC	European Coal and Steel Community
EEA	European Economic Area Agreement
EFTA	European Free Trade Area
EMA	Euro-Mediterranean Agreement
EU	European Union
GATS	General Agreement on Trade in Services
GATT	General Agreement on Tariffs and Trade
GCC	Gulf Co-operation Council
GPA	Government Procurement Agreement
GSP	Generalised System of Preferences
HS	Harmonised System Nomenclature
IMF	International Monetary Fund
MENA	Middle East/North Africa countries
MFN	Most-favoured-nation treatment
MNC	Mediterranean Non-Member Country
VAT	Value added tax
WTO	Word Trade Organisation

Chapter 1

· **Introduction** ·

1.1 **Barcelona Declaration**

In November 1995, the Foreign Ministers of the European Union (EU) and the Mediterranean Non-Member Countries (MNCs) adopted a document called the "Barcelona Declaration" (Declaration). It set out the guidelines for the future development of the political, economic and social "partnership" between the EU and the Mediterranean. Most significantly, the Barcelona participants undertook to create a Euro-Mediterranean free trade zone embracing 30-40 countries and 800 million people by the year 2010.

The European Commission (the Commission) and the Council of the European Union (commonly referred to as the Council of Ministers or the Council) intends to achieve this objective by means of bilateral free trade accords between the EU and the individual MNCs (contracting parties or parties). These accords are known as Euro-Mediterranean Agreements (EMAs). Eventually, the hope is that through a web of such agreements, a free trade zone will be created between the 15 EU Member States and the 12 MNCs (Turkey, Israel, Palestinian Authority, Egypt, Morocco, Tunisia, Lebanon, Jordan, Algeria, Cyprus, Malta and Syria).

Essentially, the Euro-Mediterranean scheme is formulated to facilitate and accelerate the economic reforms sweeping the Middle Eastern and North African countries. Once closed economies are now opening to the outside world and generating growing interest amongst foreign investors and traders. Globalisation rather than isolation is the new mantra in the region. The EMAs will make the Southern Mediterranean even more attractive to the international business community.

1.2 **Euro-Mediterranean Agreements**

Thus far, the EU has concluded EMAs with Tunisia, Morocco, Turkey, Israel, the Palestinian Authority, Jordan and Egypt. The state of implementation of these Agreements at the time of writing this book is as follows:

- The Palestinian EMA[1] is an interim agreement until the period when the peace process with Israel is finalised. It took effect on 1 July 1997.
- The Israeli EMA[2] has been concluded, but is awaiting ratification by all the EU Member States before it enters into legal force. In the meantime, an Israeli interim EMA[3] has been negotiated with the EU containing the trade and trade-related measures of the permanent EMA and it took effect on 1 January 1996. Upon ratification of the permanent EMA by all the Member States and its entry into force, the interim EMA will be subsumed into the permanent Agreement.
- The Tunisian EMA entered into force on 1 March 1998.[4]
- Unlike the other EMAs, the Turkish EMA[5] is a customs union with the EU rather than a mere free trade agreement. It entered into force on 1 January 1995. It is worth noting that the Turkish EMA builds on pre-existing agreements with the EU. First, Turkey negotiated an Association Agreement in 1970,[6] which is still in force. Then an Additional Protocol[7] was reached with the EU that supplemented the original Association Agreement which is still in force. Eventually, the customs union was concluded dealing with the trade in goods. Hence, to understand and interpret the Turkish EMA, the Association Agreement, Additional Protocol and the Customs Union Agreement must be read together. (For the sake of consistency, the Agreements are referred to collectively throughout this book as the Turkish EMA unless otherwise specified.)
- The Egyptian[8] and Jordanian[9] EMAs are awaiting ratification by all the Member States before they have legal effect. The Moroccan[10] EMA has been ratified by all the Member States

---

1   Council Dec 97/470 (OJ 1997 L187/1).
2   SEC(95) 1719 final 13 November 1995. There is also a special agreement on technical and scientific co-operation between the EU and Israel (Council Dec 99/224, OJ 1999 L83/50).
3   Council Dec 96/206 (OJ 1996 L71/1).
4   Council Dec 98/238 (OJ 1998 L97/1).
5   Dec 1/95 of the EU-Turkish Association Council (OJ 1996 L35/1).
6   Council Dec 64/732 (JO 1964 L217/368; OJ 1973 C113/1).
7   Council Reg 2760/72 (JO L293/1; OJ 1977 L361/61).
8   The text was not yet published at the time of writing.
9   COM(97) 554 final.
10 COM(95) 640 final.

and should take effect in 1999 on approval by the EU.

- The Syrian, Lebanese and Algerian EMAs are stilll being negotiated

1.3 Objectives of the book

This book has two principal objectives:

(1) To describe the commercial aspects of the Arab, Israeli and Turkish EMAs.

(2) To show how traders, businessmen and professionals may use these Agreements both as a shield and a weapon.

Hence, the different chapters outline the various commercial provisions ranging from free movement of goods to rules of origin utilising jargon-free language. In addition, there are chapters on methods of enforcement designed to bring home to the reader the best ways to enforce the EMAs so as to obtain maximum mileage out of them.

To achieve these objectives, the book attempts to inform the reader how he can take advantage of these agreements to profit from new and exciting markets in the European Union and the MNCs. Thus, several chapters include a "What if" section in a question and answer format. In others, extensive examples are used to break down complex issues into easy to understand explanations. In short, the guiding principle throughout the book is to engage the reader's interest and identify simple and practical solutions, whilst examining ways to exploit fully the opportunities inherent in the EMAs.

Cyprus and Malta have deliberately been excluded from the scope of this book. First, because the "Barcelona process" is targeted primarily towards the Arab countries, Turkey and Israel and secondly, because both Cyprus and Malta may soon accede to the European Union.

1.4 World Trade Organisation

Some parts of the EMAs incorporate provisions from the General Agreement on Tariffs and Trade (GATT) and agreements related to the

World Trade Organisation (WTO). The wording and structure of some of these provisions depend on whether or not the MNC concerned is a member of the WTO. Therefore, the list of MNCs which are members or non-members is set out below:

WTO Members	WTO Non-Members
Bahrain	Algeria (1)
Egypt	Jordan (1)
Israel	Lebanon (1)
Morocco	Palestinian Authority (3)
Qatar	Oman (2)
Turkey	Saudi Arabia (1)
United Arab Emirates	Syria (3)

Source: WTO

(1) Countries with observer status at the WTO and which have applied to join the organisation.
(2) Countries without observer status at the WTO and which have applied to join the organisation.
(3) Countries or entities which have not applied (or are unable to apply) to join the WTO.

1.5 Gulf Co-operation Council

The Gulf Co-operation Council (GCC) is negotiating a Free Trade Agreement with the European Union on behalf of its members (Bahrain, Kuwait, Oman, Qatar, Saudi Arabia and the United Arab Emirates) as one collective unit. Negotiations should be completed in 2000 or 2001; the most contentious issues revolve around steel, fishery products and the EU carbon tax. The GCC is setting up a Gulf Arab Customs Union by March 2001.

It is very likely that the Free Trade Agreement will mirror closely the provisions in the Euro-Mediterranean Agreements. Therefore, all comment and discussion in this book apply equally to the putative EU-GCC Free Trade Agreement.

1.6 Sources of material and information

A wide array of materials and sources of information were used in writing this book. However, the following sources were particularly helpful:

Peter Xuereb (ed), *Malta, The European Union and the Mediterranean: closer relations in the wider context*, European Documentation and Research Centre, University of Malta (1998).

Andrew Evans, *A Textbook on European Union Law*, Hart Publishing (1998).

Annet Blank and Gabrielle Marceau, "The history of the government procurement agreement since 1945", (1997) 4, *Public Procurement Law Review* 77-149.

Peter Thomson and Oliver Stehman, "EU-Israel Agreements on government Procurement and telecommunications procurement," (1997) 6 *Public Procurement Law Review*, 174-179.

Nicholas Zaimis, *EC Rules of Origin*, Chancery Law Publishing (1992).

Stephen Weatherill and Paul Beaumont, *EC Law*, Penguin Books (1995) (2nd ed).

The WTO website: www.wto.org.

The European Union website: www.europa.eu.int.

Chapter 2

· Free Movement of Goods ·

2.1 Introduction

The essence of all free trade agreements is to ensure the movement of goods, services, companies and capital across national boundaries without hindrance or formalities. Undoubtedly, the greatest impact of such agreements is that consumers are exposed to goods and services from across the globe, since the elimination of customs duties and other obstacles to trade enhances the mobility of products and service-providers. The ultimate beneficiaries are consumers. Expensive items, such as German cars, drop radically in price and therefore become more accessible to the public. Consumers benefit from a greater choice of products at affordable prices.

However, there is another side to the free movement coin. As trade obstacles diminish, local producers face increasing competition from their foreign rivals. The reaction generated is usually diverse: some complain and sink under the foreign pressure, others seek to influence governments to find ingenious ways to impede the access of foreign products, whilst the more enterprising adapt to the competition by improving the quality and marketability of their goods and services.

Under the EMAs, the same principles underlie the free movements of goods (Goods Provision), services, companies and capital.

2.2 Goods Provision

"Without prejudice to the provisions of the GATT:
  (a) no new quantitative restrictions on imports and measures having equivalent effect shall be introduced in trade between the [European] Community and [the MNC];
  (b) quantitative restrictions on imports and measures having equivalent effect in trade between [the MNC] and the Community shall be abolished progressively upon entry into force of this [Euro-Mediterranean] Agreement;
  (c) neither the Community nor [the MNC] shall apply to the other's exports customs duties or charges having equivalent effect or measures of equivalent effect.

The provisions concerning the abolition of customs duties on imports shall also apply to customs duties of a fiscal nature.

The Agreement shall not preclude prohibitions or restrictions on imports, exports or goods in transit justified on grounds of public morality, public policy or public security; the protection of health and life of humans, animals or plants; the protection of national treasures of artistic, historic or archaeological value or the protection of intellectual, industrial or commercial property or rules relating to gold or silver. Such prohibitions or restrictions shall not, however, constitute arbitrary means of discrimination or a disguised restriction on trade between the Parties."

The Goods Provision is composed essentially of two parts:

(1) Prohibiting the introduction of **new customs duties and equivalent charges** (usually referred to as a "standstill clause"). All charges of this type must eventually be abolished.

(2) Prohibiting the introduction of **quantitative restrictions and equivalent measures** (standstill clause). All measures of this type must also be abolished.

Each part will be discussed separately below.

2.3 **Customs duties and equivalent charges**

This prohibition covers customs duties and similar charges between the parties to the EMAs. Customs duties are defined as any charge imposed on goods by virtue of their crossing a national frontier of one of the parties, irrespective of whether it has a protectionist purpose or effect.

The Court of First Instance in the *Opel Austria*[1] case and the European Court of Justice in the *Legros*[2] and *Aprile*[3] cases have interpreted the prohibition in the same way as the identically-worded EC Goods Provision. Therefore, no charges are permissible except for two types of levies:

(1) Fees imposed to cover the costs of services that are of specific benefit to a trader.

(2) Fees imposed to cover the costs of services required under international law.

---

1 Case T-115/94 *Opel Austria GmbH v European Commission* [1997] ECR II-39.
2 Case C-163/90 *Legros* [1992] ECR I-4625.
3 Case C-125/94 *Aprile Srl* [1995] ECR I-2919.

Ford[4] is a good case, which illustrates point (1) above. In this case, the Court of Justice took the opportunity to emphasise that even if the specific nature of the necessary benefit is readily identifiable, the state will fall foul of the European Community (EC) Goods Provision unless the sum demanded is proportionate to the cost of applying the benefit. Ford received a demand for 0.165 per cent of the declared value of its cars and other goods imported into Spain. The Spanish authorities contended that the sum related to services rendered in connection with clearing the goods through customs. The Court ruled that although the specific benefit conferred on Ford could be proven, the flat-rate nature of the charge based on the value of the goods prevented a finding that the Spanish system was compatible with the EC Goods Provision. The system was evidently not fixed according to the cost of the alleged service and thus could not meet the Court's test. Clearly, a fee must be assessed according to the particular costs involved in that deal before a true bargain will be found to exist.

Asymmetrical relationship

The EMAs create a free trade area in industrial goods between the parties under an asymmetrical relationship, except for Israel and Turkey. This means that the EU markets will be opened up more rapidly to MNC traders than the MNC markets to EU traders. Hence, MNC imports into the EU are free of all customs duties/quantitative restrictions or their equivalent upon the entry into force of the EMA. On the other hand, the MNC must abolish customs duties on industrial products according to a graduated timetable which, varies according to the category of product. Some products will be allowed in duty free on entry into force of the EMA. Others will have the duty reduced over a five or a 12-year period.

By comparison, the Israeli and Turkish EMAs envisaged an immediate reciprocal elimination of all customs duties and charges on industrials products.

Agriculture

The EMAs merely liberalise trade in agriculture (including industrial goods with an agricultural component, "combined product") according

---

4 Case 170/88 *Ford España* v *Spain* [1989] ECR 2305.

to agreed schedules (or lists) in the relevant EMA. Liberalisation may include, depending on the agricultural product concerned, the reductions/elimination of customs duties or the increase/elimination of tariff quotas, or a combination of the two. It may also include first, improvements in the periods of time during the year when certain agricultural products may be marketed in another party's territory – usually connected to seasonal periods of the year – and, secondly, less cumbersome procedures for the entry of such products.

In relation to combined products, the customs duties on the industrial component will be abolished according to agreed schedules. The agricultural component (sometimes referred to as "variable component") will remain subject to either fixed duties or *ad valorem* duties (*i.e.* duties depending on the value of the product). This component is determined by adding the price of all the agricultural products used in the production of combined goods. Where the total cost of combined products imported into the EU from the MNC is higher in the EU than the MNC, then the agricultural component must reflect the differences between the price of agricultural goods on the EU market and imports from third countries. These differences must be replaced, where appropriate, by specific duties based on tariffication (*i.e.* drawing up specific tariff lists) of the agricultural component or by *ad valorem* duties.[4a]

For some combined products, the MNC may specify the agricultural component according to its own criteria.

The procedures for the entry of agricultural products across national frontiers are stipulated in the EMAs.

Fishery products

The trade in fishery products will be liberalised according to agreed schedules and therefore some of these products will remain subject to customs charges and quotas.

Review of agriculture and fishery arrangements

Arrangements for fishery and agricultural products will be reviewed in the year 2000 (or later) with a view to liberalising trade in both areas.

4a See proposal for Council Decision on EU position within EU-Tunisian Association Council concerning secondary legislation on agriculture (COM (99) 166 final).

2.4 **Quantitative restrictions and equivalent measures**

The Goods Provision also seeks to tackle direct and indirect barriers to trade of industrial goods between the EU and the MNC. These restrictions are termed in the EMAs as "quantitative restrictions".

Direct restrictions

The EMAs proscribe the parties from employing outright bans, quotas or other numerical limits in relation to the trade of industrial goods between them.

Indirect restrictions

The EMAs go further to prohibit "measures equivalent to quantitative restrictions", which is the expression used to denote indirect restrictions to trade. In other words, the expression in question deals with restrictions resulting from differing technical and regulatory standards which do not discriminate on the basis of place of production. For example, if Lebanon were to apply a new electrical standard for hair dryers different from the EU, a German manufacturer of hair dryers which wants to sell its products to Lebanon would have to meet both European and Lebanese standards. However, a local Lebanese manufacture would only have to satisfy the local standard. Hence, the German competitor would be at a distinct competitive disadvantage.

This area of the law is very controversial and has been subject to interpretation by the European Court of Justice and other courts in the context of free trade agreements concluded between the European Union and some European countries.

In the *Polydor*[5] case, Article 14 of the EU-Portuguese Free Trade Agreement (concluded before Portugal joined the European Union in 1986) prohibited the introduction of new quantitative restrictions or measures having equivalent effect on imports between the parties. It also required the abolition of existing restrictions and equivalent measures. The meaning of the latter provision was at issue.

---

5 Case 270/80 *Polydor v Harlequin Records Shops Ltd* [1982] ECR 329.

This judgment concerned the importation of gramophone records from Portugal, where they had been purchased from the exclusive licensee for that country. They were then sold in the United Kingdom without the consent of the copyright holder or his exclusive licensee in the United Kingdom. In particular, the question was whether the exclusion of such products from the United Kingdom was contrary to Article 14 of the Portuguese Agreement. The Court of Justice ruled that their exclusion was justified under Article 23 of the same Agreement on the basis of protection of intellectual, industrial and commercial property. This Article was substantially identical to the derogation in the EC Goods Provision.[6] In contrast, within the context of trade between the Member States of the EU, the "exhaustion of rights" doctrine would apply. Its application would prevent the holder of an intellectual property right from using his right to exclude from one Member State products lawfully marketed in another Member State with his consent. Hence, their exclusion would be prohibited by the EC Treaty and would not be justified under the derogation provisions of that Treaty.

Such a contrast between the operation of the free movement of goods provisions of the EC Treaty and the operation of similar provisions in free trade agreements was acceptable to national courts in non-EU countries. For example, the case of *Gramola*[7] concerned the Austrian Free Trade Agreement (concluded before Austria joined the EU in 1995). Here, the Austrian Supreme Court found that an Austrian record shop proprietor, who imported records from Germany, where they were lawfully marketed, infringed the copyrights in Austria of the Austrian music society. In so finding, the Court ruled that the creation and exercise of copyrights in the widest sense were not covered in the Austrian Agreement. This was the position in so far as the restrictions stipulated by the contract between the music society and the copyright owner were not excessive (*i.e.* they did not extend beyond the substance of the copyrights).

An approach similar to *Gramola* was adopted by the Swiss Supreme Court in the case of *Bosshard Partners*.[8] It found that a Swiss trade mark holder was entitled to prevent the importation into Switzerland of German-made detergents lawfully branded in Germany with the trade mark concerned. The court confirmed that this entitlement was unaffected by the Swiss Free Trade Agreement.

---

6 For a discussion of the derogation, see below.
7 *Gramola* [1984] 2 CMLR 626.
8 *Bosshard Partners Intertrading AG v Sunlight AG* [1980] 3 CMLR 664.

Derogation from free movement of goods

The Goods Provision permits the prohibitions or restrictions on imports, exports and goods in transit between the parties to the EMA. These grounds are:

    (i)   public morality, public policy, or public security;

    (ii) the protection of life and health of humans, animals or plants;

    (iii) the protection of national treasures possessing artistic, historic or architectural value;

    (iv) the protection of intellectual, industrial or commercial property;

    (v) rules relating to gold or silver.

It is commonly known that the Middle East and North Africa are regions with acute religious and cultural sensitivities. Therefore, where the MNCs feel that such sensitivities are undermined by certain trading activities, they are likely to impose trade restrictions especially on the grounds of public morality and public policy and will, therefore, be given a wide latitude by the European Commission for doing so.

Any imposition of prohibitions or restrictions must not, however, constitute arbitrary means of discrimination or a disguised restriction on trade between the parties. Essentially, these requirements translate into two conditions:

Proportionality principle

This principle stipulates that a measure must be no more restrictive than is necessary to secure a lawful end. Its essence is best encapsulated by the expression, "you don't use a sledgehammer to crack a nut." Thus, the restrictive measures must not simply be necessary to protect the interests with which the derogation is concerned. They must be necessary in the sense that such interests are not already protected and cannot be as effectively safeguarded by less restrictive measures on free movement. The burden on proving such necessity is on the party seeking to rely on the derogation. Account may be taken of diversity in national values in relation to the requirements of public health and public morality.

Least restrictive principle

This principle states that the national measure must be the least restrictive of trade available. In other words, if an alternative measure exists which is less onerous on trade between the parties, then the alternative one should be adopted instead.

Practical consequences of goods provision

As can be observed from the case law, the Court of Justice and other courts in Europe have given restrictive interpretation to provisions, which substantially reproduce the EC Goods Provision. The reason for the divergent interpretations was best summarised in the *Polydor* case, where the Court of Justice stated:

> "The considerations which led to that interpretation of [the EC Goods Provision] [on the exhaustion of rights doctrine] do not apply in the context of the relations between the [European] Community and Portugal as defined in the Agreement. It is apparent from the examination of the Agreement that although it makes provision for the unconditional abolition of certain restrictions, such as quantitative restrictions and measures having equivalent effect, it does not have the same purpose as the EC Treaty." (at para 18)

Simply put, the EC Treaty has sought to unify the 15 national markets of the Member States into a single market having the characteristics of a domestic market, whereas, the objective of the Portugese Agreement was merely to create a free trade area. In support of this conclusion was the fact that, unlike the EC Treaty, there were no adequate legislative instruments and institutional arrangements in the Agreement to bring about deeper integration of markets. Also, unlike the EC Treaty, there was no general obligation for liberalisation in other areas of trade, such as free movement of services and freedom of establishment (the right to set up offices in another party's territory).[9]

The practical consequences flowing from the narrow interpretation is that the Goods Provision in the EMAs is apparently interpreted merely as prohibiting one party from discriminating between its domestic products and the other party's imports on the basis of national origin. The Swiss Supreme Court favoured this interpretation in the *Brosshard* case and Court of Justice implicitly adopted it in *Kupferberg*.[10]

An example of how the Goods Provision will operate is provided by the *Eurim-Pharm*[11] case. This case turned on the interpretation of Article 13 of the Austrian Free Trade Agreement, which is identical to

---

9   For a discussion on freedom of establishment, see Chap 4.
10   Case 104/81 *Haupzollamt Mainz* v *C A Kupferberg & Cie KG* [1982] ECR 3641.
11   Case C-207/91 *Eurim-Pharm* v *Bundesgesundheitsamt* [1993] ECR I-3723.

the EC Goods Provision. Eurim-Pharm (EP) brought proceedings against the Bundesgesundheitsamt (BG) challenging its refusal to grant marketing authorisation to place a medicinal product on the German market. EP wanted to buy the product in Austria and resell it in Germany and it therefore applied to the BG for authorisation. EC law refers to products already marketed in one country which are imported into another country where they are also marketed as "parallel imports". Under German law, where an application is made to the BG concerning a product, which was previously the subject of an application, the documentation required is reduced. This procedure does not, however, apply to imports. In essence, German law discriminated on the basis of nationality, applying one set of standards to German products and different (more onerous) standards for imports (*i.e.* Austrian products). The Court ruled that Article 13 prohibited Germany from making the marketing authorisation for a pharmaceutical product originating in Austria and already authorised by the German health authority, subject to the condition that the parallel importer submit documentation already supplied by the manufacturer upon first request for marketing authorisation.

Technical barriers to trade

One major consequence of the restrictive interpretation of the Goods Provision is that most technical barriers (*i.e.* obstacles due to divergent technical and regulatory standards) between the parties are unaffected by the prohibition of measures having equivalent effect to quantitative restrictions. Such barriers will gain in importance as the relative benefits of tariff reductions decline due to the GATT successes in lowering them world-wide. Comparative advantage, whether natural or man-made, may be sufficient to outweigh the costs associated with technical barriers. However, costs of compliance may diminish or negate the advantages of economies of scale.

On an empirical level, this omission should not be exaggerated since the vast majority of the MNCs' foreign trade is with the EU. As a result, foreign companies will be able to satisfy any technical barriers, especially given that they increasingly cater to the requirements of their customers from all across the world. If anything, the elimination of high customs duties in the MNC under the EMAs should provide greater opportunities for foreign enterprises to expand their penetration of such markets.

Moreover, there is a WTO-related Agreement on Technical Barriers to Trade, which seeks to ensure that technical negotiations and standards, as well as testing and certification procedures, do not create unnecessary obstacles to trade. However, it recognises that countries have the right to establish protection, at levels they consider appropriate, for example for human, animal or plant life or health or the environment, and should not be prevented from taking such measures to ensure those levels of protection are met. The Agreement therefore encourages countries to use international standards where these are appropriate, but it does not require them to change their levels of protection as a result of standardisation.

This Agreement covers processing and production methods related to the characteristics of the product itself. The coverage of conformity assessment procedures are quite wide and the disciplines generally precise. There are notification provisions applying to local government and non-governmental bodies. A Code of Good Practice for the Preparation, Adoption and Application of Standards by standardising bodies, which is open to acceptance by private sector bodies as well as the public sector, is included as an annex to the Agreement.

Mutual recognition of standards

Potentially, an important way in which technical barriers to trade between the EU and the MNC may be reduced is by both parties recognising each other's technical standards. Mutual recognition of standards will be dependent on the conclusion of separate bilateral agreements. In particular, the parties undertake to adopt appropriate steps to promote the use by the MNC of the EU's technical rules and European standards for industrial and agri-food products and certification procedures. Eventually, when the circumstances are right, both parties may conclude agreements for the mutual recognition of certification.

2.5 Turkish EMA

The Goods Provision in this EMA goes further than all the other EMAs, in terms of both customs duties and quantitative restrictions.

Customs duties and equivalent charges

There is an additional ban on export customs duties and equivalent measures, unlike the other EMAs. It prohibits each party from imposing customs duties and equivalent charges, which discriminate against its exports. Thus, Turkey may be prohibited from levying inspection fees on its meat exporters whilst exempting EU exporters or domestic producers from such fees.

Common Customs Tariff

In contrast to the other EMAs, the Turkish EMA seeks to create a customs union between Turkey and the EU, rather than a mere free trade area. Unsurprisingly, the EMA extends the EU's common external tariff and common commercial policies with third states to cover Turkey. In general, this means that Turkey shares the same tariffs and external economic arrangements with third countries as the EU. Hence, products from third countries are considered to be in free circulation in the EU or Turkey[12] provided import formalities have been complied with and any customs duties or charges having equivalent effect which are payable have been levied by the EU or Turkey without reimbursement.

As a result, Turkey must adopt EU legal instruments dealing with external tariffs (called the Common Customs Tariff) and the common EU commercial policies applicable to third states (*e.g.* common EU rules relating to imports from third states).[13] At the same time, Turkey is bound to negotiate (and has actually negotiated some) preferential trade arrangements with third countries, which are substantially similar to the ones concluded by the EU.[14]

The Turkish EMA contains special arrangements for processed agricultural products not covered by the EC Treaty. Turkey is permitted to impose a duty on the agricultural components of processed agricultural products imported from the EU or third states. For such products, the duty is determined by adding together the quantities of basic agricultural products considered to have been used in the manufacture of the products in question multiplied by the basic amount corresponding to each of these basic agricultural products. The basic

---

12 In Case 41/76 *Donckerwolcke and Schou* [1976] ECR 1921, the European Court said that goods in free circulation are "definitively and wholly assimilated to the products originating in the Member States" (and by extension Turkey in the context of the Turkish EMA).

13 The list of EC legal instruments is stipulated in the Turkish EMA.

14 According to the Turkish EMA, Turkey will give priority to concluding preferential trade agreements with Bulgaria, Hungary, Poland, Romania, Slovakia, Czech Republic, Israel, Estonia, Latvia and Lithuania, Morocco, Tunisia and Egypt. Turkey has concluded free trade agreements with Israel and Central and Eastern European Countries and is close to concluding an agreement with Egypt.

agricultural products to be taken into account and their quantities are set out in agreed schedules. The basic amount corresponding to each basic agricultural product is the amount of charge applicable on import into Turkey of the agricultural product originating in a third country. This amount is also set out in agreed schedules.

Whilst the EMA lays a specific formula for Turkey, the EU applies to Turkey the same specific duties on the agricultural component that are applicable to third countries.

For purely agricultural products,[15] both parties undertake to negotiate more advantageous terms than existing preferential arrangements. In addition, once Turkey adopts the necessary measures in line with the EU's Common Agricultural Policy, the Association Council will adopt the necessary provisions to he achieve the free movement of agricultural products between the parties.

Quantitative restrictions and equivalent measures

The provision extends the prohibition of quantitative restrictions and equivalent measures beyond imports to exports. This only bites in the event of discrimination against exports in favour of domestic products. A good example is the leading case of *Groenveld*.[16] Dutch legislation prohibited all meat producers from stocking or processing horse meat. Groenveld, which was a Dutch firm involved in the import of and trade in horse meat, decided to extend its business activities into the field of horse meat sausages. The plan would place the firm in direct conflict with Dutch law. Groenveld argued that the Dutch legislation precluded it from manufacturing and subsequently exporting horse meat sausages and therefore contravened the ban on quantitative restrictions and equivalent measures being imposed on exports.

The Court of Justice ruled that the ban was concerned exclusively with the establishment of a difference in treatment between the domestic trade and the export trade, which was not the case in *Groenveld*. Therefore, either party may impose quality standards and other restrictions on its domestic producers, even if that policy favours domestic producers and foreign imports at the expense of its exporters provided they apply to the domestic and foreign trade.

---

15 Turkey's preferential agricultural trade regime with the EU is spelt out in Dec 1/98 of the EU-Turkey Association Council (OJ 1998 L86/1). Dec 1/97 of the EU-Turkey Association Agreement contains arrangements applicable to certain processed agricultural products (OJ 1997 L166/7).

16 Case 15/79 *Groenveld v Produktschap voor Vee en Vlees* [1979] ECR 3409.

Technical barriers to trade

In order to facilitate the free movement of goods, Turkey is obliged to adopt EU legislation into its legal order which aim to remove technical barriers to trade based on mutual recognition of standards.[17] This means both parties agree to recognise each other's standards by meeting the conditions stipulated in the requisite legislation and thereby allowing entry for one another's goods.

Some of the legislation may take a further step and harmonise standards between Turkey and the EU. In other words, the same (minimum) technical standard is applicable to both parties and naturally removes any divergence of standards with respect to certain products.

Case law

Besides legislative initiatives, EU case law may facilitate the free movement of goods between the parties, especially by eliminating technical barriers to trade. Unlike the other EMAs, the Turkish EMA incorporates EU case law of the European Court of Justice for the interpretation of all the provisions in the EMAs, which closely mimic the corresponding provision in the EC Treaty. Therefore, the restrictive interpretation of the Goods Provision by the European Court of Justice as described above is not applicable to the Turkish Goods Provision. Specifically, the Turkish EMA says:

> "The provisions of this Decision [*i.e.* EU-Turkish Customs Union Agreement] in so far as they are identical in substance to the corresponding provisions of the Treaty establishing the European Community shall be interpreted for the purposes of their implementation and application to products covered by the Customs Union, in conformity with the relevant decisions of the Court of Justice of the European Communities."

This provision has been the subject of interpretation by the Court of First Instance in relation to an identical provision in the European Economic Area Agreement (EEA) in the *Opel Austria* case. In that case, the Court said that the EEA is designed to achieve a high degree of integration with objectives, which exceed those of a mere free trade area. In light of the manifest purpose of the Turkish EMA and in

---

17 The list of the EU legislation may be found in EU-Turkey Association Council Dec 2/97 (OJ 1997 L191/1) establishing a list of EU instruments relating to the removal of technical barriers to trade and the conditions governing implementation by Turkey.

particular the objective of integration ("homogeneity" in EC legal parlance), provisions worded identically to the corresponding provision in the EC Treaty are likely to be "identical in substance". As a result, the relevant decisions by the Court of Justice apply for purposes of interpretation. Therefore, given that the Turkish EMA augurs in a customs union, a relationship that involves more integration than the EEA which is not a customs union, the reasoning of the *Opel Austria* case applies equally to the Turkish EMA.

The European Court of Justice has given a sweeping definition to the phrase "measures equivalent to quantitative restrictions". In *Dassonville*,[18] it said that the phrase encompassed "all trading rules enacted by a … State which are capable of hindering directly or indirectly, actually or potentially … trade" between the Member States (and by extension between the parties). The definition, called the "*Dassonville* formula", is extremely broad potentially catching all possible trade barriers, including those enacted by either party genuinely in the public interest.

Shortly after the *Dassonville* case, the Court in *Cassis de Dijon*[19] recognised the need for derogations from the "*Dassonville* formula" in limited circumstances where the benefits of free movement of goods are outweighed by more important objectives. In that case, the Court declared that each party has regulatory independence in a particular economic field, provided that the European Union has not legislated in that field. It went on to state that:

> "obstacles to movement resulting from disparities between national laws relating to the marketing … of products … [are allowed] … in so far as those provisions … [are] necessary to satisfy mandatory requirements relating to the effectiveness of fiscal supervision, the protection of public health, the fairness of commercial transactions and the defence of the consumer." (at para 8)

In other words, pending harmonisation of laws in a particular field at the EU level, the parties may restrict the free movement of goods if a "mandatory requirement" or public interest aim needs to be satisfied, such as the protection of health. As for the derogation clause in the Goods Provision, the "proportionality" and the "least restrictive of trade" principles must be met. What this means is that the derogation clause itself applies to rules which directly discriminate against foreign goods on the basis of national origin, whereas the *Cassis de Dijon* case applies to

---

18 Case 8/74 *Procureur du Roi v Dassonville* [1974] ECR 837, para 5.
19 Case 120/78 *Rewe-Zentrale v Bundesmonopolverwaltung für Branntwein* [1979] ECR 649.

indirect or technical barriers to trade. But, there are no practical differences because the principles underlying both exceptions are the same.

Recently, the Court of Justice has sought to reduce the ambit of the *Dassonville* formula. In *Keck*[20], it decided to "re-examine and clarify" its jurisprudence and enunciated that national provisions restricting "certain selling arangements" (*e.g.* a ban on advertising) which hinders imports are outside the scope of the Goods Provision provided:

> "that those provisions apply to all affected traders operating within the national territory and so long as those provisions affect in the same manner, in law [the first condition] and in fact [the second provision], the marketing of domestic products and of those of other Member States [and by extension the other Party]."

The *Keck* case provides two pre-conditions to bring a national measure outside the scope of the Goods Provision:

(1) The national measure must not discriminate on the basis of national origin.
(2) It does not have a greater effect, factually-speaking, on foreign products than on domestic producers (*i.e.* there is no indirect discrimination against a foreign product in the host market).

In simple terms, national rules restricting or prohibiting "certain selling arrangement" (*i.e.* circumstances in which a product may be sold) is beyond the ambit of the provision provided they do not discriminate directly or indirectly against imported goods. On the other hand, national rules affecting the physical manifestation of products (*i.e.* conditions that goods must fulfil), such as goods' packaging, presentation or weight are still caught by the provision. This interpretation of *Keck* is confirmed by the case itself:

> "In *Cassis de Dijon* … it was held that in the absence of harmonization of legislation, measures of equivalent effect prohibited by [the EC Goods Provision] include obstacles to the free movement of goods where they are the consequences of applying rules that lay down requirements to be met by such goods (such as requirements as to designation, form, size, weight, composition, presentation, labelling and packaging) to goods from other Member States [of the European Union] where they are lawfully manufactured and marketed even if those rules apply without distinction to all products unless their application can be justified by public interest objectives taking precedence over the free movement of goods." (at para 15)

---

20   Joined Cases C-267 & C-268/91 *Keck and Mithouard* [1993] ECR I-6097, paras 14,16.

The *Spilec*[21] case demonstrates the type of restrictions, which may escape the Provision, *i.e.* those affecting selling arrangements. In that case, French legislation banned television advertising to any business involved in the distribution of goods, such as supermarket chains. The Court decided that the French prohibition at issue concerned selling arrangements since it prohibited a particular form of promotion – televised advertising and a particular form of marketing products. It found that this did not discriminate between different categories of distributors or between French and non-French products, and thus was not a measure equivalent to a quantitative restriction.

On the other hand, the *Mars*[22] case is an example of restrictions still caught by the Provision, *i.e.* measures affecting the physical manifestation of goods. In this case, the Court found that the EC Goods Provision must be interpreted as preventing national legislation from prohibiting the importation and marketing of a product lawfully marketed in another EU Member State. In *Mars*, the issue was a sales promotion on Mars packaging which stated that the size of the ice-cream bar subject to the offer was increased by 10 per cent. The Court of Justice reaffirmed that national rules concerning the conditions that goods must fulfil (*e.g.* labelling and packaging) including rules on sales promotion affecting their content are not selling arrangements. It also confirmed that national restrictions on the packaging and presentation of goods imposed to satisfy mandatory requirements will only be allowed if they are proportionate to the objective pursued (in this case, consumer protection) and are incapable of being achieved by measures which are less restrictive of trade.

Intellectual property rights

Intellectual property rights[23] protected by national law may lead to restriction of trade between Turkey and the EU. National law, for

---

21 Case C-412/93 *Société d'Importation Edouard Leclerc-Spilec v TFI Publicité and M6 Publicité* [1995] ECR I-179.
22 Case C-470/93 *Verein gegen Unswen in Handel und Geweerbe Köln v Mars* [1995] ECR I-1923.
23 Turkey and other EMA countries are required to accede to, or observe obligations flowing from, international multilateral conventions on the protection of industrial, intellectual and commercial property rights. Examples of such conventions include the Patent Co-operation Treaty (1970, amended 1979 and modified in 1984) and the Paris Convention for the Protection of Industrial Property in the 1967 Act of Stockholm (Paris Union). Turkey was required to adopt intellectual property rights legislation in line with EU legislation, *e.g.* Council Dir 91/250 on the protection of computer programmes as literary work (OJ 1991 L122/1). Moreover, Jordan (and by extension MNCs without WTO membership) must provide for effective legal protection of patents for pharmaceuticals in line with the relevant corresponding WTO provisions within three years of the entry into force of the EMA.

example, entitles the holder of a trade mark to prevent the marketing by others of any products, domestic or imported, which bear the same or similar mark. Such law does not entail discrimination against exports. However, its application to imports from the other party is prohibited by the Goods Provision, unless its application can be justified on the grounds of the protection of commercial or intellectual property. According to the Provision's derogation clause, the free movement of goods does not preclude trade restrictions on such grounds.

It is also stipulated in the derogation clause that the restrictions must not constitute a means of arbitrary discrimination or a disguised restriction of trade between the parties. Where a producer uses different trade marks in different countries, there may be a disguised restriction of trade so as to partition the market along national lines.

At the same time, this derogation appears to conflict with the fact that the Turkish EMA cannot interfere in national laws on the ownership of property, such as laws protecting intellectual property rights.

To resolve the conflict between free movement of goods, the derogation clause and the non-interference of EU law in national laws on property rights, the Court of Justice has distinguished between the "existence" and "exercise" of an intellectual property right.

The Court has stated repeatedly that EU law recognises the existence of intellectual property rights and therefore the "specific subject matter" of such rights is protected under the derogation clause. The specific subject matter of a patent, for example, is the guarantee that the patentee has the exclusive right to use an invention with a view to manufacturing industrial products and putting into circulation for the first time, either directly or by the grant of licences to third parties. This also includes a right to oppose infringements. Thus a patent right in, say, Italy may be used to exclude products exported by a compulsory licensee from, say, Turkey to that state.

However, a patentee in one party's territory may not use his patent to restrict imports from the other party where he has placed the patented product on the market.

In other words, the Court has developed the "exhaustion of rights" doctrine to delineate the extent of the intellectual property rights protected under the derogation clause. According to this doctrine, for instance, where products are put into free circulation anywhere in the customs union area by the trade mark holder or with his consent, his rights are "exhausted". Hence, he may not invoke them to prevent the products being traded between the parties. For example, assume that a

Turkish inventor invented a new product. He decides to manufacture his invention in Turkey and market it in both Turkey and Germany. In those circumstances, Turkish patent laws may assist him in protecting his invention when he first manufactures and markets it in Turkey. Once marketed, his patent rights have been "exhausted," in that he cannot use them in the future to prevent imports of his invention which are marketed in Germany and then re-sold in Turkey.

2.6 **What if ?**

Q: I am a Spanish exporter of ABC product to Egypt. At the port of Alexandria, the Egyptian customs authorities levied a flat-rate one per cent charge to pay for health inspections. This charge has priced my product outside the abilities of Egyptians to pay for it. What is my legal position?

A: Under the Egyptian EMA, the parties are prohibited from imposing customs duties and charges which are equivalent to such duties unless this is mandated under an international agreement or a specific service is being provided. On the assumption that the customs authorities are providing a specific service, the law assesses whether the inspection fee is calibrated according to the costs of the benefit being provided. However, given that specific benefit conferred on you could be shown, the flat-rate nature of the charge based on the value of the ABC product prevents the Egyptian system being found compatible with the Goods Provision. The system was evidently not fixed according to the cost of the alleged service, so that inspection fee is illegal under the Egyptian EMA.

Q: I am an Israeli exporter of ABC product to France. French law requires certain technical specifications, which would add to my production costs, but are easily met by French competitors. In essence, my product is put at a competitive disadvantage in the French market. I understand from my friends that if such trade obstacles impeded German ABC product that would be contrary to EC law. What is the situation *vis-à-vis* the Israeli EMA?

A: Unfortunately, all the EMAs (except for the Turkish one) merely ban directly discriminatory trade restrictions. In other words, if the French technical specifications apply to Israeli and French ABC products alike, then there is nothing more you can do. Your friends were absolutely right that EU law disallows similar trade restrictions between Germany and France on the grounds that they are equivalent to quantitative restrictions. The reason is that the European Court of Justice and other European courts have stated that such restrictions are beyond the scope of Association Agreements, whilst they are well within the ambit of the EC Treaty.

Q: I am a Swedish patent-holder for ABC product. When I came to market this product in Turkey, I discovered that a Turkish company, XYZ Limited, was importing ABC from Spain, where my distributor lawfully markets it. Can I use Turkish patent laws to prevent XYZ from importing such a product?

A: You cannot prevent XYZ from importing such products from Spain due to the exhaustion of rights doctrine. The Court has stated repeatedly that EU law recognises the existence of intellectual property rights and therefore the specific subject matter of such rights is protected under the derogation clause. The specific subject matter of a patent, for example, is the guarantee that the patentee has the exclusive right to use an invention with a view to manufacturing industrial products and putting them into circulation for the first time, either directly or by the grant of licences to third parties. This also includes a right to oppose infringements. Thus, you may not utilise your patent to restrict imports from Spain where you have placed the patented ABC product on the market. According to this doctrine, for instance, where products are put into free circulation anywhere in the customs union area by the trade mark holder or with your consent, your rights are "exhausted". Hence, you may not invoke them to prevent the products being traded between the Spain and Turkey.

Chapter 3

· **Taxation** ·

3.1 **Introduction**

As a complement to the Goods Provision, the EMAs regulate trade obstacles of a fiscal nature in the form of discriminatory taxation designed to put foreign products at a competitive disadvantage in a national market (Taxation Provision).

3.2 **Taxation Provision**

"1. The two Parties shall refrain from any measures or practices of an internal fiscal nature establishing, whether directly or indirectly, discrimination between products of one Party and like products originating in the territory of the other Party.

2. Products exported to the territory of one of the two Parties may not benefit from repayment of internal taxation in excess of the amount of direct or indirect taxation imposed on them."

This Provision prevents each party from imposing fiscal taxes, which discriminate between local and foreign goods possessing identical characteristics.

3.3 **Relationship between the Goods and Taxation Provisions**

Both provisions are complementary, yet mutually exclusive. Both are concerned with the control of fiscal charges imposed on goods by the relevant parties, but a charge must fall under one or the other. A fiscal charge is either considered a customs duty or a charge of equivalent effect (the Goods Provision), or else it forms part of a general system of internal taxation (the Taxation Provision). The distinction is vital. A charge caught by the Goods Provision is unlawful, whereas a charge that falls to be considered under the Taxation Provision is lawful, except to the extent it contains an element that discriminates according to nationality. The demarcation is not always easy to make.

According to EU case law, any pecuniary charge, which is imposed unilaterally on domestic or foreign goods by reason of the fact that they cross a frontier constitutes a charge having equivalent effect to a customs duty. The Goods Provision is then applicable where the levy is triggered by the fact of border crossing. On the other hand, the Taxation Provision applies to a general system of internal dues applied systematically to categories of products using objective criteria irrespective of the origin of the products. If the charge in question can be accommodated within the internal structure, as well as being based on criteria that are of general application to aspects such as quality or function rather to the fact of crossing a border, then the matter should be dealt with by the Taxation Provision.

Consequently, even a charge levied in respect of a procedure carried out at a border is capable of assessment in the light of the Taxation rather than the Goods Provision, provided the system applies generally and systematically. Thus, a fee attached to a border control may exceptionally be part of a general system of internal taxation if the same procedure is undertaken in the light of the same criteria in respect of home-produced goods.

3.4 **Prohibition of discriminatory taxation**

The Taxation Provision only prohibits taxes that discriminate directly on the basis of national origin. Imported products, which are being discriminated against, must share the same features and characteristics as the competing home-produced products. This is reminiscent of the language in Article III of the GATT, which prohibits the imposition of discriminatory taxation.

In the *Kupferberg*[1] case, German taxation put port wine from Portugal at a competitive disadvantage to German alcoholic products. The Court of Justice had to interpret Article 21(1) of the Portuguese Free Trade Agreement, worded identically to the Taxation Provision. According to the European Commission, only effective discrimination rather than the mere fact of difference of taxation was prohibited. Hence, the taxation of port from Portugal was not affected by the Agreement, because no similar products were made in Germany. In contrast, Germany would not be

---

1 Case 108/81 *Hauptzollamt Mainz v C A Kupferberg & Cie KG* [1982] ECR 3641.

permitted under the EC Taxation Provision to impose any tax on port from an EU Member State if it put this product at a disadvantage in relation to competing national products capable of being protected by this tax. Such a tax would only be permissible where there was no national product capable of being protected by a tax on products imported from another EU Member State.

In the case of *Metalsa*[2] the Court of Justice confirmed the *Polydor*[3] judgment. This case concerned a decision by the Italian authorities to seize aluminium imports imported from Austria by Metalsa for the failure to pay the value-added tax (VAT) due on importation. Italian law makes a distinction between offences concerning the payment of VAT on imports and offences concerning the payment of VAT on domestic transactions. The latter offence is treated more leniently than the former. Metalsa argued that this was contrary to Article 18 of the EU-Austrian Free Trade Agreement (the Taxation Provision) and that the case law concerning EC Taxation Provision should be applied, which prohibits such divergence in the Italian law. The Court applied the rule from the *Polydor* case and compared the objectives of the Agreement and the EC Treaty. It decided that the purpose of the former was to consolidate and to extend the economic relations between the EU and Austria and to ensure, with due regard for fair conditions of competition, the harmonious development of their commerce and to create a free trade area. The latter on the contrary seeks to create a single market reproducing as closely as possible the conditions of a domestic market. The Court therefore concluded that the Agreement did not prohibit different punishments for similar offences.

In summary, the Provision only covers tax rates that discriminate based on the place of production of a product. Matters ancillary to tax rates, such as penalties for non-payments of taxes, are outside the remit of the EMAs.

3.5 Discriminatory refund of taxation

It is sometimes necessary to examine refunds of internal duties in order to uncover disguised export subsidies. If the exporting domestic industry is supplied with resources refunded out of a tax levied on all products, the effect is no different from a subsidy that favours export goods to the

---

2 Case C-312/91 *Metalsa Srl* [1993] ECR I-3751.
3 Case 270/80 *Polydor v Harlequin Records Shops Ltd* [1982] ECR 329.

detriment of producers in the other party's territory. Therefore, the Taxation Provision states that products exported to the territory of the other party may not benefit from repayment of internal taxation in excess of the amount of direct or indirect taxation imposed on them.

3.6 **Turkish EMA**

The Turkish EMA prohibits directly discriminatory taxation to a greater extent than the other EMAs. Those areas outside the scope of non-Turkish EMAs (*e.g.* penalties relating to tax offences) are regulated. More ambitiously, the Turkish Taxation Provision prohibits taxes that discriminate indirectly against the other party's products.

The ban on discriminatory taxation also includes products originating in third countries, which are in free circulation within the EU or Turkey.[4]

Direct discrimination

The Turkish EMA provides that neither party is allowed to impose, directly or indirectly, on the products of the other party any internal taxation of any kind in excess of that imposed directly or indirectly on similar domestic products. For the purposes of this paragraph, products are similar when they come within the same customs, fiscal or statistical classification or when they have similar characteristics and meet the same needs from the point of view of the consumer. Only taxation, which directly discriminates against imports in favour of domestic products and is similar in this sense, is prohibited by this paragraph. The mere possibility of such discrimination may be sufficient to bring the prohibition into play, as may conditions in the application of the tax. However, taxation differentiating between products by criteria other than their national origin and applying equally to domestic and imported products is unaffected by this paragraph.

Indirect discrimination

Another paragraph of the Turkish Tax Provision provides that neither contracting party may impose on the products of the other party any

---

4 Case 193/85 *Cooperativa Co-Frutta* [1987] ECR 2085.

internal taxation of such a nature as to afford indirect protection to other products. This paragraph applies where there are no domestic products similar to imported products.

The paragraph covers all forms of indirect tax protection in the case of products, even though dissimilar, are nevertheless in (partial, direct or potential) competition with certain products of the importing party. Thus, it prohibits taxation, which does not directly discriminate between domestic products and imports but has the effect of putting the latter at a competitive disadvantage. For example, if a party has a system of taxation imposed on the sale of cars which is graduated so that the highest rate is paid by the largest cars and no such cars are produced in that party, there may be a violation of this paragraph. Consequently, indirect discrimination may be deduced where measures are found having a protective effect in favour of domestic goods relative to imports.

According to EU case law, it is the competitive effect of a tax difference, which determines whether the difference amounts to such discrimination. Therefore, to be prohibited, taxation must have the effect of reducing potential consumption of imports to the advantage of domestic products. The mere fact that imports may be restricted by tax measures does not necessarily mean the tax measures are prohibited.

This paragraph seeks to eliminate all forms of protectionism resulting from the application of internal taxation, which discriminates against one party's products or is protectionist in scope. In other words, it aims to guarantee generally the neutrality of the systems of internal taxation with regard to trade between the parties whenever an economic transaction brings about the chargeable event giving rise to a fiscal charge within the context of such a system.

If a distortion of competition contrary to this guarantee is not established, national taxation arrangements are unaffected by the paragraph. For example, the *Schul*[5] case concerned the imposition of Dutch VAT on the importation into the Netherlands of a second-hand pleasure boat purchased by a private individual resident in the Netherlands from another private individual in France. The Court of Justice ruled that the adoption of the "destination principle" for taxation purposes (*i.e.* taxing products according to the destination, rather than origin, of the product concerned) was a political choice for the European Parliament. The importing EU Member State merely had

---

5 Case 15/81 *Gaston Schul Douane Expediteur BV v Inspecteur der Inverrechten en Accijnzen, Rosendaal* [1982] ECR 1409.

to reduce the VAT charged on imported goods by the amount levied in the exporting EU Member State. Provided they did so, there would be no breach of the EC Taxation Provision.

Moreover, this paragraph does not aim to place imports in a more privileged position in relation to domestic products. Hence, a party is not required to exempt imports from its tax system simply because there are no domestic products burdened by a given tax.

On exports, the Court of Justice has extended the provision to cover fiscal discrimination against exports, that is taxation of exports at a higher level than goods destined for the home market. In the *Kontrol*[6] case, the Court insisted that EU law include a general principle of tax neutrality with regard not only to imported goods, but also to goods for export. Consequently, a state that seeks to restrain the export of a valuable scarce commodity through tax disincentives acts in violation of the Provision.

Reverse discrimination

The Turkish Taxation Provision does not prohibit the imposition on national products of internal taxation in excess of that on imported products. Such disparities result from the special features of national laws, which have not been harmonised, in spheres for which the Parties are responsible. In other words, "reverse discrimination" is not prohibited by the Turkish Provision, which is choosing to levy a higher tax on home-produced goods than is demanded of imports.

Objective differentiation

The Turkish Provision does not prohibit either party's tax laws from differentiating between products according to objective criteria. This is subject to the relevant party:

(1) Pursuing objectives compatible with the requirements of the Turkish EMA and EU secondary legislation connected to the EMA.
(2) Formulating detailed rules of implementation that avoid discrimination or protection.

Thus, economic or social policy goals may be pursued.

---

6 Case 142/77 *Statens Kontrol med Aedle Metaller v Preben Larsen* [1978] ECR 1543.

In principle, the identification of social/economic policy goals is a matter of choice for the parties. The choice can only be subject to supervision by the EU and Turkey at an official level whenever the concept of social/economic policy is distorted. As a result, measures may be enacted possessing objectives and effects, which lie outside the scope of the concept.

France[7] is a good example of a case where the Court of Justice found national rules to be objectively justifiable despite an indirectly discriminatory effect on grounds of nationality. In that case, the European Commission failed to convince the Court that a French system that taxed sweet wines produced in a traditional and customary fashion at a lower rate than liqueur wines was contrary to the EC Taxation Provision. The criterion for classification within the lower rate was in principle available to all products irrespective of origin and was not closed to imports. There was consequently no direct discrimination on the grounds of nationality. Once it was shown, if anything, indirect discrimination was an issue, it was open to France to demonstrate objective justification for the preferential treatment offered to natural sweet wines. It was shown that natural sweet wines tend to be produced in areas of low rainfall and poor soil, where the economy is unusually dependent on wine output. It was consequently found to be objectively justifiable to confer tax concessions on such products in order to support economically weak areas. It was thus accepted that the prohibition on discrimination under the provision still permits a state to use its tax system as a means of regional policy. However, such concessions must be available to all products, not just domestically produced goods.

3.7 **What if ?**

Q: I am a Dutch maker of ABC product who aims to take advantage of the Algerian EMA and sell my product to Algeria. However, I soon realised that the Algerian authorities imposed higher taxes on my product which, although not produced in that country, competes against Algerian-made CDE product with similar features and characteristics to ABC. Can I do anything about this?

A: The short answer is no. The Taxation Provision in the Algerian EMA bans discriminatory taxation between domestic and imported

---

7 Case 196/85 *Commission v France* [1987] ECR 1597.

products identical in terms of features and characteristics. Similarity between ABC and CDE is not sufficient. Since no directly competing product exists, the Algerian authorities have the right under the EMA to impose differential taxation, even if that potentially harms imports.

Q: I am a Turkish manufacturer of ABC product where my main foreign market is Luxembourg. The tax authorities of that country announced a new tax proposal, which effectively puts my exports at a competitive disadvantage compared to CDE product produced in Luxembourg. ABC and CDE are dissimilar to one another. Is this tax proposal legal, if enacted?

A: In principle, the answer to your question is no. The Turkish EMA provides that neither Luxembourg nor Turkey may impose on the products of the other party any internal taxation of such a nature as to afford indirect protection in favour of domestic products. This paragraph applies where there are no domestic products similar to imported products. It covers all forms of indirect tax protection in the case of products, even though dissimilar, are nevertheless in (partial, direct or potential) competition with certain products of the importing party. Thus, it prohibits taxation, which does not directly discriminate between ABC and CDE products but has the effect of putting the former at a competitive disadvantage relative to the latter.

According to EU case law, it is the competitive effect of the tax difference, which determines whether the difference amounts to such discrimination. Therefore, to be prohibited, the proposed taxation must have the effect of reducing potential consumption of ABC to the advantage of CDE. The mere fact that imports may be restricted by tax measures does not necessarily mean the tax measures are prohibited. This paragraph seeks to eliminate all forms of protectionism resulting from the application of internal taxation, which discriminates against a party's goods or is protectionist in scope. In other words, it aims to guarantee generally the neutrality of the systems of internal taxation with regard to trade between the EU (in your case Luxembourg) and Turkey whenever the prospective tax is triggered.

If you cannot establish that there is distortion of competition contrary to the EMA, then the proposed tax proposals in Luxembourg are perfectly legal.

So, you need to have proof in the form of economic reports etc to demonstrate that this tax proposal potentially reduces the consumption of your ABC product to the advantage of CDE. In other words, the proposal alters the nature and structure of competition in the relevant market so that CDE benefits at your expense.

Chapter 4

Free Movement of Services and Establishment Rights

4.1 Introduction

The provision on the free movement of services is designed to supplement the Goods Provision, namely by extending the principles of free movement to the trade in services (Services Provision). This extension includes rights of establishment, *i.e.* the right of one party's firms to set up on the other party's territory.

4.2 Services Provision

"1. The Parties agree to widen the scope of the [Euro-Mediterranean] Agreement to cover the right of establishment of one Party's firms on the territory of the other and liberalisation of the provision of services by one Party's firms to consumers of services in the other.

2. The Association Council will make recommendations for achieving the objective described in paragraph 1.

   In making such recommendations, the Association Council will take account of past experience of implementation of reciprocal most-favoured-nation treatment and of the obligations of each Party under the General Agreement on Trade in Services annexed to the Agreement establishing the WTO [World Trade Organisation], hereinafter referred to as the 'GATS', particularly Article V of the latter.

3. The Association Council will make a first assessment of the achievement of this objective no later than five years after the Agreement enters into force.

   ...   In accordance with the GATS, [most-favoured-nation] treatment shall not apply to:

   (a) advantages granted by either Party under the terms of an agreement of the type defined in Article V of the GATS or to measures taken on the basis of such an agreement;

   (b) other advantages granted in accordance with the list of exemptions from most-favoured-nation treatment annexed by either Party to the GATS."

Pursuant to the Services Provision, the Association Council will make recommendations to the parties for taking the necessary steps to extend the coverage of the EMAs to free movement of services and establishment rights, subject to exceptions allowed under the General Agreement on Trade in Services (GATS). In essence, this amounts to enacting measures granting one party's service-providers the right to supply services or establish firms in another party's territory under the same laws, rules and regulations accorded to domestic suppliers or firms. That is, such "foreign" suppliers are not to be discriminated against directly on the basis of nationality.

As can be seen above, the Association Council must take into account the GATS upon recommending any measures implementing the Provision. Therefore, this chapter will briefly outline the GATS. But, before doing so, first, it is important to define the words "services" with respect to the free movement of services, and "firms" and "establishment" in relation to establishment rights and, secondly, to discuss the exceptions allowed from the Provision.

Services

This term is likely to cover economic activities, which are intangible and involve an element of commercial motivation, such as transport, advertising and the transmission of television signals (but not films, which are considered as goods). On the other hand, state education is not a service nor are sports provided on considerations of purely sporting interest.

Firm and establishment

"Firm" is likely to cover a company or firm, which has its registered office, central administration or principal place of doing business in the territory of a party to an EMA under its national laws. If a company or firm has its registered office in one party's territory, its operations must possess a "real and continuous link" with the economy of that party. This means the business concerned would have to enjoy legal status in the territory in the EMA country of origin, and its activities would need to relate to activities in the country of origin. However, it would not appear that it would have to maintain, for instance, personnel in the country of origin unless this were a prerequisite of its legal status under the country of origin's national law. Thus, for example, a company set up in Egypt and undertaking all its activities in Sudan is not regarded as a company or firm within the scope of the Services Provision.

In respect of firms or companies, "establishment" means the right to take up and pursue economic activities by means of setting up and managing subsidiaries, branches and agencies. "A subsidiary" means a company, which is effectively controlled by the parent. "Economic activities" include activities of an industrial or commercial character, activities of craftsmen and activities of professionals.

4.3 **Derogation**

It is likely that the recommmendations by the Association Council implementing the Services Provision will allow for exceptions on the grounds of public policy, public security or public health. Moreover, it will not apply to activities connected, even occasionally, with the exercise of official authority, such as the administration of justice. It is arguable that these exceptions will be interpreted restrictively, just like the derogation from the Goods Provision as discussed in Chapter 2, paragraph 2.4.

4.4 **GATS in a nutshell**

GATS (sometimes referred to as the Services Agreement) is the first multilateral agreement covering trade in all services sectors, except those provided in the exercise of governmental authority. The basic principles of the Services Agreement are similar to those of the GATT, namely:

- **national treatment**: each WTO member should not treat foreign services and service-suppliers less favourably than its nationals;
- **most-favoured-nation treatment** (MFN): each WTO member should not discriminate between other WTO members in terms of the treatment accorded to their service-suppliers;
- **transparency**: relevant policies, including barriers to market access and discriminatory restrictions, must be published; and
- **progressive liberalisation**: binding commitments on the negotiated levels of market access and national treatment make the process of liberalisation irreversible, and provide the basis for future rounds of negotiations.

Unlike the GATT, however, the Services Agreement covers not just cross-border trade, but every means by which services can be traded. Four types of supply are included:

(1) Cross-border supply;

(2) Consumption abroad (*i.e.* foreign nationals consuming services in the territory of a WTO member);

(3) Supply through commercial presence, meaning the supply of a service in a foreign country through a commercial presence established there; and

(4) Supply through the movement of natural persons working abroad to supply a service.

The GATS is organised in two parts: the framework agreement (with sectoral annexes dealing with specific services like financial and maritime) and the national schedules of specific commitments on market access and national treatment for all services or specific sectors undertaken by each member government. The Final Act contains 95 certified schedules (the European Union has submitted a common schedule on behalf of its Member States, indicating specific commitments at the national level, where applicable). It provides explicitly for future rounds of negotiation with a view to achieving a progressively higher level of liberalisation.

Nature of the commitments

In its national schedule each member government inscribes the service sectors and activities to which it will apply the market access and national treatment obligations of the GATS. In addition, it must indicate any limitations, which it intends to maintain on market access and national treatment for those sectors or activities. Every such indication in a schedule is a binding commitment to allow supply of the services in question on the terms and conditions specified, and not to impose any new measures that would restrict entry into the market or operation of the service. Commitments can only be withdrawn or modified after the agreement of compensatory adjustments with affected members. The schedules thus provide economic operators trading or investing in a foreign market – and domestic customers of foreign service-suppliers – with the assurance that the conditions of entry and operation in the market will not be changed to their disadvantage.

The national schedules all conform to a standard format, which is intended to facilitate comparative analysis. In nearly all schedules commitments are split into two sections: "horizontal" commitments applying in all sectors included in that schedule, such as a restriction on a purchase of land by foreigners; and secondly, "sector-specific" commitments applying to particular services or activities. Any evaluation of the access provided for any given service must take into account both horizontal and sector-specific commitments. In assessing commitments undertaken in national schedules, two considerations are of special relevance: the sector coverage (*i.e.* the sectors, sub-sectors and activities included in the schedule) and depth of a particular commitment (*i.e.* whether or not it is subject to limitations).

Derogation from basic principles

GATS provides for three exceptions to its basic principles:

(1) Governments can choose the services in which they make market access and national treatment commitments.

(2) They can limit the degree of market access and national treatment they provide (for example, the EU's audio-visual exception).

(3) They can take exception even from the MFN, although it is a general obligation applicable to all measures affecting trade in services. Measures inconsistent with this obligation can be maintained – in principle for not more than 10 years and subject to review after five years. Such measures are specified in national lists of MFN exemptions.

General derogation

The GATS does not cover government procurement of services for non-commercial purposes nor national measures which are:

- necessary to protect public morals or to maintain public order;
- necessary to protect human, animal or plant life or health;
- necessary to secure compliance with laws or regulations which are consistent with the Services Agreement. This includes the prevention of deceptive and fraudulent practices, dealing with the effects of a default on services contracts, the protection of individual privacy and safety;

- inconsistent with the national treatment principle, provided that the difference in treatment is aimed at ensuring the equitable or effective imposition or collection of direct taxes in respect of services or service-suppliers of other members; and
- inconsistent with the MFN principle, provided that the difference in treatment is the result of an agreement on the avoidance of double taxation or provision on the avoidance of double taxation in any other international agreement or arrangement by which a member is bound.

Any derogation measure must not constitute a means of arbitrary or unjustifiable discrimination between countries where like conditions prevail, or a disguised restriction on trade in services.

There is a broad exemption for services related to issues of national security and the military.

Article V GATS Agreements

Article V of the GATS permits members to enter into an agreement liberalising trade in services between or among the parties to such an agreement, provided that it:

- has substantial sectoral coverage (this condition is understood in terms of the number of sectors, volume of trade affected and modes of supply. In order to meet this condition, agreements should not provide for the *a priori* exclusion of any mode of supply); and
- provides for the absence or elimination of substantially all discrimination in the sectors outlined in sub-paragraph (a) of Article XVII of the GATS (*e.g.* transport) by prohibiting new discriminatory measures and/or eliminating existing ones;

either at the entry in force of that agreement or on the basis of a reasonable time-frame.

4.5 Jordanian EMA and non-WTO members

All the EMAs where both parties are WTO members make two essential commitments.

(1) The parties re-affirm their reciprocal obligations under the GATS, and in particular the MFN obligation (although subject to both the

general and specific exemptions under the GATS itself and the parties' schedules to it).

(2) The parties will aim to widen the scope of the EMA to liberalise trade in services.

Jordan is not a member of the WTO, and so rather than merely referring to and re-affirming the MFN non-discrimination commitment found in the GATS, the Jordanian EMA puts in place a similar legal framework. Under this EMA, MFN treatment will apply reciprocally to the establishment of firms, except in the air, inland waterways and maritime transport sectors. There is also a national treatment commitment in relation to subsidiaries of Jordanian firms established within the EU, in respect of their operations. This applies to firms already established within the EU at the time of the EMA coming into force and to firms established thereafter once they are established. The effect therefore is that the national treatment commitment does not extend to establishment itself but only to the regulation of the business operations once the firm is established. It is also subject to the proviso in relation to the needs of prudential supervision. There is an additional commitment not to introduce further restrictions on establishment and to the possibility of taking steps towards mutual recognition of qualifications. All these provisions are fully reciprocal.

As far as services are concerned, the parties agree to use their best endeavours to allow progressively the supply of services, acting on recommendations of the Association Council. After five years, the parties will consider the possibility of negotiating an Article V GATS agreement, taking into account the "approximation" (*i.e.* the alignment) of laws that has taken place in relation to the relevant activities.

4.6 **Turkish EMA**

The free movement of services and establishment rights in the Turkish EMA are similar to the other EMAs and therefore all the comments in this chapter apply with equal force and effect. However, in one aspect the EMA goes further: the rights of establishment extend to individuals. This means Turkish and EU nationals have a right to take up economic activities (*i.e.* of a commercial, industrial or professional nature) as self-employed persons and to set up undertakings[1] which

---

1 The term "undertakings" has been defined in Chap 7, para 7.3.

they effectively control. Moreover, the scope of this right includes the ability to enter the other party's territory and set up as a self-employed person. At the same time, the motive or intention of the person who wishes to be self-employed is irrelevant. However, the right does not include seeking or taking employment in the labour market or confer a right of access to the labour market of the other party.

In the case of *Asscher*,[2] the Court of Justice defined self-employment as the situation where a person is not subordinated to another person or organisation, but is performing services for remuneration.

4.7 **What if ?**

Q: I am a Finnish provider of ABC services who wants to establish an office in Jordan. Will the Jordanian EMA make it easier for me to achieve my objectives?

A: The Jordanian EMA ensures that the MFN principle relating to rights of establishment of firms applies to you, so that any advantages that it has conferred to other trading countries are extended to you. In respect of the national treatment principle (*i.e.* the application of domestic laws on establishment to you), Jordan undertakes to take the necessary steps to achieve this endeavour in the future, (including the possibility of Jordan recognising Finnish qualifications and vice versa).

The latter position is also true for the provision of services. Jordan and the EU may conclude in five years' time an agreement to liberalise the supply of services between them (*i.e.* an Article V GATS agreement). Essentially, this means that both parties are likely to extend the national treatment principle to the other party's service-providers.

Under present circumstances, once you have set up a company in Jordan, the Jordanian EMA guarantees that you are governed by the same rules as those applicable to your Jordanian rivals.

---

2 Case 107/94 *Asscher* [1996] All ER (EC) 757.

Chapter 5

Free Movement of Capital and Payments

5.1 Introduction

For the last few decades, most Middle Eastern and North African countries, and quite a few EU Member States, had strict controls on the free movement of capital and current payments. For instance, foreign investors had to go through complex government procedures to repatriate profits they earned on their investments. However, the recent tide of liberalisation of capital movements/current payments have swept away much of this labyrinth of Byzantine controls in favour of free or relatively free movements of such capital/current payments. Even Egypt, a country renowned for its controls, has replaced them with a free regime, which has done much to attract foreign portfolio and direct investments. Now, the EMAs have codified liberalised capital/current payments regime between the parties (Capital Provision).

5.2 The Capital Provision

"Subject to the provisions [below], the Parties undertake to allow all current payments for current transactions to be made in a freely convertible currency.

1. With regard to transactions on the capital account of the balance of payments, the [European] Community and [the MNC] shall ensure, from the entry of this [Euro-Mediterranean] Agreement, that capital relating to direct investments in [the MNC] in companies formed in accordance with current laws can move freely, and that the yield from such investments and any profit stemming therefrom can be liquidated and repatriated.

2. The Parties shall consult each other with a view to facilitating, and fully liberalising when the time is right, the movement of capital between the Community and [the MNC].

Where one or more Member States of the Community, or [the MNC], is in serious balance of payments difficulties, or under threat thereof, the Community or [the MNC], as the case, may, in accordance with the conditions established under the General Agreement on Tariffs and Trade [GATT] and Article VIII and XIV of the Articles of Agreement of the International Monetary Fund [IMF], adopt restrictions on current transactions which shall be of limited duration and may not go beyond what is necessary to remedy the balance of payments situation. The Community or [the MNC], as the case may be, shall inform the other Party forthwith and shall submit to it as soon as possible a timetable for elimination of the measures concerned."

Under this Provision, the parties promise to permit the free movement of current payments and capital relating to direct investments, and in time this should embrace all types of capital. Also, current payments for current transaction may be made in a freely convertible currency (*e.g.* the Euro). However, they may impose temporary restrictions on current transactions in the event of a balance of payments crisis by following the conditions of Articles VIII and XIV of the GATT and the IMF Articles of Agreement. These Articles essentially require that any restrictions for balance of payments purposes must be of limited duration and should be done in the least trade disruptive manner. Restrictions should favour price-based measures, like import surcharges and import deposits, rather than quantitative restrictions, like quotas. There are procedures for consultations by the GATT Balance of Payments Committee as well notification of the balance of payments measures.

5.3 Turkish EMA

The Capital Provision in the Turkish EMA is very similar to the above provision and therefore all comments in this chapter apply with equal force and effect.

5.4 What if ?

Q: I am a Belgian multinational company and I have invested about Euros 300 million in Syria. What impact will the Capital Provision have on me?

A: This Provision will ensure that you will be able to repatriate freely current payments, capital relating to your direct investments and profits out of Syria. In other words, it removes capital controls without the risk of re-imposition by Syria, except in well-defined circumstances involving a balance of payments crisis and for a limited period of time.

Chapter 6

(Un)free Movement
of Persons

6.1 Introduction

Without any doubt, the most illiberal provisions in the Euro-Mediterranean Agreements relate to the movement of persons. Europeans exhibit a strong desire to restrict the entry of Mediterranean peoples for a variety of reasons. Moreover, the EMAs are dissimilar regarding the rights granted to such peoples: the Maghreb and the Turkish EMAs grant more rights to their citizens than the other EMAs. This chapter will discuss the provisions on the movement of persons as found in the Maghreb EMAs as a group, the Turkish EMA separately and the rest of the other EMAs grouped together.

6.2 Maghreb EMAs

The Maghreb EMAs have granted essentially the same rights to their workers as those in the previous Maghreb Co-operation Agreements. These rights on working conditions, remuneration and dismissal are reciprocal, thus benefiting Maghreb citizens employed in the EU and EU citizens employed in a Maghreb country.

Working conditions

Maghreb EMAs contain a provision on non-discrimination as regards working conditions, remuneration and dismissal for those who are legally employed within the EU (illegal migrants are specifically excluded). The European Court of Justice considered this provision in depth in *El-Yassini*[1]. It involved a Moroccan who was given "leave" (*i.e.* permission) to enter the United Kingdom as a visitor with a restriction

---

1 Case C-416/96 *El-Yassini v UK Secretary of State for the Home Department*, judgment of 2 March 1999, printed on the EU web site www.europa.eu.int

prohibiting employment. Subsequently, the UK government refused to extend his leave to remain in the country. El-Yassini later married a British national, as a result of which his employment restriction was removed and his leave to remain was extended for 12 months. He was in gainful employment until he separated from his wife. The UK Immigration Adjudicator found that the case included no marriage of convenience or sham arrangement to enable El-Yassini to obtain leave to remain in the United Kingdom. He later applied for a further extension of his leave under the above provision contained in the EU-Moroccan Co-operation Agreement (the predecessor to the Moroccan EMA).

The Court found that this provision was directly effective.[2] It also said that an EU Member State is not prevented in principle from refusing to extend the residence permit of a Moroccan national where the original reason for the grant of his leave to stay (*e.g.* marriage) has expired by the time the residence permit expires. The situation would be different only if that refusal were to affect the right to engage in employment duly granted by the competent national authorities for a period exceeding that of his residence permit. It is for the national court to determine whether that is the case.

It should be noted that workers who have been allowed to undertake paid employment within an EU Member State "on a temporary basis" are entitled to equal treatment with regard to working conditions and remuneration.

Social security

These EMAs prohibit discrimination against Maghreb workers and members of their families living with them in the field of social security, a provision that was ruled to be directly effective in the *Kziber*[3] case. In that case and *Yousifi*,[4] the Court of Justice applied its case law on Council Regulation 1408/71[5] to the interpretation of the provision on social security. Moreover, it construed the term "worker" as including those who have permanently left the labour force as a result of retirement, illness or injury.

---

2 For an explanation of "direct effect", see Chap 19, para 19.2 (6).
3 Case C-18/90 *ONEM* v *Kziber* [1991] ECR 199.
4 Case C-58/93 *Yousifi* v *Belgium* [1994] ECR I-1353.
5 On the application of social security schemes to employed persons and their families moving within the EU (JO 1971 L149/2). This Regulation is the primary source of the EU's rules on social security entitlement. It guarantees that nationals from one Member State working in another Member State have equal access to social security schemes upon the same terms as nationals of the host state.

In *Krid*[6] the Court also gave a wide interpretation of "workers and members of their families living them" ruling that the term applies to a member of family who continued to live in a Member State after the death of a migrant worker. A further significant aspect of the *Krid* case is its insistence that "workers and the members of their families" are entitled to the same rights. The Court refused to make a distinction between "personal" rights of the worker and "derived" rights (*i.e.* those to which the person is entitled not in their own right but as a family member of a "worker"). This view was further endorsed in the case of *Babahenini*.[7]

The provision on social security has essentially two elements. First, there is the equal treatment clause:

> "…workers of [Maghreb] nationality and any members of their families living with them shall, in the field of social security, enjoy treatment free from any discrimination based on nationality relative to nationals of the Member States in which they are employed."

The term "social security" has been defined in conformity both with Regulation 1408/71 and the Court's case law. It includes sickness and maternity benefits, invalidity, old-age and survivors' benefits, industrial accident and occupational disease benefits and death, unemployment and family benefits.

There are three other specified rights:

(1) The of right of "aggregation"[8] of periods of insurance, employment and residence in various Member States for the purposes of entitlement to social security benefits (including sickness and maternity benefits, invalidity and survivors' benefits, pensions and annuities) and medical care for workers and family resident in the EU.

(2) The right to family allowances for family members resident in the EU.

(3) The right to transfer pensions and other benefits (including invalidity resulting from industrial accident or occupational disease) to the state of origin.

Implementing rules are to be adopted by the Association Council and these are likely to have direct effect.

---

6 Case C-103/94 *Krid v CNAVTS* [1995] ECR I-719.
7 Case C-113/97 *Henia Babahenini v Belgium* [1998] ECR I-183.
8 See definition of "aggregation" below.

The meaning of aggregation

The collective nature of social insurance co-ordination rules is reflected in the principle of aggregation, which requires the competent authorities of a Member State to take into account rights earned in another Member State when computing certain benefits guaranteed by Regulation 1408/71. This principle applies to a Member State whose legislation makes the acquisition, retention or recovery of the rights to benefits conditional upon completion of periods of insurance, employment or residence. It must treat such periods completed in another Member State as if they were periods completed under its own legislation. The result is the verification of the entitlement to a given benefit.

6.3 **Turkish EMA**

The EU-Turkey Association Agreement provides that the:

> "Contracting Parties agree to be guided by Articles 48, 49 and 50 of the Treaty establishing the Community[9] [the EC Treaty provisions dealing with the free movement of workers] for the purposes of progressively securing freedom of movement of workers between them."

To that end, the Additional Protocol lays down the timetable for the progressive attainment of freedom of movement for workers between the EU Member States and Turkey and provides that the Association Council is to decide the rules necessary to that end. The Protocol also provides that EU Member States cannot discriminate as regards conditions of work and remuneration between Turkish workers employed in the Community and workers who are nationals of other EU Member States.

Decision 1/80

The EU-Turkish Association Council, on the basis of the Association Agreement and Additional Protocol, passed Decision 1/80[10] concerned with rights to Turkish workers already legally resident and employed within the Community, but not conferring rights of entry into the European Union.

---

9   The numbering of Arts, 48, 49 and 50 of the EC Treaty has changed to Arts 39, 40 and 41 respectively since the Amsterdam Treaty took effect on 1 May 1999.
10 Dec 1/80 was never published in the *Official Journal*.

A Turkish worker duly registered as belonging to the labour force of a Member State is entitled in that state, after one year's legal employment, to the renewal of his work permit for the same employer. After three years' legal employment, such a worker is entitled to respond to another offer of employment for the same occupation made under normal conditions and provided he is registered with the employment services of the relevant Member State. However, this right is subject to the priority given to workers from the Member States. If the worker has been in four years' legal employment in the relevant Member State, he enjoys free access to any paid employment of his choice in that State.

The *Bozkurt*[11] case declared very clearly that the term "worker" does not include those who have permanently left the labour force as a result of retirement, illness or injury. This concept was further elaborated in *Birden*[12]. It is defined in accordance with the objective criteria, which distinguish the employment relationship, by reference to the rights and duties of the persons concerned. In order to be treated as a worker, a person must pursue an activity, which is genuine and effective, to the exclusion of activities on such a small scale as to be regarded as purely marginal and ancillary. The essential feature of an employment relationship is that for a certain period of time a person performs services for and under the direction of another person in return for which he receives remuneration. By contrast, the nature of the legal relationship between the worker and the employer is not decisive for the purposes of determining whether a person is a worker.

What happens if there are interruptions during a Turkish worker's legal employment? The Decision says that annual holidays and absences shall be treated as periods of legal employment. Periods of involuntary unemployment duly certified by the relevant authorities and long absences on account of sickness shall not be treated as periods of legal employment.

The European Court of Justice so as to imply a right of residence has extended the employment rights mentioned above. In the case of *Sevince*[13], the Court found that the EU rules on the renewal of work permits could not be fully effective without the renewal of residence permits, provided that the person concerned was in a stable position on

---

11 Case C-434/93 *Bozkurt* [1995] ECR I-1475.
12 Case C-1/97 *Birden*, judgment of 26 November 1998, printed on the EU web site: www.europa.eu.int; OJ 1998 C20/7.
13 Case C-192/89 *Sevince* [1990] ECR I-3461.

the employment market. In *Kus*[14], the Court ruled that the obligation to renew a Turkish worker's work permit also presupposed the renewal of his residence permit, even if the marriage through which the right was acquired was subsequently dissolved.[15] In other words, a Turkish right to reside in a Member State exists as a corollary of their right to work permits.

Being duly registered as belonging to the labour force

The *Birden* case interpreted this concept as whether the legal relationship of employment of the person concerned can be located within the territory of a Member State. In addition, it includes an employment relationship, which retains a sufficiently close link with that territory. This determination should take into account in particular the place where the Turkish national was hired, the territory on or from which the paid activity is pursued and the applicable national legislation in the field of employment and social security law. The concept must be regarded as applying to all workers who have complied with the requirements laid down by the laws and regulation of the Member State concerned.

Legal employment

The Court has sought to clarify the concept of "legal employment". In *Ertanir*[16], it ruled that a Turkish national who has been lawfully employed in a Member State for an uninterrupted period of more than one year and is duly registered as belonging to the labour force of that state should be regarded as legally employed there. In addition, the calculation of the one-year period must include short periods during which the Turkish worker did not hold a valid residence or work permit in the host Member State, provided its competent authorities have not called into question the legality of the residence of the worker on that ground.

In the case of *Günaydin*[17], the Court stated that a Turkish worker lawfully pursuing a genuine and effective economic activity and employed in a Member State for three years could seek renewal of his

---

14   Case C-237/91 *Kus* [1992] ECR I-6087.
15   According to Council Reg 1612/68 (JO 1968 L257/2) the family members of an EU worker (*e.g.* his spouse) exercising his freedom of movement have the right to enter and reside with him and the right to take up employment.
16   Case C-98/96 *Ertanir* [1997] ECR I-5179.
17   Case C-36/96 *Günaydin* [1997] ECR I-5143.

residence permit. This should be the outcome notwithstanding that he obtained the residence and work permits solely to prepare for employment in a Turkish subsidiary of a specific employer. In other words, the specific purpose, which the paid employment sought to achieve, cannot deprive a Turkish worker's rights under the Decision. Moreover, this case supported the contention that the Decision does not make the recognition of the right it confers on Turkish workers subject to any condition connected with the reason for which the right to enter, work or reside was granted. In *Eker*[18], the Court ruled that the extension of a Turkish worker's residence permit in the host Member State is subject to his having been employed continuously for one year with the same employer.

Further, the *Birden* case decided that a Turkish worker who has lawfully pursued a genuine and effective economic activity and satisfied the requirements in the Decision is entitled to demand the renewal of his work permit even if his employment was financed by public funds.

Has the Court spelt out the situations which should not be regarded as "legal employment" and therefore outside the ambit of the Decision? In *Sevince*,[19] the Court declared that the legality of the employment presupposes a stable and secure situation as a member of the labour force of a Member State and, by virtue of this, implies the existence of an undisputed right of residence. Hence, a Turkish worker was not in stable employment during a period in which a decision refusing him the right of residence was suspended as a consequence of his appeal against that decision. Pending the outcome of the dispute, he obtained authorisation on a provisional basis. This dispute related his rights to reside and be employed in the Member State in question.

Likewise, in *Kus*, the Court found that a Turkish worker fails the stability test where his right of residence is only due to the effect of national legislation allowing a person to provisionally reside in the host country pending the final outcome of the procedure for granting him a right of residence.

The case of *Kol*[20] has also specified that periods in which a Turkish national was employed under a fraudulently obtained residence permit, which led to a criminal conviction, are not secure and stable. This is in view of the fact that during those periods, the person concerned was not legally entitled to a residence permit.

---

18 Case C-386/95 *Eker* [1997] ECR I-2697.
19 See fn 13.
20 Case C-285/95 *Kol* [1997] ECR I-3069.

It seems, however, that the longer the period of employment, the more lenient the Court of Justice becomes in its interpretation of what constitutes stability in the labour force of a Member State. In *Recep Tatik*[21], the Court ruled that a Turkish worker who has been legally employed for more than four years in a Member State may decide to leave voluntarily in order to seek new work in that state. He enjoys a right of residence for a reasonable period for the purpose of finding new paid employment, even if he is unable to find a new employment relationship. Throughout this period, the worker must be duly registered as belonging to the labour force of the relevant Member State complying with any requirements of the legislation in force in that state. One example of such a requirement would be registering as a person seeking employment and making himself available to the employment authorities. It is for the Member State to fix such a reasonable period, which must be sufficient not to jeopardise (factually-speaking) his prospects of finding new employment.

Family members

Family members of a Turkish worker are entitled to certain employment rights under Decision 1/80. According to the Decision, such members who have been authorised to join a Turkish worker are entitled to respond to any offer of employment after they have been legally resident for at least three years in the Member State. However, this is subject to the priority given to workers of the European Union. After five years of legal residency in the Member State, they enjoy free access to any paid employment of their choice.

The Court of Justice in *Selma Kadiman*[22] interpreted the above provision. It found that Member States are entitled to enact measures to ensure that the family members who claim their rights under the Decision must be with the Turkish migrant worker on the grounds of family unity conducive to the lasting integration of the worker into the host Member State. Accordingly, in order to avoid the risk that Turkish nationals might use sham marriages to benefit from the above provisions, Member States are allowed to demand evidence of actual cohabitation in the household with the relevant worker. Objective circumstances, such as distance from the place where the family

---

21   Case C-171/95 *Recep Tetik* [1997] ECR I-329.
22   Case C-351/95 *Selma Kadiman* [1997] ECR I-2133.

member works or is undergoing training, may justify him living separately from the Turkish migrant worker.

Moreover, the case stated that the family member who has joined a Turkish worker in pursuit of family unity must have resided in the relevant Member State without interruption for three years under the same roof. However, short interruptions of cohabitation not intended to detract from residence together in the host Member State must be assimilated to the periods during which the family member concerned has actually lived with the Turkish worker. This will apply to holidays or visits to the family of the person concerned in his country of origin or an involuntary stay of less than six months in that country. Similarly, in view of the fact that the rights are granted regardless of a specific administrative document (*e.g.* residence permit), account must be taken of any period during which the person concerned did not possess a residence permit for the purpose of calculating the three-year period. This applies especially to the situation where the competent authorities of the host Member State did not claim that due the lack of a residence permit, the person concerned was not legally resident, but on the contrary issued a new residence permit to him

Children of Turkish workers

Children of Turkish workers who have completed a course of vocational training in the host Member State may respond to any offer of employment, irrespective of the duration of their residency, provided one of their parents has been legally employed in Member State concerned for at least three years. In the case of *Eroglu*[23], the Court of Justice declared that children who complete vocational training are automatically entitled to work, which includes a right to reside.

In *Haydar Akman*[24], the Court of Justice found that a Turkish child who has completed a vocational training course in the host Member State was entitled to respond to any offer of employment there. Consequently, he must be issued with a residence permit when one of his parents has in the past been legally employed in that state for at least three years. However, it is not required that the parent in question should still work or be resident in the Member State in question when his child wishes to gain access to the employment market there.

---

23 Case C-355/93 *Eroglu* [1994] ECR I-5113.
24 Case C-210/97 *Haydar Akman*, judgment of 19 November 1998, printed on the EU website: www.europa.eu.int.

Decision 3/80

The EU-Turkey Association Council passed Decision 3/80.[25] This measure set out to co-ordinate the Member States' social security schemes with a view to enabling Turkish workers employed or formerly employed in the EU, members of their families and their survivors to qualify for benefits in the traditional branches of social security. To that end, the provisions of the Decision refer for the most part to Council Regulation 1408/71[26] on the application of social security schemes and their families moving within the Community. Also, they refer, albeit less frequently, to Council Regulation 574/72[27] which lays down the implementing measures and procedural rules for implementing Council Regulation 1408/71.

Consequently, the Decision requires Member States to co-ordinate their laws and policies on social security to allow Turkish workers and their families equal, non-discriminatory access as EU citizens would be entitled under Regulation 1408/71. The entitlements include maternity benefits, invalidity benefits, old-age benefits and death benefits (pensions), benefits in respect of accidents at work and occupational diseases, and death grants, together with family benefits and allowances. References in the Decision to Regulation 574/72 set forth the principle of the aggregation of such benefits for Turkish workers and their families. However, the supplementary implementing measures of the kind contained in that Regulation cannot be found in the Decision. In other words, the Decision does not have the detailed procedural rules necessary for its implementation.

The European Commission submitted a proposal in 1983 for a Council Regulation[28] implementing Decision 3/80 modelled largely on Regulation 574/72. To that end, it embodies detailed rules with a view to the application of the provision of the Decision in respect of each category of benefits coming within its scope. They also contain particulars relating to the prevention of overlapping benefits, determining the applicable legislation and aggregation of periods, together with financial and transitional provisions. The Council has not adopted the proposal.

In the *Taflan-Met*[29] case, the Court of Justice decided that a provision adopted by an Association Council, set up by an Association

---

25 Dec 3/80 was never published in the *Official Journal*.
26 Council Reg 14084/71 (Spec Ed OJ 1971 (I) 159).
27 Council Reg 574/72 (Spec Ed OJ 1972 (II) 461).
28 OJ 1983 C110/60.
29 Case C-277/94 *Taflan-Met* [1996] ECR I-4085.

Agreement to implement its provision might be directly effective.[30] This occurs when the wording of the provision and the purpose and nature of the Agreement itself are taken into account and the provision is found to contain a clear and precise obligation which is not subject, in its implementation or effects, to the adoption of any subsequent measure. That case concerned the right of Turkish migrant workers employed successively in more than one Member State, or the right of survivors of those workers, to certain social security benefits on the basis of technical provisions for the co-ordination of different national laws. The Court found that Decision 3/80, by its nature required the adoption of supplementary measures, just like Regulation 1408/71 which sought to co-ordinate the different social security legislation of the Member States, required the adoption of Regulation 574/72. In other words, the nature of the Decision needs to be supplemented and implemented by the Community by a subsequent act of the Council.

It follows that without the supplementary measures essential for implementing the Decision like the Commission proposal discussed, much of the Decision does not have direct effect in the Member States and therefore does not entitle individuals to rely upon it before the national courts.

Not all the provisions of Decision 3/80 lack direct effect. According to one provision, Turks resident in the territory of one of the Member States are subject to the same obligations and enjoy the same benefits under the legislation of any Member State as nationals of that State.

The European Court of Justice in the *Sürül*[31] case ruled that a Member State should not require a Turkish national authorised to reside in its territory to possess a residence entitlement or a residence permit in order to receive family allowances for his child, whilst nationals of that state are only required to be resident there. This must be the outcome irrespective of whether a Turkish worker only has a conditional residence authorisation issued for a specified purpose and for a limited duration.

The Court also ruled that the direct effect of this provision may not be relied on in support of claims relating to benefits prior to the date of the judgment (4 May 1999). There is one exception: those persons who before that date instituted legal proceedings or made an equivalent claim.

---

30 For a discussion of "direct effect", see Chap 19, para 19.2(6).
31 Case C-262/96 *Sema Sürül*, judgment of 4 May 1999, printed on the EU website: www.europe.eu.int.

6.4 **Other EMAs**

The rights of free movement in the other EMAs are far more limited in their coverage of workers' rights than the Maghreb EMAs and the Turkish Association Agreement. In the Israeli EMA, for example, there is no provision on equal treatment, either in relation to working conditions or in relation to social security. As far as social security is concerned, it does, however, provide for aggregation of periods of insurance, employment and residence, for transfer of pensions and benefits and for family allowances.

The Jordanian EMA is even more limited than the Israeli EMA in this area – which is also true of the Egyptian EMA. It does not contain any equal treatment provisions at all, either in relation to employment conditions or in relation to social security; nor does it contain the aggregation and transfer rules found in the Israeli EMA. There is merely a Joint Declaration referring to "fair treatment" and the possibility of future reciprocal agreements:

> "The Parties reaffirm the importance they attach to fair treatment of foreign workers legally resident and employed in their respective territory. The Member States agree that, if Jordan so requests, they are each prepared to consider negotiating bilateral reciprocal agreements relating to working conditions and social security rights of Jordanians and Member State workers legally employed and resident in their resident territory."

6.5 **Summary**

There exists a wide divergence in the levels of commitment in this field:

- the Maghreb EMAs contain an obligation of equal treatment with regard to working conditions and social security benefits, together with aggregation and transfer in relation to social security;
- the Turkish Association Agreement extends equality of treatment in the fields of working conditions and remuneration. Such treatment is somewhat lacking in the area of social security, since the necessary implementing legislation (*i.e.* supplying the procedural rules) has not been promulgated. Upon continuous employment with the same employer for specified periods of time, Turkish workers are entitled to the

extension of their work and residency permits, and eventual unimpeded access to the relevant Member States' labour market. These rights are non-transferable, meaning that Turkish workers moving from one EU Member State to another must satisfy those conditions all over again in the second state. For instance, Turkish workers moving from Germany to France must fulfil the conditions again in France before they could enjoy the rights under the Turkish Association Agreement in France. In other words, the rights obtained in Germany do not "move" with them to France;

- the Israeli EMA provides only for the aggregation and transfer in relation to social security benefits. Equal treatment provisions are not included;
- the Jordanian EMA embodies only a Declaration on the possibility of further negotiations on both working conditions and social security rights for migrant workers – which is also true of the Egyptian EMA .

A common characteristic shared by all the EMAs is that none of them regulate the rights of entry into a Member State, or access to its labour market. These are subject to the national laws and regulations of the individual Member States, and EU law (where applicable). Even the employment and residency rights conferred on Turkish workers only accrue by virtue of existing employment in a Member State, *i.e.* initial entry and access to the labour market is left to the discretion of that State.

6.6 **What if ?**

Q: I am an American manufacturer of ABC product with production facilities throughout the Middle East and North Africa. I wish to expand my operations into Germany, France and other EU Member States. Over the years, my Middle Eastern employees have accumulated much knowledge and experience in the production of ABC and so I want to employ them in the EU. Do the EMAs facilitate the movement of such employees?

A: No. In practical terms, these Agreements have no legal effects on the rights of entry into the Member States, or access to their labour markets. The national laws of those states and EU law (where applicable) govern these areas. You are best advised to ascertain the immigration laws of the various States and find out to what extent EU law may assist you. Alternatively, you may have to employ EU workers given the time, expense and difficulty of hiring employees from the MNCs.

Turkish workers are in the most advantageous position of all. They enjoy guaranteed rights to work and residency permits, provided they remain in continuous employment with the same employer for specific periods of time. But these rights only affect Turkish workers who are already employed in an EU Member State. In other words, rights of initial entry and access to a Member State's labour market depend on its national immigration laws and EU law (where applicable).

Chapter 7

· **Cartels** ·

7.1 **Introduction**

The Euro-Mediterranean Agreements include provisions prohibiting cartels and other collusive behaviour between two or more companies (Cartel Provision). To a large extent, those rules mimic the EC Cartel Provision. So, for example, companies are not allowed to fix prices or carve-up markets amongst themselves. These provisions are a potent weapon in the hands of exporters and investors whenever they face private arrangements between companies at the importing country which impede the marketing opportunities for their products and services.

7.2 **Cartel Provision**

"1. The following are incompatible with the proper functioning of the [Euro-Mediterranean] Agreement, in so far as they may affect trade between the [European] Community and [the MNC]:

(a) all agreements between undertakings, decisions by associations of undertakings and concerted practices between undertakings which have as their object or effect the prevention, restriction or distortion of competition;

2. Any practices ... shall be assessed on the basis of criteria arising from the application of Article 85.[1]

3. The Association Council shall, within five years of entry into force of the Agreement, adopt by decision the necessary rules for the implementation of paragraph 1."

According to paragraph 2 of the Cartel Provision, anti-competitive conduct must be assessed according to the rules and principles governing the EC Cartel Provision. In other words, the competitive effects of commercial practices are to be determined in accordance with

---

1 The numbering of Art 85 EC has changed to Art 81 EC since the Treaty of Amsterdam took effect on 1 May 1999.

the decisions of the European Commission (including Notices and Practice Statements), the Court of First Instance and the European Court of Justice. Therefore, reference will be made to EU law to explain the various elements of the Cartel Provision.

In the same regard, reference will also be made to secondary legislation. Paragraph 3 declares that the Association Council will promulgate the rules essential to implement the Provision. Since, no such rules have yet been passed under any EMA, resort (where necessary) will be had to those rules connected to the Central and Eastern European Association Agreements (cartel implementing rules).

Paragraph 1(a) prohibits:

- **undertakings** from anti-competitive **practices and conduct;**
- which **distorts competition;**
- and has an **effect on trade between the EU and the MNC.**

7.3 **Undertakings**

"Undertakings" has not been defined in the EMAs or in the Treaty of Rome. However, Advocate-General Roemer defined it in *Italy*[2] as entities pursuing economic or commercial activity irrespective of their legal form, which includes non-profit making bodies and co-operatives of individuals.

By contrast, subsidiaries may lack the autonomy from their principal company to be covered. Furthermore, bodies carrying out purely social functions and responsibilities, such as the administration of the public social security system, are not "undertakings".

7.4 **Practices and conduct**

Paragraph 1(a) targets agreements, decisions of associations of undertakings and concerted practices. The following concepts have been broadly interpreted and in reality they usually overlap:

---

2 Case 32/65 *Italy* v *Council and Commission* [1966] ECR 389.

1. Agreements between undertakings

Most types of agreements are covered ranging from "gentleman's agreements" to written or oral agreements expressed to be informal and binding. It is immaterial whether the agreement has been signed or that consent to its terms has been formally given. Thus, it need not contain all the terms decided between the parties; implied terms are also caught. Any motive underlying the agreement is irrelevant.

2. Decisions of associations of undertakings

The activities of trade associations are capable of control as either "agreements between undertakings" or "decisions of associations of undertakings". The Commission and the Court have tended to use both notions interchangeably and differentiation is therefore unnecessary.

3. Concerted practices

This is a broad concept, which basically deals with the situation where undertakings collaborate or co-ordinate their activities to replace the risks of competition or independent conduct in reaction to competitive pressures. It is sufficient that there is an intention to concert, even if there is no actual effects. So, for example, if two car manufacturers exchange information on pricing strategies or co-ordinate marketing campaigns, this constitutes concerted practice.

However, there exists the problematic issue of distinguishing between legitimate parallelism and unlawful concertatation. In oligopolistic markets in which a few enterprises dominate the market, it is quite natural for one enterprise to match the conduct of the other. The question arises of how to determine whether the first enterprise is copying the actions of the second, or whether both enterprises are concerting. According to the Court of Justice in the *Compagnie*[3] case, parallel conduct provides evidence of concertation where concertation is the only plausible explanation for such conduct. Consequently, undertakings are not penalised for reacting rationally to the actions of competitors.

---

3 Joined Cases 29 & 30/83 *Compagnie Royale Asturienne des Mines SA and Rheinzink v Commission* [1984] ECR 1679.

7.5 **Distortion of competition**

The Cartel Provision bans practices which "have as their object or effect the prevention, restriction or distortion of competition". Commission and Court practice shows that "prevention, restriction or distortion" are not independent concepts, but rather interchangeable terms with "distortion" being the key word.

What needs to be demonstrated is that the practice has as its object or effect the distortion of competition. "Object or effect" are both disjunctive; either will suffice on its own. Taking the "object" criterion first, the determination of the object or intended purpose behind an agreement depends on an objective assessment against its aims and structure, notwithstanding that the purpose may be diametrically opposed to the contractual parties' actual intentions. If the required object is missing, then all that needs to be shown is that the agreement has a nominal effect on competition; actual effect is not vital.

Distortion of competition entails that the nature and structure of competition in the relevant market has been altered by the existence of an anti-competitive agreement.

Examples of anti-competitive practices

Besides price-fixing and carving-up markets, there are many other practices that the Commission and the Court have declared to be anti-competitive; that is the state of competition in the relevant market is different than it would have been had the collusive practices (whether vertical[4] or horizontal[5]) been absent. Other prohibited practices include:

- product distribution agreements compartmentalising markets along national lines;
- the exchange of sensitive information between rival companies to secure markets;
- agreements linking the sale of one item to the sale of others.

Where the state promotes anti-competitive practices, then the Cartel Provision applies to the undertakings concerned. On the other hand, state measures strengthening such practices themselves violate the Provision.

---

4   "Vertical practices" refers to those arrangements between companies at different levels of the supply chain, such as between a distributor and a retailer.
5   "Horizontal practices" refers to those arrangements between companies at the same level of the supply chain, such as between two retailers.

7.6 **Effect on trade between EU and MNC**

Practices of undertakings that distort competition are prohibited, provided they affect trade between the EU and the MNC. This means that agreements between undertakings must be capable of constituting a threat, either direct or indirect, actual or potential, to freedom of trade in a manner which might harm the attainment of a Euro-Mediterranean free trade area. In other words, this requirement applies to agreements, which may alter the pattern of trade between the parties in such a way as to prejudice the attainment of this objective.

Although trade between the parties must be affected, it is unnecessary that the goods and services which are the subject matter of an agreement are themselves traded between the parties. In addition, such trade may cover the movement of suppliers as well goods and services.

De minimis issues

Agreements with a minor impact on trade and competition between the parties escapes the purview of the Cartel Provision. Its impact is dependent on whether a real, as opposed to theoretical, possibility exists that competition in such trade is distorted. The cartel implementing rules provides guidance on ascertaining if an agreement has minor trade ramifications. There is a refutable presumption that anti-competitive activities are minor if:

- the aggregate annual turnover of the "participating undertakings" is 200 million Euros; and
- the goods and services, the subject-matter of the relevant agreement, do not constitute 5 per cent or more of the total EU/MNC market for such goods or services.

Domestic agreements

Restrictive agreements between undertakings located within the same contracting party are covered by the Cartel Provision, where they make the inter-penetration of the domestic market more difficult for undertakings from the other party. For example, in *Delimitis*[6], an agreement that is part of a network of local agreements having a

6 Case 234/89 *Stergios Delimitis v Henninger Bräu AG* [1991] ECR I-935.

cumulative effect on competition in the relevant market falls foul of the Provision. Alternatively, agreements with effects localised within one party (*e.g.* within a particular region) are not covered. Factors such as the market position of the undertakings concerned and the agreement's impact on imports are necessary to enable such a determination to be made.

7.7 **Exemptions from the Cartel Provision**

Anti-competitive agreements may be exempted from the strictures of the Provision. This flexibility allows certain agreements to remain valid since either their anti-competitive effects are minimal or their positive effects in terms of technological progress and consumer welfare are greater.

Individual exemption

When an agreement is notified to the Commission[7] and the MNC competition authority an individual exemption may be granted, in effect declaring that the provision does not apply to it, provided four conditions of the EC Cartel Provision are satisfied.

(1) The agreement must contribute to improving the production and distribution of goods or to promoting technical progress. Commission practice suggests such a benefit must exceed any other benefit that would otherwise result from undistorted competition.

(2) Consumers should be allowed a fair share of the resulting benefits. The Commission tends to assume that the second condition is met whenever the first condition is satisfied, in the event that a sufficient degree of competition endures in the relevant market.

(3) Restrictions must not be imposed on the undertakings concerned, which are not indispensable (*i.e.* not vital) to the attainment of the

---

7 The Commission's procedures used in competition cases are contained in Council Reg 17/62 (JO 1962 204/62). There are many proposals, which can be found on the EU website www.europa.eu.int, involving overhauling the EU procedure for administering EU competition law. The heart of these proposals is that administration will be decentralised to the Member States with the power to exempt "routine" competition matters, whereas important competition questions will be dealt by the European Commission Competition Directorate-General. These proposals may take effect by 2002/2003.

objectives of the first condition.

(4) The undertakings must not be afforded the possibility of eliminating competition in respect of a substantial part of the free trade area.

Group exemptions

Group exemptions can be found in "block Regulations" for:

- exclusive distributorship agreements;[8]
- exclusive purchasing agreements,[9]
- patent licensing agreements;[10]
- specialisation agreements;[11]
- research and development agreements;[12]
- air transport arrangements[13] and co-operation;[14]
- franchise agreements,[15]
- know-how licensing agreements;[16]
- insurance;[17]
- maritime transport;[18]
- motor vehicle distribution and servicing agreements;[19] and
- technology transfer agreements.[20]

Agreements meeting all the conditions stipulated by these Regulations are exempted without prior notification to the relevant competition authority. According to the cartel implementing rules, the parties must apply the exemptions in full. Where an agreement fails to meet the conditions, an individual exemption can still be sought. The Commission has recently expressed an intention to replace by the year 2000 all

---

8 Commission Reg 1983/83 (OJ 1983 L173/1).
9 Commission Reg 1984/83 (OJ 1983 L173/5). A Commission Notice (OJ 1984 C101/2) deals with both types of agreements.
10 Commission Reg 2349/84 (OJ 1984 L219/15).
11 Commission Reg 417/85 (OJ 1985 L53/1).
12 Commission Reg 418/85 (OJ 1985 L53/5).
13 Commission Reg 3976/87 (OJ 1987 L374/9); Commission Reg 83/91 (OJ 1991 L10/9); Commission Reg 3652/93 (OJ 1993 L333/37).
14 Commission Reg 1617/93 (OJ 1993 L155/3).
15 Commission Reg 4087/88 (OJ 1988 L359/46).
16 Commission Reg 556/89 (OJ 1989 L61/1).
17 Commission Reg 1534/91 (OJ 1991 L143/1).
18 Commission Reg 479/92 (OJ 1992 L55/3) and Commission Reg 3652/93 (OJ 1993 L333/37).
19 Commission Reg 1475/95 (OJ 1995 L145/25).
20 Commission Reg 240/96 (OJ 1996 L31/2).

block exemptions (except the motor vehicle block exemption) with one all-encompassing exemption dealing with "vertical restraints" (*i.e.* anti-competitive restrictions in agreements involving contractual parties at different stages of the supply chain). The proposed changes mean that the Commission will adopt a more economic based approach to the assessment of vertical restraints. It will promulgate new legislation to confirm that:

- certain "hardcore" restrictions will always infringe the Cartel Provision irrespective of the market shares of the contractual parties involved and can never be exempted. The list will include restrictions imposing fixed or minimum resale prices and the restriction or prevention of "passive sales" (*i.e.* selling products to customers without active solicitation);
- agreements for both sale of goods and services will not normally infringe the Provision where the parties have a market share not exceeding 30 per cent and can therefore be block exempted;
- agreements which contain only certain types of restriction or combination of such restrictions can be similarly exempted where the market shares of the parties are between 20-30 per cent; and
- above 30 per cent no general presumption of exemption can be made. The Commission will however issue a detailed guideline on how it will apply the provision and in what circumstances it will grant an individual exemption.

Rule of reason

The Court of Justice introduced a "rule of reason" into EU competition law so that agreements promoting fair competition in structural terms and enabling new entrants to participate in a unified market are outside the scope of the Provision. For instance, the European Court has found in *Viho*[21] that both franchise agreements and selective distribution agreements can include clauses which select distributors on the basis of qualitative (such as the technical knowledge of staff) rather than quantitative criteria (*e.g.* the level of sales). Such criteria, however, must not be unduly restrictive and "parallel importation" (the importation of a product from one party

---

21   *Viho/Toshiba*, Commission Dec 91/532 (OJ 1991 L287/37).

to the other, even though both are lawfully marketed in both contracting parties) must not be prohibited.

7.8 **Intellectual property rights**

The exercise of intellectual property rights must not distort competition. Conversely, EU law respects the "specific subject matter" of such rights. The subject matter of a patent, for example, is the guarantee that the patent-holder has the exclusive rights to use an invention with a view to manufacturing industrial products and putting them into circulation for the first time, either directly or indirectly by granting licences to third parties. It also includes the right to oppose infringements.

The Cartel Provision does not generally interfere with the "existence" of the rights, except where the specific subject-matter is abused. However, the anti-competitive exercise of such rights is prohibited. For instance, the exercise of trade mark rights in a restrictive agreement designed to exclude imports bearing a similar mark to the products at issue is unlawful.

7.9 **Coal and steel industries**

The EMAs extend the principles of the Treaty on European Coal and Steel Community (ECSC Treaty), and related secondary legislation, to the regulation of competition in the coal and steel sectors.[22] Generally, the applicable principles and derogations are similar to the ones described above.

7.10 **Agriculture**

The Cartel and Monopoly Provisions[23] apply generally to all agreements, decisions and practices, which relate to the production or trade in

---

22 Turkey has concluded a free trade agreement with the ECSC covering ECSC products. It includes provisions similar to those in the Turkish EMA but specific to the coal and steel sectors. Examples of such provisions are the Goods Provisions, Cartel Provision, rules of origin etc (OJ 1996 L227/3).
23 The Monopoly Provision is discussed in Chap 8.

agricultural products in accordance with Council Regulation 26/62.[24]

However, there is one main exception. The Cartel Provision does not apply to agreements, decisions and practices, which form an integral part of a national market organisation of the agricultural market or are necessary for the attainment of the following objectives:

(1) Increasing the agricultural productivity by promoting technical progress and by ensuring the rational development of agricultural production and the optimum utilisation of the factors of production, in particular labour.

(2) Ensuring a fair standard of living for the agricultural community, in particular, by increasing the earnings of persons engaged in agriculture.

(3) Stabilising markets.

(4) Assuring the availability of supplies.

(5) Ensuring that supplies reach consumers at reasonable prices.

In particular, the Cartel Provision does not apply to agreements, decisions and practices of farmers, farmers' associations or associations of such associations belonging to a single country which concern:

- the production or sale of agricultural products; or
- the use of joint facilities for the storage, treatment or processing of agricultural products

as long as there is no obligation to charge identical prices and that the objectives 1 to 5 above are not jeopardised.

7.11 **Turkish EMA**

The wording of the Cartel Provision in the Turkish EMA is an exact replica of the EC Cartel Provision and is therefore slightly different from the wording in the EMAs. However, these differences are not too significant. Therefore, everything mentioned above applies to Turkey.

---

24 JO 1962 993.

7.12 **What if ?**

Q: I am a Finnish producer of ABC product with Tunisia being my biggest export market. Recently, XYZ Limited and 123 Limited, Tunisian producers and distributors of ABC respectively, concluded a verbal agreement to prevent me from using 123's extensive distribution network. This leaves me with little alternative since this is the only viable network. Is this illegal under the Cartel Provision?

A: Yes. All the elements of the provision are satisfied. First, two undertakings have concluded an agreement. The fact that it was unwritten is immaterial. Secondly, this agreement distorts competition since the nature and structure of the competition in the Tunisian ABC market has been altered by the existence of the agreement. Lastly, there is clearly a demonstrable effect on the pattern of trade between Tunisia and the EU. However, you will need to ensure that the agreement is not exempted under the rules on *de minimis* or the distribution block exemption.

Q: I am a Syrian manufacturer of ABC product and I have concluded an anti-competitive exclusive purchasing agreement with XYZ Limited which does not come within the exclusive purchasing block exemption and it is not *de minimis*. Can I seek an exemption for this agreement?

A: Yes, provided the relevant Syrian competition authority is satisfied that you have adequately complied with the four conditions stipulated under the EC Cartel Provision in accordance with EC law. You should note that you might not find it easy to comply with these conditions, as EU law allows for exemptions in exceptional circumstances only; generally where the consumer benefits greatly outweigh the anti-competitive effects of the agreement. You should also note that an exemption might be granted with conditions attached to minimise the latter effects.

Chapter 8

· Monopolies ·

8.1 Introduction

The promotion of competitive markets may be an elusive objective if the EMAs solely prohibited cartels. Unsurprisingly, the regulation of monopolies is an essential ingredient to enable foreign producers and service providers to enter or compete in new or existing markets. Therefore as a counterpart to the Cartel Provision, the EMAs also incorporate a provision controlling the behaviour of monopolies (Monopoly Provision). Both provisions work in tandem with a view to eliminating market-partitioning activities in the Euro-Mediterranean marketplace.

8.2 Monopoly Provision

> "1. The following are incompatible with the proper functioning of the [Euro-Mediterranean] Agreement, in so far as they may affect trade between the [European] Community and [the MNC]:
>
> (b) abuse by one or more undertakings of a dominant position in the territories of the Community or of [the MNC] as a whole or in a substantial part thereof.;
>
> 2. Any practices ... shall be assessed on the basis of criteria arising from the application of Article 86[new Article 82].
>
> 3. The Association Council, shall within five years of entry into force of the Agreement, adopt by decision the necessary rules for the implementation paragraph 1."

Like the Cartel Provision, paragraphs 2 and 3 entail respectively that reference will be made to EU law and the implementing rules (where necessary). The rules are the same ones as for the cartel implementing rules.

As can be seen from paragraph 1(b), monopolistic behaviour is only prohibited where:

- one or more **undertakings**;
- in a **dominant position** in the Community or the MNC;
- **abuse** this dominance;
- which has an **effect on trade** between the parties.

8.3 **Undertakings**

"Undertakings" has the same definition as provided in Chapter 7, paragraph 7.3.

8.4 **Dominant position**

Conduct attributable to an undertaking enjoying a dominant market position (*viz* the ability of an undertaking to operate independently of its competitor's actions) is regulated by the Provision. The determination of this dominance depends on the size of the particular market; the larger the market, the less likely the undertaking in question is in a dominant position. For instance, ABC Limited, a prominent manufacturer of telephones, is more likely to dominate the specific telephone market than the general market for communications equipment. It is evident, therefore, that the definition of the size of the relevant market is of crucial importance for the determination of dominance. Definitions of market size are based on geographical and economic considerations.

Geographical considerations

This refers to the territory in which all the traders concerned are exposed to objective conditions of competition that are similar or sufficiently homogenous. For example, XYZ Limited, an Italian company, sells pasta in Italy and Tunisia where the competitive pressures are so similar that ABC faces severe competition from other pasta producers in both markets; in this case the pasta market encompasses Italy and Tunisia. But, 123 Limited decides to export pasta to Egypt, a country with an indigenous pasta maker, which is preferred by the local people to imports. In this situation, the nature of the competition in Egypt is dissimilar to Italy; the former has a dominant producer, the latter a vibrant competitive market. Therefore, the pasta market would exclude Egypt.

Economic considerations

The definition of the relevant market includes goods or services that are substitutable with the goods or services of the undertaking in question. Their substitutability (or interchangeability) depends fundamentally on their objective characteristics, by virtue of which they appropriately satisfy the needs of consumers. Another important factor is the structure of supply and demand, including the conditions of competition, in the market under consideration. Two prominent EU competition cases illustrate the interplay of both factors.

In *United Brands*[1], the issue was whether there was a distinct market for bananas separate from the market for fresh fruit generally. According to the Commission, there was little cross-elasticity of demand (*i.e.* substitutability), since only banana tasted like banana. After much agony, the European Court of Justice agreed with the Commission, observing that bananas were a vital source of nutrition to babies, the elderly and sick because, unlike many other fruits, it was produced all year round and was easy to peel.

In *Continental Can*[2], the issue was whether there was a separate market for meat tins, fish tins, metal closures for glass jars distinct from the general market for tins. The Court of Justice examined the substitutability of production and found that that no distinct market for the former existed. Although Continental Can was a major manufacturer of tins, it was not considered as a dominant producer.

Assessment of dominance

Once the size of market is defined, it is important to determine whether the undertaking dominates the market: is it able to behave independently of competitive pressures, in accordance with the test outlined by the *United Brands* case? This is simply a matter of economic power. One of the strongest indicators of dominance is market share. In *United Brands*, for example, 40-45 per cent of the market in which the company was operating was sufficient to give it dominance, given the fragmented nature of the market. Other indicators include the ability of an undertaking to discriminate on pricing (*Michelin*[3]) and existing barriers to market entry by new undertakings (*ECS/AKZO*[4]).

1 Case 27/76 *United Brands* v *Commission* [1978] ECR 207.
2 Case 6/72 *Continental Can* v *Commission* [1973] ECR 215.
3 Case 322/81 *Michelin NV* v *Commission* [1993] ECR I-3461.
4 *ECS/AKZO*, Commission Dec 85/609 (OJ 1985 L374/1).

8.5 **Abuse**

The notion of abuse is a nebulous concept without definition in the EC Treaty or the EMAs. However, the case law appears to imply that abuse entails conduct which is objectionable in itself to the detriment of final consumers. Moreover, the Provision states clearly that dominance itself is not unlawful but rather the abuse of such dominance. In effect, leading companies bear a special responsibility not to distort the conditions of competition on the market. A fundamental rule of thumb is that a dominant undertaking must not act beyond the legitimate boundaries of a commercial transaction.

There are four broad categories of conduct considered abusive, though the list below is far from exhaustive:

1. Unfair pricing.
2. Discrimination.
3. Consolidation of a dominant position.
4. Commercial acceptability.

1. **Unfair pricing**

The European Court regards excessively high (or low) price by dominant undertakings as abusive and unfair (*General Motors*[5]).

2. **Discrimination**

Discrimination on the basis of nationality or pricing may be abusive. This happens where a dominant undertaking favours some undertakings over others on the basis of national origin. For instance, in the case of *Sacchi*[6], the matter in dispute was the legality of the exclusive right of the Italian state to operate television. The Court found that discrimination as to access to television advertising between the undertakings and products of one Member State and those of another Member State is abusive. In other words, the Italian state-owned television station could not grant more favourable access to advertising to, say, German cars over, say, British cars.

---

5 Case 26/75 *General Motors v Commission* [1975] ECR 1367.
6 Case 155/73 *Giuseppe Sacchi* [1974] ECR 409.

3. Consolidation of a dominant position

This deals with the situation where a dominant undertaking takes steps to maintain and enhance its market dominance at the expense of effective and open competition. A typical example is the refusal of a prominent undertaking to supply a certain product essential for the exercise of a given activity, in that there is no actual or potential substitute. In the *Hilti*[7] case, Hilti was a leading producer of fastening nail guns in Europe which refused to supply cartridges to Profix Distribution Limited, a manufacturer of nails intended for the Hilti guns. Profix complained that Hilti was trying to exclude them from the market by refusing to supply cartridges other than those designed for a certain quantity of nails. Without these cartridges, the nails could not be sold. Both the Commission and the Court of First Instance found this conduct to be abusive and therefore contrary to the EC Monopoly Provision.

4. Commercial acceptability

Commercially acceptable conduct in a given industry/market or certain state of circumstances is not abusive. Hence, dominant undertakings may charge differential prices if justified by objective and commercially viable reasons. For example, a dominant Tunisian textile company may charge higher prices for clothes according to the complicated nature of the industrial processes and quality standards of the material used.

It seems that commercial practice/usage is an important factor. In the case of *BP*,[8] the Court of Justice ruled that in an international oil shortage it was not abusive to cut supplies to occasional customers more than in the case of special or contractual customers. Once the state of affairs cease or differential pricing is based on subjective factors (*e.g.* the identity of the customer), then the conduct becomes abusive.

8.6 Effect on trade

This concept has the same meaning as provided in Chapter 7, paragraph 7.6. In the case of *Alsatel*,[9] there were telephone system

---

7 Case T-30/89 *Hilti* v *Commission* [1991] ECR II-1439.
8 Case 77/77 *BP* v *Commission* [1978] ECR 1583.
9 Case 247/86 *Alsatel* v *Novasam NV* [1988] ECR 5987.

and rental agreements between Alsatel and its customers. The Court noted that only contractual terms restricting imports of telephone equipment from other Member States affected trade between them. No such evidence existed and so Alsatel's conduct was not unlawful.

8.7 **Intellectual property rights**

The exercise of, or (sometimes) the acquisition of intellectual property rights, may be prohibited by the Monopoly Provision. For instance, refusal to license materials to third parties protected by copyright (*RTE*[10]) or the imposition of arbitrarily fixed and unfairly high royalties for such materials (*Tournier*[11]) might be contrary to the Provision.

8.8 **Coal and steel industries**

The EMAs extend the principles of the ECSC Treaty and related secondary legislation, to the regulation of competition in the coal and steel sectors. Generally, the applicable principles and derogations are similar to the ones described above.

8.9 **Turkish EMA**

The wording of the Monopoly Provision in the Turkey Agreement is an exact replica of the EC Monopoly Provision and is therefore slightly different from the wording in the EMAs. However, these differences are not too significant. Therefore, everything mentioned above applies to Turkey.

8.10 **What if ?**

Q: I am a British exporter of ABC product (or an independent trader in ABC product) and I tried to export ABC to Egypt. However, the local producer of ABC, XYZ Limited, a dominant company owned by the state, refused to allow me to sell my goods through its

---

10 Case T-69/89 *RTE* v *Commission* [1991] ECR II-485.
11 Case 395/87 *Ministère Public* v *Jean-Louis Tournier* [1989] ECR 2521.

distribution network. In effect, my product was excluded from the Egyptian market, since XYZ had an exclusive distribution network for ABC product in Egypt. Is the company's conduct regulated by the Monopoly Provision?

A: Yes. The fact that XYZ is owned by the state is immaterial. XYZ is an "undertaking" for the purposes of the Monopoly Provision even though it is state-owned, since the producer is an entity carrying out commercial or economic activities. To decide whether the provision prohibits the exclusion of the marketing and sale of your product, you need to determine whether XYZ is abusing its dominant position, thereby affecting the trade of ABC between the EU and Egypt. There is a strong indication that XYZ is in a dominant position because it possesses the sole distribution network for ABC product in Egypt. In addition, XYZ seems to be abusing its dominance by refusing to sell your product potentially harming the interests of Egyptian consumers. Also, XYZ's conduct clearly alters the pattern of trade between Egypt and the EU because your product is unable to penetrate the Egyptian market.

Q: I am a Tunisian manufacturer of ABC product, which I primarily sell in Lyons, France. XYZ Limited, a French producer of DEF material which is essential (though not vital) for the production of ABC, will only supply me with DEF on the condition that I do not sell ABC in Lyons. What should I initially do to compel XYZ to supply me with DEF?

A: Here, the fundamental issue is the size of the market for ABC product. On the assumption that XYZ's conduct may affect Tunisian exports of ABC into France, you must define the market in which XYZ operates using economic and geographical considerations to ascertain if XYZ is in a dominant position. The bigger the market, the less likely that XYZ is in a dominant position. Taking economics first, your comment that DEF is important, but not vital, for the production of ABC suggests that there are adequate substitutes for DEF, so that the market would be likely to include substitute materials, thereby making the size of the market larger. On the second factor, the main issue is to what extent are the Tunisian and EU markets for DEF considered similar. You need to ask questions, such as: what is the level of competition for DEF in the EU and Tunisia? The greater the similarity of market conditions for DEF, the larger it becomes since that would embrace both Tunisia and EU. Once the market is defined, you should also look at such indicators of dominance as the market share of XYZ so that the likelihood of it being dominant increases. You should try to define the market as narrowly as possible. It may be advisable to instruct consultants to study the whole question of the size of the market.

Q: I am a Moroccan exporter of ABC product to Italy. I am certain that XYZ, an Italian producer, dominates the Italian market. XYZ has signed distribution agreements with Italian village shops. My economic experts assure me that the terms of the agreements affect only a small number of villages in Southern Italy and do not in anyway restrict the sale of Moroccan-made ABC product. Can the provision assist me in any way?

A: No. First, your experts admit that the agreements do not affect imports so trade between the EU and Morocco is not affected. Secondly, it is possible that those agreements are accepted commercial practice in the relevant industry, and if this is so, then XYZ's conduct is not abusive.

Chapter 9

· **State Aid** ·

9.1 **Introduction**

State aid to local enterprises is a type of anti-competitive conduct where the hand of government is most visible. In the Middle East (and Europe to a smaller extent), the state tends to provide financial or other type of assistance to public and private undertakings deemed worthy of such assistance. The EMAs would have created a noticeable omission if state aid were not controlled, especially since subsidised imports unfairly damage local producers. Unsurprisingly, there are extensive provisions in the Euro-Mediterranean Agreements (State Aid Provision) to ensure public funds are not misused to the disadvantage of imports.

9.2 **State Aid Provision**

"1. The following are incompatible with the proper functioning of the [Euro-Mediterranean] Agreement, in so far as they affect trade between the [European] Community and [the MNC]:

(c) any state aid which distorts or threatens to distort competition by favouring certain undertakings or the production of certain goods with the exception of cases in which derogation is allowed under the Treaty establishing the European Coal and Steel Community.

2. Any practices contrary to this Article shall be assessed on the basis of criteria arising from the application of the rules of Article 92 [new Art 87] and in the case of products falling within the scope of the European Coal and Steel Community, the rules of Articles 65 and 66 of the Treaty establishing that Community, and the rules relating to state aid, including secondary legislation.

3. The Association Council shall within five years of the entry into force of this Agreement, adopt by decision the necessary rules for the implementation of paragraphs 1 and 2.

Until these rules are adopted, the provisions of the Agreement on interpretation and application of Articles VI, XVI and XXIII of the General Agreement on Tariffs and Trade shall be applied as the rules of the implementation of paragraph 1(c) and related parts of paragraph 2.

4. (a) For the purposes of applying the provisions of paragraph 1(c), the Parties recognize that during the first five years after the entry into force of the Agreement any state aid granted by [the MNC] shall be assessed taking into account the fact [the MNC] shall be regarded as an area identical to those areas of the Community described in Article 92(3)(a) of the Treaty establishing the European Community [new Art 87(3)(a)...

The Association Council shall ... decide whether the five years should be extended.

(b) Each Party shall ensure transparency in the area of state aid, *inter alia* by reporting annually to the other Party on the total amount and the distribution of the aid given and by providing, upon request, information on aid schemes. Upon request by one Party, the other Party shall provide information on particular individual cases of state aid

7. Notwithstanding any provisions to the contrary adopted in accordance with paragraph 3, the Parties shall exchange information taking into account the limitations imposed by the requirements of professional secrecy."

There are special arrangements dealing with state aid to the coal, steel, agriculture and fishery industries.

Although much of the Provision is self-explanatory, there are some complications in the Provision. According to paragraph 3, the Association Council must enact secondary legislation to implement the Provision (state aid implementing rules). At the time of writing, no such legislation has been negotiated between the EU and the MNCs. Therefore, resort (where necessary) will be made to the Central/Eastern European implementing rules.[1]

During the interim stage, Articles VI, XVI and XXIII of the GATT will govern state aid. Once implementing rules are passed, the EU control regime takes over. Hence, both stages are discussed below.

9.3 Articles VI, XVI and XXIII of GATT

These articles and related agreements make up the Agreement on Subsidies and Countervailing Duties (Subsidies Agreement). Its aim is to regulate the use of subsidies by WTO members by applying certain

---

1 Dec 1/98 of the EU-Czech Association Council (OJ 1998 L195/21).

disciplines only to "specific" subsidies (both domestic and export). These are subsidies available only to an enterprise, industry, group of enterprises or group of industries in the country that gives the subsidy.

A complaining country can use the WTO dispute settlement procedure to seek the withdrawal of the subsidy, or it can launch its own investigation and ultimately charge extra duty (known as "countervailing duty") on subsidised imports that are found to be damaging domestic producers.

The Subsidies Agreement applies to all agricultural goods as well as industrial products, except when the subsidies conform to the WTO Agricultural Agreement. The definition for subsidies encompasses three categories:

1. Prohibited subsidies.
2. Actionable subsidies
3. Non-actionable subsidies.

1. Prohibited subsidies

These are subsidies that require recipients to meet certain export targets at the expense of imported goods. They are prohibited because they are specifically designed to distort international trade, and are therefore likely to damage other countries' trade. They can be challenged using the WTO dispute settlement procedure where they are handled under an accelerated timetable. If the dispute settlement procedure confirms that the subsidy is prohibited, it must be withdrawn immediately. Otherwise, the complaining country can take counter measures. If domestic producers are damaged by imports of subsidised products, countervailing duty can be imposed.

2. Actionable subsidies

In this category the complaining country has to show that the subsidy has an adverse effect on its interests. Otherwise, the subsidy is permitted. The Subsidies Agreement includes three types of damage they can cause. One country's subsidies can damage a domestic industry in an importing country. They can damage rival exports from another country when the two compete in a third country. And domestic subsidies in one country can damage exporters trying to compete in the subsidising country's domestic market. If the Dispute

Settlement Body rules[2] that the subsidy does have an adverse effect, the subsidy must be withdrawn or its adverse effect must be removed. Again, if domestic producers are damaged by imports of subsidised products, countervailing duty can be imposed.

3. Non-actionable subsidies

These can either be non-specific subsidies, or specific subsidies for industrial research and non-competitive development activity, assistance to disadvantaged regions, or certain types of assistance for adapting existing facilities to new environmental laws or regulations. Non-actionable subsidies cannot be challenged in the WTO's dispute settlement procedure, and countervailing duty cannot be imposed on subsidised imports. But the subsidies have to meet strict conditions.

Countervailing duties and other disciplines

Countervailing duty can only be charged provided the importing country has conducted a detailed investigation. There are detailed rules for deciding whether a product is being subsidised (sometimes a very difficult calculation), criteria for determining whether imports of subsidised products are damaging (*i.e.* causing injury to) domestic industry, procedures for initiating and conducting investigations. In addition, there are rules on the implementation and duration (normally five years) of countervailing measures. The subsidised exporter can also agree to raise its export prices as an alternative to its exports being charged countervailing duty.[3]

Least-developed countries and developing countries with a gross national product of less than US $ 1,000 per capita are exempted from disciplines on prohibited export subsidies. Other developing countries are given till 2003 to get rid of their export subsidies. Least-developed countries must eliminate import-substitution subsidies (*i.e.* subsidies designed to help domestic production and avoid importing) by 2003. For other developing countries the deadline is 2000. Developing countries also receive preferential treatment if their exports are subject

---

2 For a discussion of the Dispute Settlement Body and the WTO dispute settlement mechanism, see Chap 19, para 19.5.

3 The European Commission has published helpful guidelines for the calculation of the amount of subsidies in countervailing duty investigations (OJ 1998 C394/6).

to countervailing duty investigations. Transition economies must phase out prohibited subsidies by 2002.

9.4 **EU state aid regime**

According to paragraphs 3 and 4 of the State Aid Provision, once state aid implementing rules have been enacted, the EU state aid regime applies and in particular the rules and principles of Article 92 EC.[4]

As can be seen from paragraph 1(c) above, state aid only applies where it:

- is being provided by one of the parties;
- **favours** certain goods or undertakings;
- **distorts competition;**
- has **effects on trade between the contracting parties.**

9.5 **Definition of state aid**

State aid (loosely) is the provision of direct or indirect financial assistance by any level of government to a private or state-owned undertaking. Such assistance entails a benefit for the entity and a burden for the state, in that the former does not give anything in exchange for the assistance of the latter. Usually, there is a specific purpose connected to the provision of assistance.

Besides the direct supply of funds, EU law considers the following to be examples of state aid:

1. Credit

This concerns the supply of credit, including export credit, assistance with the costs of obtaining credit, and interest rates thereon, as well as a grant of a loan with inadequate security.

2. Guarantees

The provision of state guarantees, including comfort letters assuring lenders that the government stands behind an undertaking, constitutes aid.

---

4   The numbering of Art 92 EC changed to Art 87 upon the Treaty of Amsterdam entering into force on 1 May 1999.

3. Tax concessions

Aid may arise where the government reduces public charges imposed on undertakings through tax concessions. For instance, such concessions may entice a bank to finance a project which others are unable or unwilling to finance.

4. Social security concession

Assistance is provided where the state reduces social security burdens on entities, such as those under employment legislation or collective bargaining agreements with trade unions.

5. Low returns

The failure of the state to maximise returns on its capital may constitute aid. For example, a public authority grants aid when disposing an asset to a commercial interest trading in the EU or the associated country at below market price.

Coercive measures

The State Aid Provision deals exclusively with the state use of financial resources rather than with the state regulation of the use of such resources by others. This, however, does not mean that aid must be financed from state resources. For instance, the imposition of a levy by a public authority on a specific group of undertakings which is then used to favour certain goods or undertakings constitutes aid.

In *Kirasammer-Hack*[5], the Commission argued that the exemption of small companies from unfair dismissal legislation in Germany is state aid. However, the Court of Justice ruled that no aid was present, because the exemption only concerned the framework of legislative relations in small companies. This meant that the state was regulating the use of financial resources by others, which does not equate to the provision of state aid.

---

5   Case C-189/91 *Kirasammer-Hack v Sidal* [1993] ECR I-6185.

General state interventions

An important issue is to demarcate general state interventions through fiscal rules and social measures etc from the grant of aid. The established position is that the State Aid Provision does not demarcate general state measures of intervention by reference to their causes or aim but defines them in terms of their effects. Thus, the exemption of a particular industrial sector from the obligations under the social security system amounts to the grant of state aid, provided there are no justifications for the exemption in the nature or general scheme of the system.

Nationalisation

The nationalisation of a particular undertaking is outside the scope of the Provision where this resembles state investment. Conversely, the granting of assistance by public authorities for the public good is state aid.

The Commission distinguishes between the two characterisations by using the "private investor test" – whether the private investor would have provided the finance associated with state participation. In the *Belgium*[6] case, public authorities provided capital subscriptions to a Belgian producer of equipment for the food industry. Here, the Court of Justice accepted the Commission's characterisation of the subscriptions as aid, unless a private shareholder that disregards social or political considerations and concentrates on the probability of obtaining a return on capital (and ultimately profits) would have provided such assistance. With time, the private investor test has evolved, such that it is not about the "model" private investor, which would entail discrimination of the public sector's concerns for social/political considerations unrelated to profit. Rather, the test has more to do with the "reasonable" investor or entrepreneur who takes into accounts both profit-related and the wider social concerns.

Privatisation

The Commission generally favours privatisation since the reduction in the state sector enhances transparency in the grant of aid and may lead

---

6 Case 234/84 *Belgium v Commission: Meura* [1986] ECR 2263.

to increased competition. Its practice is elaborated in guidelines regarding privatisation.[7] For example, stock market flotation is generally assumed to take place on market conditions, whereas direct share sales is otherwise.

9.6 **Favouritism**

The Provision requires that certain undertakings or the production of certain goods must be favoured. This essentially means that there must be an element of discrimination or selection in the grant of aid. Moreover, aid that is formally available to undertakings generally may be treated as particularly favouring a sector or undertaking. An example would be that a greater reduction in social charges for female than male employees tends to favour undertakings with a disproportionate number of females.

9.7 **Distortion of competition**

In ascertaining whether there is a distortion of competition, the Commission tends to take into account the:

- direct and immediate impact of aid on the market position of the recipient;
- effects for potential competitors;
- "downstream" effects on competition in industries which purchase goods from the aided undertaking;
- consequences of aid provided for the production of raw materials on the costing of the final product or profit margins; and
- "upstream" effects where aid to the purchaser affects competition between producers.

There are usually two other considerations of vital importance:

1. Theory of the second best

This theory holds that aid, which merely corrects inefficient allocations associated with market imperfections, may not be regarded as

---

7 European Commission, *Twenty-Third Report on Competition Policy* (1994) Brussels, 255-256.

distorting competition. For example, an undertaking may be unable to appreciate the benefits of infrastructure and training, and so the market imperfectly provides them. Aid given to remedy this imperfection, provided it is not given for the exclusive benefit of certain undertakings, may not distort competition.

2. Market integration

This consideration holds that there is a connection between supervision of state aid and promotion of market integration, in that state subsidies to undertakings tends to partition markets. For instance, in the case of *Philip Morris*,[8] a Dutch aid scheme had been approved by the Commission, subject to the condition of prior notification of individual grants. One such grant was for Phillip Morris to close a cigarette factory in one location in the Netherlands and to expand capacity in another. Phillip Morris expected the project to lead it to half the manufacturing capacity of cigarettes in the Netherlands and expected that more than 80 per cent of its Dutch production would be exported to other EU Member States. The Court of Justice noted that the aid strengthened the position of one undertaking compared with other undertakings competing in trade between Member States. In particular, it reduced the cost of converting the production facilities and thereby gave the recipient a competitive advantage over manufacturers who had completed or intended to complete at their own expense a similar increase in the production capacity of the plant. The Court of Justice considered these effects sufficient to justify the Commission decision that the aid threatened to distort competition.

9.8 Effect on trade between contracting parties

Aid to economic sectors with "cross-border characteristics" may affect trade between contracting parties. This is because producers from the different parties may be in effective competition or the aid recipient is engaged in trade between the parties.

There are other factors usually taken into account. These include:

- aid strengthening domestic enterprises to the disadvantage of imports;

---

8 Case 730/79 *Phillip Morris v Commission* [1980] ECR 2671.

- absence of international trade in a product or lack of "trading infrastructure" by reason of high transport costs so that aid has minimal trade effects; and
- evolution of trading conditions, in that the more integrated the product markets are between the parties, the greater is the likelihood of the trade impacts of the aid given.

De minimis aid

There is a refutable presumption in the state aid implementing rules permitting aid programmes or individual aid awards, which do not involve export aid and which are limited to a total amount of aid per firm over a three-year period of Euros 100,000. Such awards have a "negligible effect on competition and trade between the parties."

This presumption does not cover the coal and steel industries, shipbuilding, transport, agriculture or fisheries. Moreover, the Association Committee must decide on maximum aid intensities and specific regional coverage of areas eligible for national regional aid.

9.9 Derogation from state aid provision

Paragraph 4(a) of the Provision, in accordance with Article 93(3)(a) EC,[9] allows aid which promotes economic development in areas where the standard of living is abnormally low or where there is serious underemployment.

The Arab MMCs will be regarded as such an area for the first five years of entry into force of an Arab EMA, unless the relevant Association Council agrees to extend the time period. The Commission has recently published guidelines on the implementation of the derogation.[10]

Compensatory justification

In pursuing a derogation from the Provision, the relevant monitoring authority must apply the principle of "compensatory justification".

---

9   The numbering of Art 93(3)(a) EC has been changed to Art 88(3)(a) since the coming into force of the Treaty of Amsterdam on 1 May 1999.
10   Guidelines on National Regional Aids (OJ 1998 C74/1).

According to this principle, aid falling foul of the Provision may only be authorised where it is necessary to accomplish one of the goals included in the derogation. This means aid will only be permitted if the market, unaided, would not produce the desired objective.

The national interests of a contracting party or the benefits obtained by the aid recipient do not in themselves justify an authorisation. Rather, the aid must contribute to the attainment of objectives, which under normal market conditions, the recipient firms would not attain by their own actions.

The rationale for this principle is that aid, which distorts competition will be authorised only to accomplish the objectives of the EMA and only in the presence of market failure. If market forces will accomplish the objectives without aid, and the aid will distort competition, then it will be prohibited. In other words, microeconomic inefficiency will only be accepted to the extent that it is necessary to alleviate macroeconomic problems.

9.10 Coal and steel industries

The EMAs extend the principles of ECSC Treaty and related secondary legislation,[11] to the regulation of state aid in the coal and steel sectors. Generally, the applicable principles and derogations are similar to the ones described above.

All the MNCs, except for Turkey and Israel have been granted a limited exception for granting aid to the steel industry. For the first five years of the entry into force of the EMA, the MNC may grant aid for restructuring purposes, provided that:

- it leads to the viability of the recipient firms under normal market conditions at the end of the restructuring period;
- the amount and intensity of such aid is strictly limited to what is absolutely necessary in order to restore such viability and is progressively reduced; and
- the restructuring programme is linked to a comprehensive plan for rationalising capacity in the MNC.

---

11   The related secondary legislation is Commission Decs 3855/91 (OJ 1991 L362/57) and 3632/93 (OJ 1993 L328/12).

The Association Council is empowered to extend the exemption period beyond five years.

9.11 **Agriculture**

The State Aid Provision does not apply to the production of or trade in agricultural products.

9.12 **Turkish EMA**

The Turkish EMA contains a clause similar to the State Aid Provision, though there are other derogations that are not contained in the other EMAs.

It is provided in the EMA that four categories of aid are compatible within the customs union. Aid falling within one of these categories is authorised as of right, provided that it is established that aid does so fall. Moreover, this type of aid should not be misused. The four categories are:

1. Social aid

This is aid with a social character and is granted to individual consumers, provided that it is granted without discrimination related to the origin of the products concerned.

The acquisition of wheat by the state and its subsequent resale at a discount, which has the effect of reducing bread prices, may be an example of aid covered by this category. Tax relief for individual consumers purchasing cars fitted with pollution reduction devices may be a further example.

2. Disaster aid

Aid to make good damage caused by natural disasters or exceptional occurrences is compatible with the functioning of the EU-Turkey customs union.

Earthquakes, volcanic eruptions, flood and weather of an exceptional and short-term character may be treated as such a disaster, where the damage suffered attains a certain severity at individual level. Apparently, temporary aid to re-establish the equilibrium disturbed is envisaged. Thus, aid to irrigation, granted even during "normal" weather conditions, is not covered by this derogation.

Exceptional occurrences for the purposes of this derogation may cover man-made damage, such as that associated with a strike, war serious internal disturbances, explosions or catastrophic mine accidents, or religious or social persecution.

3. Aid to Germany

The Turkish EMA provides that aid to the economy of certain areas of the Federal Republic of Germany affected by the division of Germany is compatible with the customs union, in so far as such aid is required to compensate for economic disadvantages caused by that division.

Deletion of this category is envisaged and the European Commission is apparently content to secure its strict interpretation and the gradual phasing out of the aid concerned, as a result of the re-unification of Germany.

4. Aid to less developed regions

Turkey may give aid to less developed regions for five years provided that such aid does not adversely affect trading conditions between the EU and Turkey to an extent contrary to the common interest.[12]

Discretionary aid

There are five categories of aid that may be considered as compatible with the customs union. In other words, the Commission and Turkish monitoring authority must exercise their discretion as to whether such aid should be authorised. In exercising this discretion, the regulators should consider whether:

- the aid promotes a project that is in the interest of the customs union area as a whole;
- the aid is necessary for the achievement of the outcome envisaged; and
- the duration, intensity, and scope of the aid are proportional to

---

12 According to Advocate-General Rozès in the *Tobacco* case, this condition is quite broad: *EC Commission v Italy: State monopoly of tobacco* [1983] ECR 1955.

the importance of the outcome.

These categories are:

1. Aid to peripheral regions

This was discussed in paragraph 9.9 above.

2. Aid to projects of common European interest and to remedy a serious disturbance

This paragraph provides that two kinds of aid may be considered compatible with the customs union. The first kind of aid concerned is one to promote the execution of an important project of common European interest. Such a project must form part of a transnational European programme supported jointly by a number of EU Member States and Turkey or arise from concerted action to combat a common threat, such as environmental pollution. The project must be promoted by the aid, in the sense that without aid the project would not go ahead or would only do so in such a manner that it would no longer be considered an important project of common European interest.

The second kind of aid is to remedy a serious disturbance in the economy of an EU Member State or Turkey. This disturbance must be cyclical rather than structural, and there must be an abnormal situation by reference to the cyclical fluctuations, which may be expected in the sector concerned. The disturbance must be serious by Turkish and EU standards. Apparently, a disturbance is not considered serious if it lacks national significance. At the same time, the aid must be of the appropriate scale and scope to remedy the disturbance. Hence, aid to a particular sub-sector, such as tomato farming, is not covered.

3. Aid for structural adjustment purposes

Aid may be given to achieve any structural economic adjustment necessitated by the establishment of the customs union. For instance, Turkey may able to grant aid to a specific industrial sector to fund projects designed to restructure that industry due to increased competition from EU companies as trade obstacles are dismantled. Such aid may only be given during a period of five years after the signing of the Turkish EMA. However, after that period, the Association Council will review the application this paragraph.

4. Aid for regional or sectoral development

This paragraph provides that aid to facilitate the development of certain economic activities or certain economic areas may be compatible with the customs union. However, the aid must not adversely affect trading conditions to an extent contrary to the common interest. These concern sectoral aid and aid to the "central regions".[13]

In considering whether to authorise such aid, the European Commission or the Turkish monitoring authority may have regard to considerations of international competitiveness and to any special rules for aid to the relevant sector. Special rules may apply to various sectors, including:

- agriculture;[14]
- fishing;[15]
- transport;
- shipbuilding;[16]
- textiles;[17]
- synthetic fibres;[18] and
- motor vehicles.[19]

Special rules also apply to aid to the coal[20] and the steel industries,[21] which are applicable to all the EMAs.

5. Cultural aid

This paragraph provides that aid to promote culture and heritage conservation may be compatible with the customs union. However, the aid must not affect trading conditions and competition in the customs union to an extent that is contrary to the common interest. It is likely

---

13 See para 9.9 above and Guidelines for state aid for undertakings in deprived urban areas (OJ 1997 C146/6).
14 Communication regarding state aid for investments in the processing and marketing of agriculture (OJ 1996 C29/4).
15 Communication for the examination of state aid to fisheries and aquaculture (OJ 1997 C100/12).
16 Commission Reg 1013/97 on aid to certain shipyards under restructuring (OJ 1997 L148/1).
17 Framework for aid to textiles (*Competition Law in the European Communities*, ii: *Rules Applicable to State Aids* (EC Commission, Brussels, 1990)).
18 Code on aid to the synthetic fibres industry (OJ 1992 C346/2).
19 Framework on state aid to the motor vehicle industry (OJ 1997 C279/1).
20 Commission Dec 3623/93 establishing EU rules for state aid to the coal industry (OJ 1993 L329/12).
21 Commission Dec 2496/96 establishing EU rules for state aid to the steel industry (OJ 1996 L338/42).

that Commission practice regarding aid to the Greek film industry will be followed.[22]

Moreover, Turkey is likely to be bound by guidelines concerning aid granted in pursuit of "horizontal" policies, that is policies not limited by region or industrial sector (*e.g.* research and development).

Additional derogation

The EU-Turkey Association Council may specify additional categories of aid which may be exempted from the State Aid Provision.

Coal and steel industries

The Turkish State Aid Provision applies to the ECSC Treaty products. However, Turkey may exceptionally grant public aid till 31 August 2001 regarding ECSC products on a case-by-case basis for conversion or restructuring purposes, provided that transparency is ensured by full and continuous exchange of information on the restructuring programme. Such information must include the amount, intensity and the purpose of the aid, and a detailed restructuring programme.

The restructuring programme must be linked to rationalisation not involving an overall increase in the capacity of hot-rolled products. It should also lead to the viability of the steel sector determined according to the usual viability criteria implying modernisation with the sole aim of improving efficiency of the benefiting firms under normal market conditions at the end of the restructuring programme. The amount of aid must not be out of proportion to its objectives and must be limited strictly in amount and intensity to what is absolutely necessary to restore viability.

Turkey must notify the EU in sufficient time of any aid proposed that it will grant under this derogation. The EU will have the right to raise reasoned objections in respect of aid, which does not comply with the above criteria.

If during this period of time, imports of specific steel in one party causes or threatens to cause serious injury to domestic producers of like products or serious disturbances to the steel markets of the other party, both contracting parties must consult one another immediately to find a

---

22 Commission Dec 89/441 on aid granted by the Greek government to the film industry for the production of Greek films (OJ 1989 L208/3)
23 For a discussion on "safeguard measures", see Chap 20, paras 20.2 and 20.4(2).

solution. Pending such a solution, the importing party may adopt in exceptional circumstances "safeguard measures",[23] namely quantitative restrictions (*i.e.* quotas) or other solutions. Such action may include quantitative restrictions limited to one or more regions that are affected by imports of these products in question.

9.13 **What if ?**

Q: I am a Jordanian producer of ABC product. I tried to export ABC to Spain, but I discovered that the Spanish government gives subsidies to my Spanish competitor, XYZ Limited, to my disadvantage. What shall I do?

A: Since the EU-Jordanian state aid implementing rules have not been passed yet, you must determine whether the WTO anti-subsidy rules apply. If they do, you should follow WTO procedures.

Once the implementing rules are enacted in the future, you will then need to ascertain if the subsidies come within the definition of state aid and if the other parts of the Provision, such as distortion of competition and effects on trade between the contracting parties, are met.

Chapter 10

· **Public Undertakings** ·

10.1 **Introduction**

Both the EU and MENA economies are dominated by public enterprises performing several social and economic functions. Naturally, such enterprises may have a profound effect on the condition of competition and trade in an economy as a result of the decisions they take. Therefore, the Euro-Mediterranean Agreements seek to regulate the decisions of public undertakings insofar as they do not distort trade from the other contracting party by means of subjecting such undertakings to certain obligations stipulated in the EMAs (Public Undertakings Provision).

10.2 **Public Undertakings Provision**

> "With regard to public enterprises and enterprises which have been granted special or exclusive rights, the Association Council shall ensure, from the fifth year following entry into force of the [Euro-Mediterranean] Agreement, that no measure which disturbs trade between the [European] Community and [the MNC] in a manner which runs counter to the interests of the Parties is adopted or retained. The provision shall not impede the performance in fact or law of the specific functions assigned to those enterprises."

The Provision obliges the Association Council to ensure that upon the fifth year of an EMA's entry into force, **public undertakings** cannot adopt a **measure**, which **disturbs trade** between the parties.

10.3 **Undertakings covered**

Public undertakings are those over which a state may exercise a dominant influence. For instance, a government's social security authority or exclusive private providers of telecommunications services are undertakings over which the state has much influence.

Generally, authorities acting in the public interest without a commercial objective are considered to be public undertakings.

10.4 Measure

The expression "measure" is broadly interpreted. It not only covers legally binding measures adopted by public authorities, but also non-binding "requests" from governments to undertakings covered by the Provision.

However, it appears from the *Macrotron*[1] case that a party does not violate the Provision simply by allowing conduct contrary to it. This case concerned the activities of the recruitment firms, which were tolerated by the German Federal Office for Employment in derogation from its own exclusive right of employment procurement. The European Court of Justice ruled that the EC Undertakings Provision would only be violated where a Member State created a situation in which an EU undertaking covered by the Provision could not avoid acting contrary to the requirements embodied in the Provision.

10.5 Disturbance of trade

The Cartel and Monopoly Provisions govern public undertakings with a commercial character. This means these undertakings must comply with those Provisions, including the ones integrated in the state administration system. However, public bodies exercising powers typically those of a public authority are outside the scope of these Provisions. In such circumstances, the party's actions are scrutinised under the Public Undertakings Provision.

The parties must ensure that their public authorities do not enact measures, which disturbs trade between them and runs counter to their interests. This Provision is very specific: what needs to be demonstrated is that actions of a public authority resulting from measures adopted by the relevant party must actually and directly, as opposed to nominally or indirectly, alter the pattern of trade between the parties. There must be explicit evidence demonstrating such trade effects. If evidence cannot be adduced showing actual trade ramifications, then the party is not in violation of the Provision.

---

1 Case C-41/90 *Klaus Höfner v Macrotron* [1991] ECR I-1979.

10.6 **Derogation**

The Provision clearly states that public undertakings are only subject to it insofar as they do not obstruct in law or in fact the specific functions assigned to the undertaking. This derogation is interpreted very strictly under EU law, which requires that the relevant function must be entrusted to a specific undertaking and must not arise from the application of general rules. Moreover, its performance must be put in jeopardy from the economic point of view and not simply made more difficult. Therefore, there must be no suitable alternative system.

At the same time, the activity of a public undertaking is strictly defined. For instance, in *Nungesser*[2], the European Court of Justice ruled that the derogation would not apply to the marketing arrangements of a public body established to promote research activity. While a public monopoly may be justified by reason of the need for cross-subsidies, the derogation does not apply to specific services separable from the service of general interest.

Subject to such strict interpretation, the derogation has been found to cover the grant of exclusive rights as regards the collection, carriage and distribution of mail. It may also cover state aid. The sole purpose of the aid must be to offset the additional costs incurred in performing the particular task assigned to the undertaking entrusted with the operation of a service of general economic interest. Moreover, the aid must be necessary to enable the undertaking to perform its public service obligations under conditions of economic equilibrium.

10.7 **Turkish EMA**

The Public Undertakings Provision in the Turkish EMA goes further than the other EMAs. It requires Turkey to enforce the principles of the EC Public Undertakings Provision, related EU secondary legislation and case law.

This means that both the EU and Turkey must not adopt measures infringing the Cartel and Monopoly Provisions in relation to public undertakings. Thus, public bodies are prohibited from restricting competition or abusing a dominant position. For instance, the Turkish social security office is prohibited from co-operating with Turkish firms

---

2 Case 258/78 *Nungesser v European Commission* [1993] ECR I-2553.

providing actuarial services to shut out similar firms from the EU. Such co-operation is contrary to the Cartel Provision and therefore in breach of the Public Undertakings Provision.

In addition, Turkey is obliged to comply with EU legislation promulgated to enhance the application of the Public Undertakings Provision in specific sectors, such as telecommunications.[3] There is a derogation similar to paragraph 10.6 above concerning undertakings entrusted with the operation of services of general economic interest or having the character of a revenue-producing monopoly.

10.8 **What if ?**

Q: I am a Lebanese provider of ABC services and the British Department for Social Security (DSS) is my principal customer. Unfortunately, the DSS has adopted an unofficial policy to avoid non-European ABC service-providers for no legitimate reason. I have specific evidence in the form of a well-researched study that this policy reduces trade flows between Britain and Lebanon. I think it is inconceivable that this policy is necessary for the operations and functions of the DSS. What is my legal position?

A: There are two potential Provisions which may assist your position: the Monopoly and the Public Undertakings Provisions. The Monopoly Provision is not applicable because the DSS as a public authority acts in the public interest (*i.e.* it has social responsibilities) without any "economic objects".

On the other hand, the Public Undertakings Provision may be applicable. The provision is designed for such undertakings as the DSS. The British government has adopted a "measure", even though it is not an official rule. You have specific evidence showing that the DSS policy actually reduces trade between Lebanon and Britain (and by extension the EU). It appears that the derogation from the Provision is inapplicable. The functions and responsibilities of the DSS (*i.e.* the Provision of social security services) are entrusted to it by specific legislation rather than by general laws. However, the measure is not vital for the performance of is functions. The DSS employed your services before the policy

---

3 Commission Dir 88/301 (OJ 1988 L131/73) on competition in the markets in telecommunications terminal equipment.

was enacted. This suggests that from an economic standpoint, its performance would not be put into jeopardy if the policy were revoked.

Chapter 11

· State Trading Monopolies ·

11.1 Introduction

A dominant feature of many MENA economies, and some European ones, is the prevalence of state-owned monopolies engaging in commercial activity. Their economic decisions have a noticeable impact on the level of trade between the EU and MENA. As a result, the EMAs regulate the activities of state trading monopolies so as to minimise the potential ramifications on EU-MENA trade (State Trading Provision).

11.2 State Trading Provision

> "The [EU] Member States and [the MNC] shall progressively adjust, without affecting commitments under the GATT, any state monopolies of a commercial character so as to ensure that the by the end of the fifth year of this [Euro-Mediterranean] Agreement, no discrimination regarding the conditions under which goods are procured and marketed exists between nationals of the Member States and [the MNC]. The Association Council will be informed about the measures adopted to implement this objective."

This Provision obliges EU Member States and the MNC to implement national measures eliminating discriminatory practices in the way goods are bought and sold by state trading monopolies. In simple terms, such monopolies must purchase and sell goods without resorting to considerations of national origin.

11.3 Objective and application of the Provision

The State Trading Provision concerns any body through which a contracting party, in law or in fact, either directly or indirectly, supervises, determines, or appreciably influences imports or exports between the parties. It applies to bodies, which have as their object transactions regarding a commercial product capable of being the subject of competition and trade between the parties and play an effective part in such trade.

Essentially, the purpose is to ensure that the sales policy of a public monopoly is subject to the requirements of the free movement of goods and the equality of treatment in the terms granted for the products concerned. Thus, this Provision only covers activities intrinsically connected with the specific business of the relevant monopoly. For example, a monopoly operating in one of the parties' territory would be prohibited from enjoying an exclusive right to import from the other party in relation to a specific product.

Existence of monopolies

The Provision does not necessarily require the abolition of state monopolies. It only seeks to control the practices of public monopolies that they do not subvert the objectives of the EMA, namely the Goods Provision.

A monopolist with exclusive rights to a certain product may invariably adopt sales policies favouring domestic producers at the expense of producers from the other contracting party. Therefore, the existence of state monopolies and the grant of exclusive rights to them may be permitted. However, the exercise of these rights is limited by the EMAs. Problems arise where the existence of such rights is, in practice, inseparable from the monopolist and thereby inherently discriminatory. In particular, an exclusive right of sale is considered intrinsically likely to cause discrimination within the meaning of the State Trading Provision.

In the case of *France*,[1] there was a French challenge to the legality of Council Directive 88/301 on competition in the markets in telecommunications terminal equipment. The Court of Justice found that an exclusive right to import and market, which deprived economic operators of the possibility of selling their products to consumers, to advise consumers or to guarantee the quality of the products, might be prohibited. This prohibition applied particularly where there was a wide range of technically different products, to such an extent that the monopolist might not be able to offer the whole range of products existing on the market. It seems the Court was exemplifying the scope of the prohibition of exclusive rights to import and market.

---

1 Case C-22/88 *France v Commission* [1991] ECR I-1223.

11.4 **Turkish EMA**

The only difference between the Turkish EMA and the other EMAs is that there is a bigger element of coercion on Turkey to adopt the State Trading Monopoly Provision, in the sense that the Association Council will enact measures stipulating conditions and timetables for the implementation of the Provision. On the other hand, the Association Councils in the other EMAs merely examine the national measures taken by each party to implement the Provision.

11.5 **What if ?**

Q: I am British seller of ABC product to Turkey, where the government has conferred on its state-owned monopolist, XYZ, an exclusive right to purchase and sell the product in Turkey. I am under the suspicion that this exclusivity may discriminate against me on the basis of my nationality (*i.e.* British) in favour of Turkish sellers and producers of ABC product. Can I challenge this exclusivity?

A: Yes, you can. The State Trading Provision ensures that publicly-owned monopolists treat Turkish and British nationals equally in the purchase and sale of ABC product, *i.e.* XYZ must be neutral as to considerations of nationality. Therefore, XYZ cannot adopt a purchase policy tailored to favour Turkish companies at your expense.

The Court of Justice has made it clear that while public monopolies are legal, an exclusive right of sale is considered inherently likely to cause discrimination within the meaning of the State Trading Provision. That is, XYZ exclusive rights to ABC will by itself discriminate between British and Turkish nationals. Consequently, this exclusivity may be illegal under the Turkish EMA.

Chapter 12

· **Public Procurement** ·

12.1 **Introduction**

Liberalisation of the public procurement market (*i.e.* where governmental entities award contracts to suppliers of goods or services) is one of the most contentious trade issues faced by the WTO. For the last 50 years, countries have attempted to open up this market at multilateral forums like the GATT and its successor, the WTO, with some success by striking delicate political compromises. The same features are also evident in the EU-MENA discussions to liberalise the procurement markets to each other's suppliers. Although the size of MENA governments (and European ones to a lesser extent) are shrinking as most states implement deep free market and structural reforms, government still remains a powerful actor in these economies. Therefore, the opening of government procurement markets may provide new commercial opportunities to foreign suppliers. As such, the EMAs contain a provision on public procurement (Public Procurement Provision).

12.2 **Public Procurement Provision**

> "1. The Parties [to the EMA] shall take as their aim a reciprocal and gradual liberalization of public procurement contracts.
>
> 2. The Association Council shall take the steps necessary to implement paragraph 1."

There is no timetable in the Provision for the "reciprocal and gradual" liberalisation of the procurement markets, but merely an obligation on the Association Council to enact measures to accomplish this aim. At the time of writing, Israel was the sole party to agree to such measures with the EU; two bilateral agreements were reached to liberalise the government and telecommunications sectors. These arrangements provide a strong indication of what type of procurement agreements the EU may conclude with other MENA countries in the future. Consequently, each agreement will be discussed below.

12.3 **EU-Israel Government Procurement Agreement**

The EU and Israel concluded an agreement to open government procurement[1] (Government Agreement) in the context and framework of the WTO Government Procurement Agreement (GPA). Hence, there is a link between the Government Agreement and the GPA. For a better understanding of the terms and implications of the latter, a brief survey of the former is given below.

12.4 **GPA in a nutshell**

The GPA was signed on 15 April 1994 in Marrakesh, Morocco alongside the signing of the Final Act embodying the results of the Uruguay round of GATT trade liberalisation talks. The European Union, Canada, United States of America, Israel, Norway and the Republic of Korea signed the GPA; Singapore applied for accession in December 1995 and eventually became a member (Signatories). This agreement came into force on 1 July 1996.

Objective

The new GPA establishes an agreed framework of rights and obligations with respect to laws, regulations, procedures and practices regarding government procurement. Its primary aim is to liberalise government procurement markets to industry in all its Signatory countries while at the same allowing governments to procure in a rational way. In essence, the GPA promotes non-discriminatory tendering procedures (such as the removal of national preference rules), subject to whatever general measures consistent with GATT or General Agreement on Trade in Services. Hence, the GPA covers the act of purchasing in its widest form but measures applicable to imports of goods or trade in services is beyond its coverage.

Fundamental principles

The GPA incorporates the fundamental principles of national treatment, non-discrimination (commonly referred to as most-

1 Council Dec 97/474 (OJ 1997 L202/72).

favoured-nation principle) and transparency to suppliers and to product and services of the other Signatories.

National treatment entails that laws and regulations of a Signatory country on the award of procurement contracts shall apply equally to foreign and domestic suppliers. This means that national law must not favour local suppliers over their foreign competitors. GPA makes an interesting link with investment policy, in that it stipulates that locally-established suppliers shall not be treated less favourably than other similar suppliers, on the basis of foreign affiliation or ownership, or on the basis of country of production of the good or service being supplied.

Non-discrimination is the principle where special procurement arrangements between two Signatories must be extended to other Signatory countries. In other words, government procurement rules in one Signatory country must not differentiate between one Signatory and another.

Transparency (*i.e.* opening procedures to public scrutiny) requires the Signatory countries to encourage their procuring entities to indicate any terms or conditions, including deviations from competitive tendering procedures, under which tenders will be entertained from suppliers located in non-Signatory countries by applying tendering rules assuring transparency. Also, this obliges the procuring entities to keep the procurement process open from the moment of inviting bids, through selection to the award of the procurement contracts so that suppliers can verify that correct procedures have been followed.

Scope and coverage

The GPA applies when four criteria are satisfied:

(1) The purchasing entity must be from a Signatory country.

(2) The procurement must be for products (excluding those which are defence-related) or for those services and construction services which are specifically indicated in the Signatory's Annexes to the GPA (Annex 4 lists non-construction services and Annex 5 construction services).

(3) The procurement must be carried out by entities specifically listed for each Signatory in its Annexes to the GPA. Annex 1 lists the central government entities. Annex 2 the sub-central government entities, such as the states, provinces and municipalities and Annex 3

lists other entities, such as public undertakings or public authorities (*e.g.* utilities) or federal enterprises.

(4) The contract value must be above a financial threshold, which each Signatory indicates in a specific Annex. The GPA only addresses procurement contracts above a certain value (threshold value).

Operational provisions of the GPA

The GPA implements the fundamental principles by stipulating detailed operational rules and providing four methods of tendering:

1. Open

Under open procedures all interested suppliers may submit a tender.

2. Selective tendering

Under this procedure only those suppliers invited to do so by the entity may submit a tender. To ensure optimum effective international competition, purchasing entities are required to invite tenders from the maximum number of foreign suppliers. There are safeguards to ensure that the procedures and conditions for qualification of suppliers do not discriminate against suppliers of other Signatory countries. For example, any conditions for participation in tendering procedures by suppliers shall be limited to those that are essential to ensure the firm's capability to fulfil the contract and shall not have a discriminatory effect. Entities using the selective tendering method are required once a year to publish their lists of suppliers in a publication specified in the GPA. They must also specify the period of validity of those lists and the conditions that need to be met for inclusion of interested suppliers in the lists.

3. Limited tendering

Under the limited tendering procedure the entity contacts potential suppliers individually. The GPA closely circumscribes the situations in which this method can be used. Examples of instances when this method may be used is in the absence of tenders in response to an open tender or selective tender or in cases of collusion. Also, this method may be used when only a particular supplier can supply the product or service, or for reasons of extreme urgency brought about by events unforeseeable by the entity.

4. Negotiations

Entities may hold negotiations with suppliers making tenders, provided this is indicated in the initial tender notice or it appears from the tender evaluation that no one tender is the most advantageous and subject to safeguards to ensure that such negotiations do not discriminate between suppliers.

Procurement procedures

There are detailed rules on a range of matters, such as technical qualifications, tender notices and their publication, time limits for tendering and delivery, tender documentation, opening of tenders and on the awarding of contracts.

All operational rules are based on considerations of non-discrimination between a foreign potential supplier and a domestic potential supplier while at the same time ensuring immediate and efficient procurement. Consequently, tendering must be done in such a way as to give the foreign supplier the same chance to win the contract as the domestic supplier. This is in line with the GPA's objective to create commercial opportunities domestic and abroad.

Furthermore, the GPA aims at ensuring a degree of transparency both at the stage of the invitation to tender and after the award has been made through its obligation to publish, in a publicly accessible publication, the tender notice and the award notice. The purchasing entity is required to set out the evaluation criteria for awarding the contract in the tender documentation which it submits to the interested bidders and must respond to reasonable queries once the award has been made. However, the purchasing entity may withhold information, which it considers confidential.

Derogation from fundamental principles

The GPA is based on reciprocity and allows for country-differentiated coverage. The Signatory countries negotiated with one another country-specific and sector-specific reciprocity clauses derogating from the non-discrimination principle by means of "notes" attached to each

Signatory's "schedules" (or lists) of entities and services covered by the GPA. There are provisions in the Signatories' schedules enumerating the economic sectors outside the ambit of the GPA. In addition, the schedules included reciprocity provisions on services within the GPA. Therefore, Israel has one agreement with the EU determining what services and public entities each side has access to, whilst both countries have different bilateral arrangements with the United States. For example, during the pre-GPA negotiations, Israel would study the EU's offer of access for Israeli companies to European procurement markets in terms of the number of services and public entities covered by the GPA. The EU would reciprocate and make a counter-offer to Israel and both sides would bargain till an agreement was reached. This bargaining process was repeated with (and between) the other Signatory countries. In essence, each Signatory decided individually on how far they wanted to be governed by the GPA.

Another derogation from non-discrimination is the use of "offsets" by developing countries. Offset is the extent to which an entity in considering the qualification of a supplier or in the award of a contract may seek or impose conditions itself, such as local content, licensing of technology, etc. The entity may also take into account such conditions proposed by the potential supplier as part of the bid. Developing countries may negotiate offset requirements at the time of joining the GPA in only well-defined cases for the purposes of qualification to participate in the procurement process and not as criteria for awarding contracts. So far, only Israel has negotiated the use of offsets.

Limitations of the GPA

The GPA confers rights and obligations on governments, not on private companies. This means that the GPA can only be invoked for breach of the procurement rules by the procuring entities and not because of anti-competitive behaviour, such as collusive bidding, by competing suppliers. Problems of collusion, monopolistic behaviour etc are the domain of competition law and not the GPA.

All procurement financed through "tied aid" is excluded from the rules of the GPA. Such aid is given to a recipient country upon the condition that the aid must be used to purchase goods and services from the donor country. There is an evident incompatibility between this type of aid and the GPA's objective to open government procurement to international competition.

Another exclusion from the obligations of the GPA is based on non-economic reasons, such as to protect national security interests, public morals, order or safety, human, animal or plant life or health or intellectual property etc.

An apparent limitation of the GPA is that there are procedures that can be employed by each Signatory to remove a listed entity being privatised from its entity list and therefore outside the coverage of the GPA. These procedures require that the Signatory country compensate the other Signatories for the withdrawal by including another procuring entity to its entity lists with a comparable level of procurement, taking into account the market-opening effects of the privatisation. Privatisation in this context is where "government control or influence over … [the entity] … has been effectively eliminated". Where a Signatory challenges a removal, there are dispute settlement procedures to resolve such disagreements.

12.5 **Details of Government Agreement**

The Government Agreement covers government procurement. It mostly complements and broadens the scope of commitments under the GPA. The contracting parties agree to notify such additional commitments to the WTO and incorporate them into the GPA. As a result, these commitments would be supported by the WTO's dispute settlement mechanism. Some limited commitments are outside the ambit of the GPA.

Israel's GPA offer to Europe includes several exclusions regarding products, the coverage of sub-central entities and services. Under "category A" (central entities), its Ministry of Health excludes products like insulin and infusion pumps, medical dressings, intravenous solution etc. Under "category C", Israel has exceptions for the procurement of cables, electro-mechanic meters, transformers etc.

Israel also operates an offset enabling it under certain conditions to require local content of up to 35 per cent of the contract or transfer of technology. Over a period of nine years (from 1996) this upper limit will be reduced to 20 per cent, while thereafter Israel will review its offset policy in consultation with the other Signatories. Under the bilateral Government Agreement, Israel has committed itself to expand market-opening in urban transport, services, medical equipment and sub-central government procurement. The EU would open those same sectors to Israel on a reciprocal basis.

The principal elements of the Government Agreement are as follows:

1. Urban transport

Israel agreed to add urban transport (except buses) to its GPA offer thereby completing coverage of the utilities sector in the GPA. EU suppliers will be able compete on an equal footing as Israel and/or municipalities develop a metro system. The EU resolved to disapply Article 36 of the Utilities Directive[2] against tenders comprising products of Israeli origin.

Article 36 applies to tenders comprising products originating in non-EU countries with which the EU has not concluded an agreement ensuring comparable and effective access for EU undertakings to the markets of those non-EU countries. Such tenders may be rejected provided the proportion of the products originating in these countries exceeds 50 per cent of the total value of the tender. Where two or more tenders are equivalent, preference has to be given to those tenders which are below this 50 per cent threshold.

Disapplication of Article 36 would guarantee Israeli companies full access to the EU market in the urban transport sector.

2. Services

Israel agreed to expand its list of services covered by the GPA by adding maintenance and repair services, building-cleaning services and publishing and printing services. As strict reciprocity underpins the GPA, the addition by Israel of three services which are already contained in the EU's GPA Annex, increases mutual coverage.

3. Product coverage

Israel consented to the removal of a product coverage exception in the field of medical equipment (a certain type of bandage).

4. Sub-central entities

Israel undertakes to require hospitals, outside the GPA's coverage, not

---

2 Council Dir 93/38 (OJ 1993 L199/84).

to discriminate against EU products, services or suppliers. It also agreed to grant EU suppliers national treatment above a specified threshold (550,000 SDR)[3] beyond the scope of the GPA. This entails that Israel disapply domestic "price preferences" for EU suppliers, thereby liberalising procurement opportunities beyond the coverage of the GPA. Domestic price preferences are rules requiring local procuring entities to favour Israeli suppliers when evaluating bids on the basis of price, even where the price exceeds that of a foreign bidder by up to a specified limit.

5. Non-discrimination

The Government Agreement obliges that Israel grant to the EU on a reciprocal basis any exceptions it disapplies to the other GPA Signatories. As for the lowering of thresholds and offset requirement in GPA, Israel promised to treat EU suppliers, service providers, products and services no less favourably than competitors from the other Signatories.

12.6 EU-Israel Telecommunications Procurement Agreement

This agreement[4] (Telecommunications Agreement) aims to liberalise the procurement market for telecommunication operators (TO). It is purely bilateral and stand-alone with no impact on coverage under the GPA. During the pre-GPA negotiations, only the EU was prepared to cover the telecommunications sector. Since no other Signatory could match the EU's offer, the latter withdrew the sector shortly before negotiations were concluded. Both Israel and the EU agreed to conclude the Telecommunications Agreement bilaterally, rather than within the GPA. Therefore, enforcement is through the bilateral dispute settlement procedure in the Israeli EMA.[5]

The Agreement is broad and liberal with no product exceptions. This means that there will be mutual dismantling of domestic price preference provisions. In Israel, a price preference of 15 per cent in favour of Israeli

---

3 SDR is the Special Drawing Rights, the International Monetary Fund's international reserve unit of account.
4 Council Dec 97/474 (OJ 1997 L202/72).
5 For a discussion on enforcement, see Chap 20, para 20.2.

products will not apply to EU bidders. In the EU, the provisions of Article 36 of the Utilities Directive will be disapplied for tenders comprising products of Israeli origin. The procedures contained in the Telecommunications Agreement are similar to the ones in the GPA.

The only exception for full bilateral liberalisation of telecommunications procurement persists with respect to an Israeli offset provision, which is similar to the one in the GPA. Israel may maintain an offset provision of up to 30 per cent of the contract value expiring in five years (*i.e.* 2001). While the form of this provision is similar to Israel's offset in the GPA, it provides for better terms to the EU due to a lower ceiling as well as the shorter duration of the offset.

The Agreement guarantees national treatment for TOs above certain thresholds. Israel has a lower threshold than the EU telecommunications equipment but a higher threshold for TO-related construction services. Since mobile and cable operators on both sides operate under competitive conditions, these companies are only subject to non-discrimination obligations. Under the Telecommunications Agreement, they do not need to follow certain procedures.

12.7 Turkish EMA

The Turkish EMA includes a provision similar to the Public Procurement Provision and Turkey has not yet concluded a procurement agreement with the EU.

12.8 What if ?

Q: I am an Israeli telecommunications company specialising in electronic switches. The Austrian central government was procuring for such switches using the open procedure. However, I noticed that the government was not complying with the procedures contained in the Telecommunications Agreements. What am I to do?

A: If you find that the Austrian government has not followed the procedures correctly, you should determine whether the Telecommunications Agreement is applicable by looking at such issues as coverage, threshold levels etc. Once you deduce that the Agreement is applicable, you should follow the rules stipulated in the Agreement for rectifying the matter. You should note that since

Chapter 13

· **Anti-Dumping** ·

13.1 **Introduction**

If a company exports a product at a lower price than it would normally charge in its home market, it is said to be "dumping" the product. This is a controversial area of trade law since many governments take action against dumping in order to defend their domestic industries from "unfair competition". The relevant provisions in the EMAs do not pass judgement and its focus is how the parties can or cannot react to dumping (Anti-Dumping Provision).

13.2 **Anti-Dumping Provision**

> "If one of the Parties finds that dumping is taking place in trade with the other Party within the meaning of Article VI of the [GATT], it may take appropriate measures against the practice in accordance with the Agreement relating to the application of Article VI of the [GATT], related internal legislation and conditions and procedures laid down [in the WTO Anti-Dumping Agreement]."

The Provision requires that anti-dumping investigations by each party must comply with the WTO Anti-Dumping Agreement (WTO anti-dumping rules). A brief description of the WTO and EU rules on anti-dumping is therefore given below.

13.3 **WTO anti-dumping rules**

The WTO anti-dumping rules allows governments to act where there is a genuine (material) injury to the competing domestic industry. In order to do so the government has to be able to show that dumping is taking place, calculate the extent of dumping (how much lower the export price is compared to the exporter's home market price) and show that the dumping is causing injury.

Article VI of GATT permits countries to take action against dumping. The WTO anti-dumping rules clarify and expand on Article VI and the two operate in tandem. They allow anti-dumping actions which means charging import duty on the particular product from the particular exporting country in order to bring its price closer to the "normal value" or to remove the injury to domestic industry in the importing country.

There are many different ways of calculating whether a particular product is being dumped heavily or only lightly. The WTO anti-dumping rules narrow down the range of possible options. It provides three methods to calculate a product's normal value. The main one is based on the price in the exporter's domestic market. When this cannot be used, two alternatives are available – the price charged by the exporter in another country, or a calculation based on the combination of the exporter's production costs, other expenses and normal profit margins. The rules also specify how a fair comparison can be made between the export price and what would be a normal price.

Calculating the extent of dumping on a product is not enough. Anti-dumping measures can only be applied if the dumping is damaging the industry in the importing country. Therefore, a detailed investigation has to be conducted initially according to specified rules. The investigations must evaluate all relevant economic factors that have a bearing on the state of the industry in question. If the investigation shows dumping is taking place and domestic industry is being hurt, the exporting company can undertake to raise its price to an agreed level in order to avoid anti-dumping duty.

WTO anti-dumping procedures

Detailed procedures are set out on how anti-dumping cases are to be initiated, how the investigations are to be conducted and the conditions for ensuring that all interested parties are given the opportunity to present evidence. Anti-dumping measures must expire five years after their date of imposition, unless an investigation shows that ending a measure would lead to injury.

Anti-dumping investigations are to end immediately in cases where the authorities determine that the margin of dumping is insignificantly small (defined as less than 2 per cent of the export price of the product). Other conditions are also set. For example, the investigations also have to end if the volume of dumped imports is negligible. In other words, if the volume from one country is less than 3 per cent of total imports of that product – however, investigations can proceed if several countries, each supplying less than 3 per cent of the imports, together account for 7 per cent or more of total imports).

The WTO anti-dumping rules state that member countries must inform the Committee on Anti-Dumping Practices about all preliminary and final anti-dumping actions, promptly and in detail. They must also report on all investigations twice a year. When differences arise, members are encouraged to consult each other. They can also use the WTO's dispute settlement procedure.[1]

13.4 **EU anti-dumping rules**

EU anti-dumping rules are contained in Regulation 384/96.[2] There are five issues involved in an anti-dumping action:

1. Margins
2. Injury
3. Community interest
4. Price undertakings
5. Anti-dumping duties

1. Margins

According to the Regulation, dumping occurs where the export price of a product is below the normal value of a like product. The export price may be the actual one charged by the exporter on the EU market or may be constructed. The normal price is generally the price charged for a like product in the state of origin or exportation. If the exporter does not sell sufficient quantities of the good in his country or where the domestic price is below costs of production or otherwise unreliable, the normal value may be constructed. A like product must be identical in all respects to the product under consideration, or in the absence of such a product, another product closely resembling the characteristics of the product under consideration.

---

1 For a discussion of the WTO dispute settlement mechanism, see Chap 19, para 19.5.
2 OJ 1996 L56/1. Similarly, anti-dumping rules for ECSC products are contained in Commission Dec 2277/96 (OJ 1996 L308/11, amended by OJ 1999 L122/35).

A finding of dumping depends on a comparison of prices and the amount by which the normal value exceeds the export price constitutes the dumping margin. Where a dumping margin is found, the EU must establish whether the dumping causes "material injury" and whether the "Community interest" is involved.

2. Injury

The fact that dumping is regarded as wrongful in itself means that an investigation of injury does not require consideration of possible justifications for dumping. For example, the possibility that below-cost pricing may simply be a response to a recession is not considered once a dumping margin is found. The Regulation requires examination of the volume of the dumped products, their prices and consequent impact on the EU industry concerned, to determine the presence of injury. Where a dumping margin is found in respect of imports from several countries, the effects of these imports may be cumulated to establish injury.

The EU takes several factors into account to determine injury. A principal factor is "price cutting", *i.e.* whether the prices of the dumped product are below those of EU producers or specially constructed EU "model prices". Injury may take the form of an increase in market shares of dumped products, losses or reduced profits for EU producers, a reduction of employment, inability of EU producers to recover their full costs or prevention of price increases that would otherwise have occurred. Often emphasis is placed on secondary effects, such as injury may be found where profitable investment becomes non-viable.

EU legislation permits the imposition of an anti-dumping duty without the need to show that dumping is the principal cause of injury. In Decision 82/220[3] and in the *Cannon*[4] case, the European Commission and the Court of Justice accepted respectively that injury attributable to dumping need only be part of more extensive injury attributable to other factors. In short, injury may be found, unless the prices of dumped products or their market share produce no real impact on the market position of EU producers. Without real impacts, the EU may find that there is no injury and that there is no need to establish whether there is a dumping margin.

---

3 Terminating an anti-dumping proceeding in respect of upright pianos from Czechoslovakia, GDR and Poland (OJ 1982 L101/21).
4 Joined Cases 277 & 300/85 *Cannon* v *Council of Ministers* [1988] ECR 5731

3. Community interest

The Regulation requires that intervention against dumping must be in the "Community interest". In practice, the EU focuses attention on the position of EU producers in competition with undertakings engaged in dumping. Therefore, EU intervention against dumping found to be injurious is likely to be considered in the Community interest, unless such intervention may not protect the producers concerned.

4. Price undertakings

In the course of an anti-dumping investigation the European Commission may accept an undertaking from the exporter concerned to the effect that the dumping or its injurious effects will cease. Such undertakings usually take the form of restricting exports to certain EU Member States, limiting market shares or more generally price increases. However, undertakings are not fool proof since the Commission may re-open the anti-dumping investigation and impose duties due to a change in circumstances underlying the undertaking.

5. Anti-dumping duties

If no satisfactory undertaking can be secured, anti-dumping duties can be imposed on the exporter. The European Commission provisionally imposes them, and the Council of Ministers may impose definitive duties or reject them. These duties may be *ad valorem* (*i.e.* according to the value of the product concerned); variable based on a minimum price for the product concerned; a combination of the two; or fixed amount per unit, weight or measure.

The EU takes several factors into account when fixing the level of duty, such as the costs/prices of the EU producers, the protection of average EU producers from serious price competition from imports and the stimulus produced by the dumped imports towards the restructuring of EU industry. Such duties, however, must be no higher than necessary to remove the injury. The Regulation provides for the refunding of any duty collected in excess of the margin. Conversely, it also provides that where the EU exporter bears the anti-dumping duty, an additional duty may be levied to compensate for the amount borne by the exporter. This may occur where an EU exporter imports a product subject to an anti-dumping duty, which he subsequently uses to produce his exported product. In such circumstances, the EU exporter may bear the anti-dumping duty. A typical example is the situation involving Egyptian cotton imports subject to an anti-dumping duty which are used by EU textile producers for the manufacture of their own products for export.

Duties may be imposed even where an undertaking has been accepted because a change in circumstances may justify the re-opening of proceedings, repealing the EU decision approving the undertaking and imposing anti-dumping duties. The Regulation makes clear that such action may be taken where the undertaking has been withdrawn or where the Commission has reason to believe that it has been violated.

13.5 **Turkish EMA**

The Anti-Dumping Provision in the Turkish EMA is substantially similar to the other EMAs and therefore all the above comments are applicable.

13.6 **What if ?**

Q: I am an Egyptian producer of ABC product. The Commission has imposed 0.5 per cent anti-dumping duty on my products. Is this duty permanent and how is its level decided?

A: The Commission could only impose a provisional duty, while the EU Council of Ministers may impose a definitive duty for as long as is necessary to counteract the perceived injury caused by your dumping of ABC product in the EU market. It may also reject them.

The EU uses various methods to calculate the dumping margin, which then leads to the consideration of whether the dumping is injurious and whether the Community interest is involved. These are not usually very difficult thresholds to cross. Once injury is demonstrated, having regard to a number of factors such as "price cutting", a duty may be imposed which must be no higher than the dumping margin. Levels are assessed utilising a number of determinants, such as average costs of producers in the EU.

You could attempt to pre-empt anti-dumping duties by undertaking to the Commission to increase your prices, for example. However, such an undertaking is not fool proof since the Commission may re-open the anti-dumping investigation and impose duties due to a change in circumstances underlying the undertaking.

Chapter 14

· **Rules of Origin I** ·

14.1 **Introduction**

Rules of origin lie at the heart of all free trade agreements. These are technical and complex rules designed to determine where the goods are made. EMAs are preferential trade areas, so that only goods made in the MNC or the EU enjoy preferential treatment (as opposed to goods produced outside the preferential area) in terms of lower customs duty upon entry into the EU (and vice versa) (beneficiary or beneficiary country). This means that only those good satisfying the "preferential rules of origin" are able to benefit from the preferential trade regime associated with the free trade area. Hence, the fundamental criterion for their application is the economic nationality of the product involved. This economic nationality of the product is referred as the "origin" of the product, whereas origin rules are the specific provisions, which permit authorities to determine the country of origin of a particular product.

A certificate is issued to goods that comply with the preferential origin rules, which is comparable to a visa or passport for purposes of travel. Preferential status is usually conferred on goods which are "wholly obtained" within the free trade area (*e.g.* locally grown agricultural produce) or to products which have been substantially transformed within the free trade area. This second type of rules applies incorporating materials imported from outside the free trade area, or to use a technical term, goods incorporating "non-originating" material.

The preferential rules of origin attempt to limit the free rider problem by obliging all raw materials and components produced outside the free trade area to undergo a substantial degree of processing ("substantial transformation") within the free trade area. One very common method is to require the so-called "change of tariff heading" at the four-digit level of the "Harmonised System". In other cases the rules impose a strict ceiling on the value of such imported or "non-originating" materials. These rules may also specify processes (sometimes referred to as "technical criteria") which must be carried out within the preferential trading area. The individual "tests" may also be modified to reflect circumstances specific to particular products or industrial sectors. The possibilities are practically endless. Anyone working with an EMA has to check each chapter or four-digit heading individually.

Goods that do not satisfy these rules can only enter the free trade area against payment of duty. Duty is paid on the value of the whole product, which originates outside the free trade area.

This chapter will deal with the issues above by outlining the common features of the preferential rules of origin present in all the EMAs.

14.2 **Basic origin criterion**

"Products will originate in a beneficiary country and thereby obtain preferential origin if they:

i   are wholly obtained in that country; or

ii have undergone sufficient working or processing in that country."

The preferential origin rules specify a list of products, which are considered as wholly obtained in a beneficiary country, covering mainly primary products in their natural state such as mineral products and vegetables. These products are:

- mineral products extracted from their soil or seabed;
- vegetable products harvested there;
- live animals born and raised there;
- products obtained by hunting or fishing there;
- products of sea fishing and other products taken from the sea by their vessels;
- products made aboard their factory ships exclusively from products of sea fishing and other products taken from the sea by their vessels;
- used articles collected there fit only for the recovery of raw materials, including used tyres fit only for retreading or use as waste;
- waste and scrap resulting from manufacturing operations conducted there;
- products extracted from marine soil or subsoil outside their territorial waters provided that they have sole rights to work that soil or subsoil; and
- goods produced exclusively from products specified from any of the above.

If non-originating materials[1] are used in the manufacture[2] of a product, then these must undergo sufficient working or processing for the finished product to originate in the beneficiary country.

As a general rule, non-originating materials are considered to be sufficiently worked or processed when the resulting product is classifiable under a customs heading (four-digit code) which is different from the headings under which the non-originating materials used in its production are classifiable.

A common feature of the EMA preferential origin rules therefore is that they interpret the notion of sufficient working or processing through the imposition of an across-the-board "tariff classification rule".

There are obvious benefits from defining what "sufficiently working or processing" is through the introduction of a clear and relatively easy-to-apply origin rule. Parties to a preferential agreement would not want to see difficulties arising in the implementation of the agreement because of conflicting interpretations on the precise meaning of the vague criterion.

Tariff classification rule

All products when imported into the European Union or an MNC are classified under a tariff code of the Combined Nomenclature (CN). The purpose of this classification is the establishment of the appropriate customs duty and/or other charges levied on products by reason of their importation into the EU or the MNC as well as the application of commercial policy measures such as quotas and anti-dumping duties. The CN is divided into 21 sections and 99 chapters. Each chapter is further divided into headings (four-digit codes) and sub-heading (six-digit codes) where all products are classified. Products are grouped into sections, chapters and headings in a coherent manner on the basis of their technical and/or physical characteristics – for example, vegetable products, mineral products, textiles, electrical products etc.

The tariff classification test (sometimes referred to as the "tariff heading" test) implies a change in the classification of the resulting product under the CN, as opposed to the classification of the raw materials or parts used in the manufacture.

---

1 "Materials" covers any product, ingredient, component or part used in the manufacture of a product.
2 "Manufacture" covers any kind of working or processing including assembly or specific operations with the exception of simple operations.

If the resulting product is classified under a different heading than the raw materials or parts used in its manufacture, then a substantial operation is deemed to have taken place. Similarly, if the resulting product is classified under the same heading of the CN as the raw materials or parts used its manufacture, then the manufacturing process or operation is not deemed to be substantial or confer origin on the resulting product.

It should be stressed that the tariff classification test applies to a change in heading (that is, the four-digit code, *e.g.* CN heading 8529 to 8528) and not in sub-headings (that is, the six-digit code). Any changes in sub-headings which do not also involve a change in headings such as, for example, a change in sub-headings within the same heading (CN heading 851890 to 851810) do not satisfy the test.

List of exceptions

The basic classification rules, does not, however, interpret the notion of sufficient working or processing with sufficient precision for all products. For some products this rule may be particularly onerous while for others it may be totally inadequate. More accurate origin rules need therefore to be established in respect of these products. Such product specific rules impose additional conditions to the basic tariff classification rule which must also be satisfied, or to establish alternative rules.

Originally, these rules were set out in two separate lists, which were attached to the origin rules (Lists A and B). List A specified a list of products which, although they were classified under a tariff heading different from that of the material used in their production, did not, by that fact alone, enjoy originating status. Products covered by List A also had to satisfy some other additional requirements in order to obtain preferential origin. In contrast, List B set out rules which, if satisfied, would result in the products achieving originating status even though the working or processing operation would not be sufficient to result in a change of tariff heading. In other words, a product listed in List A had to satisfy further conditions in addition to the change in tariff heading, while a product covered in List B had to satisfy some other conditions instead of a change in tariff heading.

The system of these two types of lists gave rise to complexities, especially with regard to products, which were covered in both Lists A and B. It was therefore decided to merge the two lists into a single list (the list of exceptions) whilst providing at the same time detailed guidance on how this list should interpreted.

The change of product classification under the Co-operation Council Nomenclature to the new classification under the Harmonised System Nomenclature (HS) and the merger of the two lists into one have altered the substance of some of the origin rules which were laid down in Lists A and B.

The list of exceptions itself is divided into three columns. The first and second columns in the list describe the products subject to these rules: the first column specifies the applicable customs heading or the chapter number used in the HS, while the second column sets out the specific descriptions of the product. For each entry in the first two columns, an origin rule is specified in the third, which indicates the working or processing that must be carried out on the non-originating material to enable the product to obtain preferential origin.

The origin rules contained in the third column may make it obligatory to use certain materials, to carry out several processes (*i.e.* the specific process test[3] and to meet a value added requirement (*i.e.* the added value test[4]). There may be restrictions on the use of certain materials or any combination of the above. For example, in respect of soap products covered by Chapter 34 of the HS, the third column provides that non-originating materials used must be classified under a heading different to that of the product. However, non-originating materials, which fall under the same heading as the resulting product may exceptionally be used if they represent up to 20 per cent of the ex-works price of the resulting product.

Thus, in the above example for soap products, an exception to the basic tariff classification rule is made which renders it easier to satisfy. An example of an alternative rule to the tariff classification can be found in the case of umbrellas (HS 6601). In that case, a straightforward added value rule applies under which umbrellas obtain origin if the value of the non-originating material does not exceed 50 per cent of the ex-works price of the umbrella. Similarly, for hats (HS 6505) an alternative specific process rule applies which provides that hats obtain origin if made from yarn or textile fibres.

Whenever a percentage rule is used in determining the originating status of a product obtained in the EU or the relevant MNC, the value-

3 See below, p 125.
4 See below, p 127.

added must correspond to the ex-works price of the product obtained, less the value of third-country materials imported into the EU or the MNC.

The list of exceptions is usually preceded by several Introductory Notes, which clarify the scope and the application of the rules in the list. For example, these notes make it clear that the term "material" covers any "ingredient", "raw material", "component" or "part", etc used in the manufacture of the product. Interestingly, the Introductory Notes also apply, where relevant, to all products manufactured with non-originating material even if they are not included in the list of exceptions but are subject instead to the basic tariff classification rule through the use of detailed instructions set out in the Introductory Notes.

The Introductory Notes should not be confused with Explanatory Notes which are often annexed to the preferential origin rules contained in other trade agreements concluded by the EU with non-EU countries. The latter aim to clarify the meaning and scope of certain provisions relating to the application of the preferential origin rules in general, while the former primarily deal with the product specific rules contained in the list or exceptions. For example, an Explanatory Note may specify that the scope of application of the preferential origin rules extends to the territorial waters of the Signatories to an EU trade agreement with a non-EU territory.

The product specific rules contained in the list of exceptions have to be carried out only in relation to the non-originating materials, which are used. Therefore, if a producer only uses originating material no restrictions apply. Moreover, it goes without saying that as originating materials are considered those which have acquired origin in accordance with the preferential rules of origin, if there is no specific origin rule for the material in question in the list of exceptions then the basic tariff classification rule applies.

Specific process test

This process entails the need to examine technically on a case-by-case basis the operations leading to the manufacture of the product in question. Normally, such an examination can only be made for each product and manufacturing process but invariably the same product is manufactured in different ways. However, there are usually basic operations, which must always be carried out for the manufacture of a particular product. Therefore, the test isolates the relative accuracy of the basic operations, which need to be carried out on the non-originating material for the product to obtain the origin of the country where the processing is carried out.

Thus, this test establishes a technical criterion and allows producers to concentrate for origin purposes on the manufacturing operations themselves and not on elements extraneous to production, such as added values or customs classification.

The specific process may introduce a positive standard by indicating a certain process or processes, which must be carried out on the non-originating material for the resulting material to obtain the origin of the country of processing. Alternatively, it may introduce a negative standard by indicating the process(es) which are not considered as substantial to confer origin of the country of processing on the resulting product.

In case a positive standard is established, it will indicate what is the minimum amount of processing required for the product to obtain origin by means of describing specific manufacturing operations which must be performed and/or by specifying materials which must originate in the country of processing.

A natural consequence of a positive standard is that the carrying out of more working or processing (that is, processing going beyond the minimum required) also confers origin on the product obtained; conversely, the carrying out of less working or processing cannot confer origin.

In case a negative standard is established it will indicate what is the minimum amount of processing which cannot confer origin. Naturally, it follows that the carrying out of less processing than that described in the origin rule also does not confer origin.

On the other hand, the carrying out of more processing in excess of that described as insufficient to confer origin does not automatically mean that the product will obtain origin. To do only marginally more so as to escape the description of the negative standard may not confer origin.

The question is then raised of how much processing must be carried out for the product to obtain origin. In the grey area which follows the negative standard, it may be indirectly used as a guideline of what is a "substantial operation" to confer origin. In view of this inherent weakness a negative standard may create more problems than it is called to solve. For that reason, negative standards are prohibited under the WTO Agreement on Rules of Origin unless they are used to clarify the context of a positive standard and therefore they are not used in the EMAs.

Added value test

The test determines origin on the basis of commercial value, which is added to a product in a specific country through manufacturing operations performed there. It implies that after its manufacturing a product has a certain commercial value which includes the commercial values of the materials used in its production as well as the value of the manufacturing process itself. Therefore, the objective of this test is to determine whether the value added in the country where the manufacturing operations took place exceeds a certain level in comparison to the finished product. This sometimes may also necessitate a comparison of the value added in the country in question, which was involved in the manufacture of the product in question.

Under the EMAs, ex-works price of a product is the commercial yardstick of the product, which is taken into account as the yardstick against which all the values that were added to the product in question in the various countries are compared. "Ex-works" is defined as the price paid to the manufacturer in whose undertaking the last processing or working is carried out provided the price includes the value of all the products used in manufacture. The preferential rules therefore set a floor price consisting of the value of all the materials used in the manufacture of a product, which would constitute the lowest ex-works price acceptable. Moreover, the ex-works price does not include any internal taxes, which are, or may be, repaid when the product is exported, such as Value Added Tax.

In essence, ex-works is the invoice price composed of the value of all non-originating material and the value of all originating material. In international trade practice, however, it is quite rare that an invoice is issued at the ex-works level. On the one hand, the ex-works price must not include costs incurred at the factory gate. On the other hand, invoice prices vary on the basis of the selling terms to the buyer (such as fob, cif or delivered etc). Therefore, adjustments must be made on invoice prices to net the price back to the ex-works level. For this purpose, the price will be preferred to a cif or delivered price. The calculation would be to take the fob invoice price and deduct all costs incurred after the factory gate such as transport costs, insurance, loading and unloading costs, customs agent fees, etc.

In view of the fact that the ex-works price is the price at the factory gate, it would normally make no difference whether the price reflects a sale to a related or unrelated party. The ex-works price could therefore be a transfer price (*e.g.* a parent company invoice to a selling subsidiary). However, if a transfer price is found to be unreliable the ex-works price may be reconstructed by the respective authorities determining the origin in question by means of directly taking into account the cost of manufacture plus all the other costs incurred up to the factory gate.

The ex-works price normally includes:

1. The value of all non-originating material.
2. The value of all originating material.
3. The value of the manufacturing process itself.
4. The overheads of the manufacture.
5. Profit.

As previously explained, the EMAs origin rules set a floor on what is the lowest ex-works price acceptable which comprises the total of items 1 and 2 – that is, the value of all the materials, whether originating or non-originating – used in the manufacture of a product.

The value of non-originating material may be calculated on the basis of either its ex-works invoice price or its customs value. Theoretically, the difference between the two systems is quite important as an ex-works price does not include transport, insurance, or other costs incurred after "the factory gate" while customs value includes all costs incurred in bringing the material up to the requisite national frontier. In practice, such a distinction may not be very important since the relevant national authorities for origin purposes usually accept invoice prices for materials. This makes sense, as often producers do not import non-originating material themselves and they do not necessarily obtain their supplies directly from the producers of the material in question. The invoice prices of the traders involved in these transactions are therefore usually accepted as proof of the value of the material.

The value of the originating materials is normally calculated on the basis of their invoice purchase price. There is a tendency in the European Commission to take into account for origin purposes the landed (delivered) into factory cost of material, thus including all costs the producer incurred for obtaining the material in question (*i.e.* including transport, insurance and unloading costs).

The value of the manufacturing process includes all the direct (such as labour) and indirect costs (such as supervision, power) associated with the manufacture of the product.

Overheads include the general, selling and other administrative expenses incurred for manufacturing and selling the product, such as financing costs, advertising costs. Finally, assuming that a product is sold at the factory gate level the difference between the sum of items 1, 2, 3 and 4 and the invoice price would just constitute profit.

The value added test may function in two different ways: either it imposes a minimum threshold in comparison to the ex-works price which must be achieved in the country where the process is carried out for the product to obtain the origin of that country. Alternatively, it limits the amount of non-originating material, which can be used in the manufacture of the product to the maximum permissible level in relation to the ex-works price.

Essentially, therefore, this test involves a comparison between the ex-works invoice price and the sum of all of the originating material and local value added to the product (items 2, 3, 4 and 5 above). Alternatively, it involves a comparison between the ex-works invoice price and the value of the non-originating materials (item 1 above), depending on the particular preferential origin rule in question.

14.3 **The problem of absorption**

The preferential origin rules clarify that where a product, which was made with non-originating materials and has acquired preferential origin, may count as wholly obtaining. This is particularly important where a product is used in the manufacture of a further product. For example, the EMA origin rules for video recording apparatus (VCRs) classified under the HS heading 8521, state, *inter alia*, that the value of all non-originating materials used in the production of VCR must not exceed 40 per cent of the ex-works of the VCR. This means that a maximum of 40 per cent of non-originating parts can be used in the production of a VCR to achieve origin under the EMA rules. An originating part may, however, contain some non-originating value as well: for example, a part may have been made with 70 per cent originating and 30 per cent non-originating parts. In such a case, it is provided that if the part has acquired preferential origin in accordance with its own origin rule (that is, after having satisfied the preferential origin rule applicable to VCR parts), then it will count as 100 per cent originating. Generally, under the specific EMA rule, a part is considered as originating if it does not have more than 40 per cent non-originating materials.

In the above example the part was made with only 30 per cent non-originating material and therefore has lawfully acquired preferential origin. Consequently, all its value may then count as originating when calculating the percentage of originating parts for the VCR.

Thus, preferential origin rules accept the principle of absorption of non-originating value by originating products, which are further used in the manufacture of other products.

14.4 **Insufficient working or processing (simple operations)**

The preferential origin rules contain a list of simple processing operations which may not be considered as conferring origin to non-originating product even where the basic tariff classification rule or any other rule contained in the list of exceptions is satisfied. These operations are not regarded as substantial as they do not generally involve a significant contribution on the part of the manufacturers. The simple operations under the EMA rules of origin are:

(a) operations to ensure the preservation of products in good condition during transport and storage (ventilation, spreading out, drying, chilling, placing in salt, sulphur dioxide or other aqueous solutions, removal of damaged parts, and like operations);

(b) simple operations consisting of removal of dust, sifting or screening, sorting, classifying, matching (including the making-up of sets of articles), washing, painting, cutting up;

(c) (i) changes of packing and breaking up and assembly of consignments;

(ii) simple packing in bottles, flasks, bags, cases, boxes, fixing on cards or boards, etc, and all other simple packaging operations;

(d) the affixing of marks, labels or other like distinguishing signs on products or their packaging;

(e) simple mixing of products, whether or not of different kinds;

(f) a simple assembly of parts or products to constitute a complete product;

(g) a combination of two or more operations specified in (a) to (f);

(h) slaughter of animals.

14.5 **Fishery products**

In relation to fishery products, a distinction is made in the preferential origin rules as to whether they are obtained in the territorial waters of the beneficiary country[5] concerned or in international waters. Fishery products, which are sourced from the territorial waters of the beneficiary country, will obtain the origin of that country notwithstanding the nationality of the vessel involved. On the other hand, for fishery products extracted in international waters to obtain preferential origin a vessel must have sourced them which:

- was registered in a beneficiary country;
- sailed under a flag of a beneficiary country;
- was at least 50 per cent owned by nationals of a beneficiary country or by a company with its head office in a beneficiary of which the manager(s) were nationals of a beneficiary country;[6] and of which
- the captain, all officers and at least 75 per cent of the crew[7] were nationals of a beneficiary country.

All of the above criteria must be satisfied cumulatively such that fishery products caught by a vessel which does not comply with all these provisions will not obtain preferential origin.[8]

14.6 **Territoriality requirement**

The process leading to a change in the customs heading of a product as well as the specific conditions set out in the list of exceptions must be fulfilled without interruption in the beneficiary country. In other words, the origin rules must be wholly satisfied in the beneficiary country concerned. Assume a product has been manufactured in a beneficiary country is then exported to a third country for further processing and then re-imported into a beneficiary country for final processing. In this

---

5 The term "beneficiary country" includes the EU.
6 In the case of partnerships or limited companies, at least half their capital must belong to the beneficiary country or to public bodies or nationals of that country.
7 This would include but not necessarily apply to the captain and officers, as is the case under other preferential agreements.
8 In the Algerian, Tunisian and Moroccan EMAs, the origin rules on fishery products apply to each others' vessels provided they satisfy criteria (1) to (4) and trade between the EU and each of those countries is covered by identical rules of origin.

scenario, not all the operations concerning that product which have been carried out in the beneficiary country (that is those prior to exportation to the third country and those following re-importation) will be taken into account for the purpose of applying the preferential origin rules. In such a case only the operations which occurred after re-importation will be considered in determining origin and therefore that part of the processing which took place prior to the product's exportation to the third country will be disregarded.

The reasoning for this rule is based upon the European Union's insistence that any benefits under the preferential arrangements or schemes must be limited to the beneficiary countries concerned. If third countries are involved in the manufacturing process, the risk of circumvention of the origin rules could be large. The rules, therefore, state explicitly that if products are exported from a beneficiary country to a third country and then re-imported to a beneficiary country, they will be considered as non-originating. This is the case provided the producer in the beneficiary country can prove, first, that the products returned were those originally exported and, secondly, that they had undergone any processing in that third country prior to re-importation with the exception of operations necessary to preserve the products in good condition (see para 14.7 below).

Without prejudice to the application of cumulation rules, the territoriality principle applies even if the third country of exportation of the products is also a beneficiary country under the same or similar preferential arrangements with the European Union. For example, there is a breach of the territoriality principle if products are exported from Tunisia to India for further processing and are then re-imported into Tunisia, even though both countries have preferential trading arrangements with the EU.

14.7 **Re-importation of goods (returned goods)**

If originating products exported from the EU or the relevant MNC are returned, they must be considered as non-originating unless it can be demonstrated to the satisfaction of the customs authorities that:

- the goods returned are the same goods as those exported; and
- they have not undergone any operation beyond that necessary to preserve them in good condition in that country or while being exported.

This rule does not apply to situations where cumulation rules of origin are effective.[9]

14.8 **Neutral elements**

There are some factors, which do not affect origin. For preferential origin purposes it is irrelevant whether or not the power, plant and equipment, machine and tools which are used to manufacture or process a product originate in a beneficiary country. For example, the fact that a television is manufactured in Egypt with tooling of Japanese origin will not affect the actual origin of the television. These elements are, therefore, completely neutral in the application of the origin rules. The obvious objective of such neutrality is to avoid hindering investment and/or transfer of know-how or technology by foreign producers into a beneficiary country.

An exception to this rule concerns fishery products sourced outside the territorial waters (that is, international waters) of a beneficiary country which, as discussed under paragraph 14.5 above, obtain the origin of the nationality which collected them.

14.9 **Direct transport**

Apart from satisfying the preferential origin rules, products will, as a general rule, only benefit from preferential treatment if they are transported directly from a beneficiary country to the European Union (or from the EU to the beneficiary whenever this applies). This rule implies that the product must be transported to the EU without passing through the territory of a third country.

The direct transport rule has been introduced to reduce the risk of fraud and circumvention of the preferential origin rules. In particular, it seeks to ensure that no substitution occurs in the products during transportation and to prevent third countries from taking advantage of the preferential treatment granted to a beneficiary country by re-exporting to the European Union products, which were originally intended for their domestic markets.

To obtain preferential treatment, exporters must produce evidence showing compliance with the direct transport rule to the satisfaction of

---

9 For a discussion on cumulation rules of origin, see Chap 17, para 17.3(3).

the customs authorities in the importing country concerned. This will include such items as the bill of lading, airway bill or similar transport document showing the carriage of the products from the exporting MNC to the EU (and vice versa). Other evidence could be a certificate by the customs authorities of the country of transit evidencing that the products have complied with the required conditions and/or any other substantiating documents.

Certain groups of the MNCs, which benefit from origin cumulation rules are regarded as a single export area for the purpose of satisfying the direct transport rule. The reasons for this exception are obvious. Further processing on a product may be carried out in another beneficiary country within the same group before it is finally exported to the EU. The only consequence of such further processing relates to the allocation within the group and not the loss of the preferential originating status of the product.

Thus, products exported from one MNC country may pass through another MNC without breaching the direct transport rule even if this is not geographically justifiable. This does not, however, apply to countries in respect of which no cumulation rules apply even if they are both countries to the same preferential agreement or scheme. The only group of MNCs considered being a single export area with the EU is Algeria, Morocco and Tunisia.

Case law

The notion of direct transport and in particular, the meaning of the terms "entered into commerce" and "delivered for home use" respectively were examined by the European Court of Justice in the *Pearl Eurotool* case.[10] This was in the context of the interpretation of a similar rule set out in the EU-Yugoslavia Trade and Trade Co-operation Interim Agreement. The case concerned the importation into the EU of machine tools of Yugoslavian origin. The machine tools in question had been first exported (and invoiced) by a Yugoslavian producer to its subsidiary in Switzerland where they remained under customs surveillance. They were then re-invoiced and re-exported by the Swiss subsidiary to a related importer in France. Because of the re-invoicing in Switzerland, the French authorities considered that the machine tools had "entered into commerce" in Switzerland and that accordingly, the direct transport rule was not satisfied.

---

10 Case 156/85 *Pearl Eurotool* [1986] ECR 1595.

The Court pointed out that the aim of the EU's agreement with Yugoslavia was to limit preferential treatment solely to trade between the two parties. It stated that if products had to cross the territories of third countries it was necessary to ensure that their final destination (the EU in this case) remained unchanged. As long as this criterion was satisfied, any legal or commercial operations, such as the re-invoicing of the products, which were under surveillance of the customs authorities, could not be considered as a breach of the direct transport rule. In other words, provided that the final destination of the products is not altered, there is nothing to prevent products from being the subject of business transactions during transportation (for example, while they are in international waters).

In that respect, any change in the ownership of the products, the nationality of the parties, the currencies involved and the place of payment are irrelevant. Furthermore, the Court found support for its reasoning also from the fact that the information required from exporters to show compliance with the direct transport rules (such as the bill of lading) has no connection with any commercial operations which may take place during the transportation of the products concerned.

The judgment in that case clarifies the scope of the direct transport rule. Although it was delivered in relation to the Yugoslavian Co-operation Agreement, one can reasonably argue that the same interpretation applies to all similar provisions in the EMAs, especially as the objectives of the above rule in all the Association Agreements are basically the same.

14.10 **Split consignments**

Preferential treatment will be accorded to products when these are imported as a single consignment. If, therefore, products covered by a single certificate of origin are not presented together upon importation at the relevant customs authorities, preferential treatment may be refused or limited to the products which have been imported at that stage. An exception to this rule, however, exists in respect of certain industrial products which for transportation or production reasons may have to be products falling within Chapter 84 or 85 of the HS (mostly mechanical and electrical equipment). Such products exported in split consignments may still get preferential treatment if, at the moment of importation of the first consignment, the person declaring the products at the relevant custom authorities requests that the various consignments should be considered as a single unit. If such an arrangement is acceptable to the customs authorities a single certificate of origin may then be submitted for the products in total.

This rule may be illustrated by the following example. An exporter may wish to send a non-assembled VCR to the EU for assembly. Despite the fact that the complete VCR may satisfy the preferential origin rule for VCR, it may be composed of both originating and non-originating components. Normally, if such parts are presented separately to the relevant customs authorities, those parts originating in the beneficiary country will be exempted from duty, while the applicable customs duty will be levied on the non-originating parts. Under the split consignment rule, however, the producer may declare at the customs authorities all the parts jointly as a non-assembled VCR. In this case, by producing a single certificate of origin for the VCR, the exporter may avoid payment of customs duties on the non-originating parts of the VCR.

14.11 **Exhibitions**

An exception to the direct transport rule is also available in respect of products sent by a beneficiary country for exhibition to third, non-beneficiary countries. In particular, exporters are allowed to send originating products for exhibitions in third countries and then to re-export to the EU (or any other beneficiary country) without the products involved losing preferential treatment. The preferential origin rules define the term "exhibition" as any trade, industrial, agricultural or crafts exhibition, fair or similar public show or display which is not organised for private purposes in shops or business premises with a view to the sales of foreign products and during which the products remain under customs control.

This derogation from the direct transport rule is, however, only permitted if:

- the products have been sold (or otherwise disposed of) by the exporter to someone in the EU (or any other beneficiary country) prior to re-exportation;
- the products have not been used in the non-beneficiary country for any purposes other than the demonstration at the exhibition; and
- the products have been re-exported during or immediately after the exhibition to the EU (or any other beneficiary

country) in the original state they were sent for exhibition.

A certificate of origin must be produced to the relevant customs authorities in the normal manner indicating the name and address of the exhibition. Where necessary, additional documentary evidence of the nature of the products and the conditions under which they have been exhibited may be required.

14.12 **Accessories, spare parts and tools**

Accessories, spare parts and tools which are dispatched with a piece of equipment, machine, apparatus or vehicle and which form part of its normal equipment may, in some circumstances, be regarded as one item with the piece of equipment, etc in question.

In other words, the preferential origin rules will apply to the total entity composed of the equipment and the accessories, spare parts or tools in question. Thus, even though accessories, spare parts and tools may be non-originating, they may benefit from preferential treatment if the entity is found to be originating. For this to apply, however, the value of the accessories, spares parts and tools must be included in the price of the originating piece of equipment concerned, or in any case must not be separately invoiced. Thus, if for the piece of equipment an added value origin rule applies, the value of the accessories, spare part or tools must normally be taken into account in calculating the non-originating content of the entity.

This rule is slightly more restrictive than the one applicable under the non-preferential origin rules as it requires accessories, spare parts and tools to be despatched together with the piece of equipment. Under the non-preferential origin rules, in some instances, a presumption of origin is made for spare parts even when they are to be used with equipment, which had been imported separately at an earlier stage.

14.13 **Packing**

The packing of a product may, sometimes, play an important role in the determination of the origin of the product it contains, especially if the value of the packing is considerable. Generally, packing which contains a product may be considered as part of the product, or alternatively, may be considered as a separate product. In the former case, the origin of the packing may influence the determination of the origin of the product. That is, if the packing of the product is non-originating, then its value must be taken into account when calculating the maximum content allowed for non-originating materials for the product in question.

In order to establish whether or not packing should count as part of a product the preferential origin rules usually refer to the general rules for the interpretation of the HS – that is, the classification rules.[11] Thus, if the packing is included with the product for classification purposes, then it will also be taken into account for the purposes of determining the origin of the product.

14.14 **Sets**

Products which although classified under different tariff headings are presented as sets (that is, products comprising different rules which are to be sold together, such as a tape recorder accompanied by pre-recorded tapes and books) will be regarded as originating if all the component articles individually examined are originating products. The strictness of the above rule is, however, softened by the existence of the tolerance rule. Imagine that a set comprises both originating (such as the tape recorder and the pre-recorded tapes) and non-originating articles (such as the books). In these circumstances, the whole set will be regarded as originating provided that the value of the non-originating articles (the books) does not exceed 15 per cent of the value of the complete set. Thus, exporters may avoid paying duties on the 15 per cent non-originating articles of the set which would have been the case had the components been imported individually.

The above rules only apply to sets which, in accordance with the general rules (specifically General Rule 3) of the HS, cannot be classified together under a single customs heading. If, therefore, products can be classified as sets under one heading, in such a case the origin rule corresponding to that heading will apply. For example, cutlery sets consisting of knives, spoons and forks in equal numbers are classified under the HS heading 82.15 and are therefore subject to that heading's tariff classification rule. Consequently, the 15 per cent tolerance rule for sets will not apply to such cutlery sets.

---

11 General Rule 5 of the HS provides that cases (and similar containers) shall be classified with the product if they are specially shaped for it, suitable for long-term use and presented and normally sold with the product, unless they give the product its essential character.

14.15 **Proof of origin**

Once exporters have presented their products to the relevant customs authorities in the country of importation to obtain the benefit of preferential treatment they must prove to the satisfaction of the customs authorities that the products have preferential originating status. For this purpose a certificate (referred to as a "movement certificate" or "certificate of origin" which is issued by the appropriate governmental authority – usually the customs authority) of the exporting beneficiary country concerned must accompany products. These certificates in the context of preferential origin rules play an important dual role. First, they serve to facilitate the application of EU trade measures (such as anti-dumping duties) or for statistical purposes. Secondly, they certify that a product has been manufactured in accordance with the requirements set out in preferential origin rules and that accordingly, it may enjoy preferential treatment upon entering the EU and thus avoid the discharge of customs duties.[12]

Detailed provisions in the relevant preferential origin rules set out the type, form and content of these certificates. Specimens of certificates and of applications for their issue are also annexed to the origin rules. Moreover, the smooth functioning of the system provides for a system of checks and verifications between the authorities of the importing and exporting beneficiary countries. The main features of the administrative system are examined below.

Issue of certificates

A Eur. 1 certificate is issued by the customs authorities of the relevant exporting beneficiary country upon receipt of an application made in writing by the exporter. The application must be accompanied by any appropriate supporting documentation, which seeks to prove that the products to be exported qualify under the preferential origin rules for the issue of the certificate. The customs authorities of the exporting country have the right to ask for information and indeed to carry out any examinations which they consider appropriate for the purposes of

---

12 The importation of products under the terms of a preferential agreement at a reduced customs duty or duty free does not affect the obligation of the importer to pay other charges or duties levied on these products. Thus, although a product may not be charged with customs duties because it has obtained preferential origin it may still be charged with, say, anti-dumping duties applicable to that product.

verifying the accuracy of the application in question. To avoid a fraudulent use of the certificate it is given to the exporter as soon as the exportation is actually carried out or when the exporter provides assurances that it will be carried out.

A simplified procedure applies in respect of products that are low in value and a concise form of certificate (referred to as Form Eur.2) may be presented. The exporter himself completes this form; that is, it does not need to be stamped or signed by the authorities in the exporting country. The maximum amounts permitted under these provisions are revised periodically to take into account currency movements.

Furthermore, there are special provisions for products of very low value which are sent by post or form part of a traveller's personal luggage as well as products imported occasionally and solely for the personal use of the recipients or travellers or their families. These products do not require the production of any documentation if they are not imported by way of trade. Their nature or quantity may evidence the non-existence of a commercial purpose for their importation. The maximum amounts of the value of the products exempt from proof of origin are also revised periodically.

Retrospective issues of certificates

In exceptional circumstances, the exporting beneficiary country's customs authorities may issue a certificate after exportation of the product. This will be the case in circumstances relating to errors, involuntary omissions and other special circumstances justifying the issuance of the certificate retrospectively.

Replacement of certificates

One can replace certificates or more certificates provided that this is effected at the customs office where the products are located. This facilitates the splitting of consignments originally covered by a single certificate of origin or, conversely, the grouping into one consignment of products previously covered by several certificates of origin issued in the same beneficiary country. For example, consider the situation where the products imported into the EU through a Member State some of which are then re-exported to another Member State where preferential treatment is claimed. The customs authorities of the first Member State may issue a new certificate covering part of the products to replace the original one. This is subject to the requirement that the products to be re-exported are located in the customs office issuing the replacement certificate.

Duplicate certificates

In the event of theft, loss or destruction of a certificate, the exporter may apply to the customs authorities, which issued the original certificate for a duplicate copy. The period of validity of the duplicate certificate commences from the date on which the original certificate is issued.

Validity of certificates

Certificates are only valid for a certain period of time and products will only benefit from preferential treatment if they are imported within the period. The period of validity of the certificate is usually five months. Certificates, which are presented to the customs authorities in the country of destination of the products after the expiry of the validity period, will not normally be accepted. However, in the case of *force majeure* or other exceptional circumstances this rule may be waived. Moreover, a certificate presented to the customs authorities after its expiry may also be accepted, if the products had already been presented to the customs authorities before its expiry.

Submission of certificates

Certificates must be submitted to the customs authorities in the importing country. In addition, customs authorities have the right to ask importers to submit a declaration stating that imported products meet the conditions required for the grant of the preferential treatment.

The existence of minor discrepancies between the information in the certificate and that contained in other documentation produced to the customs authorities will not automatically render that certificate void. If it is duly established that the certificate corresponds to the products actually imported, then it will be accepted.

Verification of certificates

The customs authorities of the importing country can carry out verifications at random or whenever there exists a reasonable doubt as to the authenticity or accuracy of a certificate. If such a case arises, the importing country customs authority must return the certificate to the appropriate governmental authorities in the exporting beneficiary country and ask them to conduct an inquiry into the origin of the products in question.[13] The exporting country is under a duty to assist the importing country in such verification.

In the meantime, the importing country customs authorities may decide to suspend the tariff preference pending the results of the verification and they may offer to release the products to the importer subject to precautionary measures being taken. Such a measure could be the issue by the importer in favour of the customs authority of a guarantee covering the amount of customs duties which may be payable in respect of the products, should preferential treatment be unavailable.

The authorities in the exporting country must reply to the importing country customs authorities within a maximum of ten months. Where they do not reply within that period or, more importantly if the reply does not contain sufficient information satisfy the customs authority of the importing country then the issue will be submitted to a Customs Co-operation Committee[14] established by the parties to the EMAs. This is because the preferential rules form part of the EMAs.

If the issue is referred to the Customs Co-operation Committee pursuant to the terms of the EMA, the Committee will have the power to decide whether or not the certificate should be accepted. The Customs Co-operation Committee also pronounces in case there is a dispute between the customs authorities of the exporting country and those of the importing country. Also, it does the same if a question is raised on the interpretation of the preferential origin rules (for example, if the exporting country considers that with regard to a product the conditions for acquiring preferential origin have been met and the importing country disagrees). In such cases and until such time as the Committee resolves the dispute, the importing country should grant preferential treatment subject to precautionary measures only.

---

13 See, *e.g.* the investigation into false declarations of origin relating to textile products from Mauritius: written questions 2326/90, OJ 1991 C70/36 and 403/91, OJ 1991 C195/35.

14 For a discussion on the Customs Co-operation Committee, see Chap 18, para 18.5. It should be noted that a movement certificate is not necessary where the importer and exporter established the origin of goods using objective, irrefutable evidence, but were unable to obtain such a certificate due to circumstances beyond their control (*e.g.* anti-competitive conduct by other persons concerned): Case C-344/93 *Bonapharma GmbH* v *Hauptzollamt* [1995] ECR I-319.

As far as the timing of the verification is concerned, it can take place during importation of the products or at any later stage – that is, after customs clearance. For that reason the authorities in the exporting country must keep copies of the certificates and of any documents relating to these certificates for a period of normally two years after their issue. Thus, the fact that a product has been imported into the EU and has been cleared through customs does not prevent retrospective verifications of the certificates on the part of the EU authorities. They may conclude, if the facts so establish, that the imported products did not actually comply with the origin requirements and that the certificates in question were wrongly issued. In such case, importers will be asked to pay the relevant customs duties in full.

The possibility of retrospective verifications of certificates has been confirmed by the Court of Justice in *Acampora*[15] on the basis that systemic verifications of the origin of products would excessively delay customs transactions.

This case concerned the importation by Acampora into Italy of radios from Hong Kong under the EU's Generalised System of Preferences scheme (GSP) which covers countries ranging from Albania to Zimbabwe. The radios in question were customs cleared without the payment of customs duties as a GSP certificate of origin accompanied them. After importation the Italian authorities requested confirmation from the authorities in Hong Kong that the radios indeed complied with the GSP rules. The latter authorities replied negatively so that Acampora was required to pay the full customs duties. Acampora challenged the customs authorities on the basis that verifications could not take place after customs clearance and that in any case Acampora was in good faith thinking that it was importing products benefiting from tariff preferences in reliance on certificates which were incorrect or falsified. On the former argument the Court simply stated that the provisions on verification of the GSP origin Regulations[16] (which at the time was in force) as well as its general structure permitted retrospective verifications. An alternative decision would have meant the imposition of an obligation on customs authorities to check the origin of all products upon importation.

On the latter argument the Court pointed out that:

---

15   Case 827/79 *Amministrazione delle Finanze* v *Acampora* [1980] ECR 3731.
16   Commission Reg 1371/71 (OJ 1971 L146/1).

(1) The EU did not have to bear the adverse consequences of the wrongful acts of the suppliers of the importers.

(2) The importer could attempt to obtain compensation from the perpetrators of the fraud.[17]

(3) Prudent traders must be able to assess the risks inherent in the market they trade in and accept them as normal trade risks.

As provisions on verification similar to those examined in *Acampora* are contained in all the EMAs, the Court's judgment applies to all the EMA origin rules. As a result, the importation of products under a preferential regime does not constitute the definitive stages of the preferential procedure; importers may be asked to pay duties waived if at any stage after importation it is established that certificates were wrongly issued. In that respect, importers cannot invoke to their defence their good faith or the fact the customs authorities of the importing country had (provisionally) accepted the preferential origin of the products in question.

The preferential rules, therefore, impose a responsibility on the authorities of the exporting beneficiary countries to ensure that certificates of origin and applications for certificates of origin are duly completed. Furthermore, these authorities also have the obligation to take all steps necessary to verify the origin of the products and to check the accuracy of other statements on the certificates of origin. The preferential origin rules are therefore based on the understanding that the EU customs authorities will benefit from extensive co-operation from their counterparts in the EMA countries.

Free zones

The Member States and the MNC must take all necessary steps to ensure that products traded under the cover of a movement certificate, which in the course of transport use a free zone situated in their territory, are not substituted by other goods. They must also ensure that such goods do not undergo handling other than normal operations designed to prevent their deterioration.

However, there is an exemption concerning free zones. When products originating in either party to an EMA are imported into a

---

17 In practice, to insure against such a possibility many importers include in their contracts a clause providing for the recovery from their suppliers of the sums paid.

free zone under cover of a movement certificate and which undergo treatment or processing, the customs authorities concerned must issue a new movement certificate at the exporter's request. This is conditional upon such treatment or processing undergone being in conformity with the rules of origin in the EMA concerned.

14.16 **Division of power**

In legal terms, in establishing the origin of a product, a division of power exists between EU customs authorities and those of the exporting beneficiary countries. Even though the proper working of the preferential origin system is monitored jointly by the authorities on both sides, the origin of a product is still established by the authorities in the exporting country.

This is justified by the fact that the authorities of the exporting country are in the best position to verify directly the facts, which determine origin. Moreover, this system has the advantage of producing certain and uniform results regarding the origin of products, thus avoiding deflection of trade and distortions of competition in trade. For example, it was left to the national customs authorities of the Member States to determine whether or not a product has preferential origin, conflicting views could then ensue. Moreover, exporters would take advantage of any inconsistencies in such treatment and import their product into the Member State, which applied the origin rules in the more favourable manner.

The division of power applies with regard to the examination of all the conditions set out in the preferential origin rules, regardless of the nature of the origin test applied. For example, in cases where an added value rule applies, the customs authorities of the importing country are not entitled to substitute their own assessment of the value of non-originating materials taken into consideration by the authorities of the exporting country in order to determine origin. They are, on the contrary, under an obligation to apply the preferential treatment provided for by the EMAs to all products whose preferential origin is duly certified. If the authorities have any reasonable doubts as to the origin of the products they can, as explained above, return the certificate to the exporting country and ask it to conduct a verification process.

Case law

The above rule was confirmed by the European Court of Justice in *Les Rapides Savoyards*,[18] which involved the export of pens from Switzerland to the EU. In that case, the French customs authorities refused to apply preferential treatment to the pens concerned on the basis that the value of the non-originating (US) materials used in the manufacture of the pens exceeded the amount permitted under the European Union-European Free Trade Area (EFTA) origin rules. However, the calculations of the French customs authorities were based on the exchange rate applicable between the US dollar and the French franc on the day of importation of the pens into France. The importer challenged the French customs decision arguing that the appropriate time and, therefore, exchange rate for the establishment of the value of the non-originating material was upon importation of that material into Switzerland in accordance with the Swiss customs rules.

In its judgment, the Court confirmed the existence of the division of power between the customs authorities of the exporting and importing country respectively in the context of the preferential agreement. The Court pointed out the significance of respecting the decisions of the customs authorities of the exporting country, as this was the basis of reciprocity between the EU and Switzerland under EFTA. The Court confirmed that it was the duty of the authorities of the exporting country to establish the origin of the products intended for export to the European Union. In consequence, the customs rules (including the exchange rules) of the exporting country applied to establish whether or not the product in question could be considered to originate in the exporting country. The Court concluded that the issue of a certificate of origin for the product certified that the preferential origin of the product had been established correctly.

The division of power principle under the preferential origin rules establishes a presumption of origin whereby a product accompanied by a certificate of origin is deemed to have obtained preferential origin until the opposite is proven through the appropriate administrative procedures. This is in sharp contrast to the EU approach under the non-preferential rules of origin where the value of a certificate of origin is limited.

The difference in treatment is, of course, understandable considering that non-preferential origin rules have not been harmonised at an

---

18 Case 218/83 *Les Rapides Savoyards* [1984] ECR 3116.

international level and thus the exporting and importing country may apply different origin rules. On the other hand, the certificates of origin issued under the preferential rules relate to a single set of origin rules, which have been accepted by both the exporting and importing countries. Furthermore, to the exclusion of unilateral schemes, the preferential origin rules are the result of negotiated agreements where these issues can be discussed and settled on a reciprocal basis.

14.17 Ceuta and Melilla

To take into consideration the particular status of Ceuta and Melilla, specific origin provisions are incorporated in the EMAs between the above territories and the MNCs concerned. In this context, Ceuta and Melilla are treated as a single territory.

14.18 Internal EU procedures

For the purposes of exportation to countries with which the European Union has preferential trade agreements like the MNCs, the EU has established internal procedures that aim to facilitate the issue of certificates of origin to EU exporters. These certify that the products exported are of "Community origin" in accordance with the terms of the particular preferential agreement in question. Without the existence of such EU procedures it would be difficult for the authorities of one Member State to verify the origin of materials which were sourced from other Member States and used in the manufacture of a product for which a certificate of origin is sought. Therefore, in order to facilitate the communication of information relating to the preferential status of products manufactured in the EU, Council Regulation 3351/83[19] provides for origin declarations by suppliers of material or products (suppliers' declarations) and for the issue of information certificates.

In particular, the EU suppliers may make declarations to their customers (producers/exporters) in the EU indicating whether or not the supplied products or materials have originating status under the provisions of a particular preferential agreement.

---

19 OJ 1983 L339/19.

Example

An Italian exporter of garments to Tunisia may request his supplier of fabric established in France to confirm that the fabric had Community origin in accordance with the Tunisian EMA origin rules. Exporters may then use these declarations as evidence to support applications for the issue of certificates of origin. In addition, suppliers' declarations are useful to producers who may then check themselves whether their products meet the preferential rules in question. This applies even in cases where the material supplied does not have preferential origin. The supplier may still make out a declaration indicating the processing carried out in the European Union on the non-originating material in question. Thus, assume the fabric in the above example was made with non-originating yarn. The French supplier should still indicate this in his declaration, since further processing of the non-originating fabric into garments in Italy combined with the processing of the yarn into fabric which had already taken place in France could still confer preferential origin on the resulting garment. It is the totalities of the operations carried out in the EU, which must be taken into account to determine whether the origin rules in question, are satisfied.

Suppliers for each consignment of the products concerned must give separate declarations. These declarations are attached to the commercial invoices relating to the shipments or to annexes of invoices or delivery notes or other commercial documents relating to these shipments which describe the products concerned in sufficient detail to enable them to be identified.

Regular suppliers of products may provide a single declaration to cover subsequent shipments of the same product as long as the origin of the product remains unchanged (long term suppliers' declarations). The period of validity of a long term suppliers' declaration is one year unless the customs authorities authorise a longer period.

As a verification measure, customs authorities may request exporters (which in their turn will request suppliers) to produce an information certificate (referred to as INF4) to confirm the accuracy or the authenticity of any suppliers' declaration.

Information certificates are issued by the customs authorities of the suppliers' Member State following an application made by the supplier concerned and after verification that the information contained in it and on the application for their issue is correct. The information certificate is given to the supplier who can forward it to the buyer or to the customs office which has requested its production.

Finally, the customs authorities before issuing a certificate of origin have the power to ask for evidence and to carry out checks in order to verify the correctness of any suppliers' declarations or information certificates.

Council Regulation 3351/83 contains detailed information on the form and content of suppliers' declarations.

Chapter 15

· **Rules of Origin II** ·

15.1 **Introduction**

The previous chapter outlined the common features of the preferential rules of origin present in all the Euro-Mediterranean Agreements. This chapter will instead look at those features specific to the different EMAs.

15.2 **Non-Turkish EMAs**

There are several features, which need to be highlighted, the most significant being those on simplified administrative procedures

Simplified administrative procedures

Given the geographical proximity of the MNCs to the EU and the huge volume of trade between these areas, the EMAs provide simplified procedures for proving preferential origin.

Under these procedures, exporters who make frequent exports of products covered by preferential certificates of origin (approved exporters) may avoid the usual, relatively time-consuming procedures concerning presentation of products to the relevant customs authorities and the issue of movement certificates. Instead, approved exporters may be authorised to forgo the requirements to present the products to be exported to the relevant customs authorities at the time of export, or to submit applications for movement certificates relating to these products. Approved exporters may instead obtain the right to endorse movement certificates themselves (with a special stamp which has been approved by the customs authorities of the exporting country) or to use pre-endorsed certificates. These are blank certificates, which have been endorsed beforehand by the customs authorities (a facsimile is acceptable) – exporters only need to complete the certificate and send it to their customers in the importing country.

For an approved exporter to be able to use the simplified procedures mentioned above, he must offer, to the satisfaction of the customs authorities, guarantees with respect to the verification of the origin of his products. For example, he may be required to submit supporting documents proving that the product qualifies for preferential treatment, offering undertakings and to agree to the customs authorities inspecting his accounts, and/or checking any of the manufacturing processes etc. As an extra measure of precaution, approved exporters may need to inform the customs authorities of the exportation of the products before actual dispatch so that the customs authorities may make the necessary verifications concerning their origin.

Customs authorities have the power to withdraw the above authorisations at any time. Furthermore, they are obliged to do so when the conditions of approval are no longer satisfied or if the approved exporter no longer offers the guarantees that have been agreed with the customs authorities.

Invoice declarations

Exporters may be authorised to use invoices in place of movement certificates by means of including in the invoice a standard declaration, a specimen of which is annexed to the rules. This greatly facilitates the administrative burden for exporters who rather than complete pre-endorsed certificates only need to include in their invoices a declaration testifying that the exported products meet the conditions for obtaining preferential origin. Furthermore, the facility of using invoices for proving origin can be extended to delivery notes or other commercial documents, which (like the invoice) describe the products concerned in sufficient detail as to permit the identification of consignments and whose value does not exceed a certain limit (*e.g.* Euros 5,110 per consignment).

Drawback of customs duties

The Israeli EMA origin rules contain a provision prohibiting the "drawback" of customs duties or duties having equivalent effect. Drawback means the non-payment by a producer of customs duties or similar charges on imported non-originating material used in the manufacture of a product. Similarly, drawback also covers repayment or remission of customs duties or similar charges already paid on imported non-originating material. The reason for the non-payment of the customs duties (or for getting them back) is usually linked to the fact that the finished product is exported from the country of manufacture. If, however, the product is sold on the domestic market of the producer, no drawback is possible.

The EU-Israeli rules prohibit drawback so as to avoid giving producers competitive (cost) advantage when exporting the product to each other's markets. In the absence of such prohibition, this would occur as (say) an Israeli product is exported to Portugal on which customs duties were not paid would be cheaper in comparison to a similar product made in Israel with imported parts on which customs duties have been paid. This is because in the first case he would able to reclaim the duty paid.

Interestingly, drawback provisions are not included in the other EMAs. The reason is that the EU considered that drawback advantage given to developing MNCs could act as a further incentive to them to manufacture products for preferential export to the EU.

Proof of origin in the context of bilateral/full cumulation rules of origin

With a view to ensuring the correct functioning of the EMA cumulation rules of origin,[1] such agreements introduce provisions concerning the issue of declarations by EMA suppliers of non-originating material to EMA producers. These declarations – a copy of which is attached to the rules – aim to help both customs authorities responsible for issuing a movement certificate (known as Eur.1) for a certain product and producers wishing to make an invoice declaration. The intention is enable them to trace non-originating material used by the producer of the product for the purpose of determining whether the product in question has obtained preferential origin or not.

Moreover, the customs authorities issuing the Eur.1 may request of the supplier of non-originating material that he submit an "information certificate" – a copy of which is attached to the rules – to check the authenticity and accuracy given on the declaration or for obtaining additional information. Alternatively, the supplier may submit such a certificate to the authorities issuing the Eur.1. The customs office of the state from which the non-originating material was supplied issues the information certificates. Such certificates supplier may either send the certificate to the customs authorities issuing the Eur.1 or to the final exporter who may then forward it to the Eur.1-issuing authorities.

---

1 For a discussion of cumulation rules of origin, see Chap 17, para 17.3(3).

Most EMA rules of origin include only "bilateral" cumulation of such rules. As a result, the above procedures pertain only to the customs authorities of the EU Member States and the associated MNC. However, the Maghreb EMAs (*i.e.* Tunisia, Algeria and Morocco) additionally allow for "full" (or "diagonal") cumulation rules of origin so that these procedures extend to the other Maghreb MNCs.

Unsurprisingly, therefore, the Maghreb EMAs oblige the contracting parties to conclude administrative arrangements with the other Maghreb counterparts to enable the full cumulation rules to operate smoothly.

15.3 **Turkish EMA**

Unlike its other Mediterranean counterparts, Turkey shares a customs union rather than a free trade area with the EU. This means that Turkey applies the same tariff structure towards the goods from third countries as the EU (known as the External Customs Tariffs) as well as identical rules of origin operating within the EU (the Community Customs Code). The latter is discussed in detail in Chapter 16.

Naturally, the administrative procedures affecting trade between the EU and Turkey are also different. These procedures are contained in Decision 1/96[2] of EU-Turkish Customs Co-operation Committee.[3] The Decision covers movement certificates and "triangular traffic". Both of them are discussed below.

Movement certificates

Products from third countries are considered to be in free circulation in the EU or Turkey provided import formalities have been complied with and any customs duties or charges having equivalent effect which are payable have been levied by the EU or Turkey without reimbursement. Such formalities are complied with in the exporting state by the validation of a document necessary to enable free circulation of the products concerned.

This document is known as the A.TR and is issued by the customs authorities of the exporting state. It may only be used when the goods are transported directly from the EU to Turkey (or vice versa), *i.e.*

---

2 OJ 1996 L200/14 (amended by OJ 1997 L166/7 and OJ 1997 L249/18).
3 For information on the Customs Co-operation Committee, see Chap 18, para 18.5.

without passing through the territory of a third country. The one allowable exception is if the goods cross such territory under cover of a single transport document made out in the EU or Turkey. An A.TR specimen is annexed to Decision 1/96.

The A.TR must be submitted to the customs authorities of the importing state within three months of the date of endorsement by the customs authorities of the exporting state.

Simplified procedures

The customs authorities may authorise any person (known as approved exporter) to issue A.TR certificates without having to present them for endorsement by the relevant customs authorities at the time of exportation.

Authorisation may only be granted to persons:

- who frequently consign goods;
- whose records enable the customs authorities to check their operations; and
- who offer to the satisfaction of the customs authorities all the guarantees necessary to verify the status of the goods.

Such authorisation may be revoked if the approved exporter no longer fulfils any of the above conditions.

Division of certificates

The competent customs authorities must permit a consignment of goods and the movement certificates to be divided. Therefore, the A.TR-issuing authorities must issue an extract of the A.TR for each part of the divided consignment.

Working or processing carried out outside the EU

The Turkish EMA contains a radical exception to the territoriality principle. Its rules of origin permit products (including semi-finished products or material) to undergo further working or processing outside the customs union area and then to be re-imported with total or partial exemptions from tariffs into the customs union area for sale and/or final working or processing. This means a firm in the EU or Turkey may temporarily export parts or raw materials released for free circulation within the EU-Turkish customs union area. When the finished goods are re-imported into either party, there is partial or total relief from customs duty (or if the product concerned is subject to duty the tariff which would have been payable on the importation of raw materials is deducted from the tariff payable on the finished product).

A special "triangular traffic" for outward processing system has been introduced. "Triangular traffic" in this context means the system under which the "compensating products" after outward processing are released for free circulation with partial or total relief from import duties in one part of the customs union other than from which the goods were temporarily exported.

A person authorised for outward processing arrangements (the holder) may opt for this system at any time, except in cases where he uses the "standard exchange system with prior importation".[4]

Where the triangular traffic system is used, information sheet INF 2 must be completed by the holder and presented to the customs office at the point of temporary export of the goods for working or processing in a third country. The issue of the INF 2 constitutes consent of the holder to concede the benefit of the total or partial relief from import duties to another person (such as the importer of the processed product into the customs union area after working or processing is undertaken in a third country).

Once the goods are re-imported into the customs union area following the initial temporary export, the importer must present the INF 2 to the customs office at the point of entry. Moreover, he must also lodge at that office a declaration for release for free circulation.

Turkey and the EU have introduced common outward processing arrangements for textiles and clothing.[5] However, the EU-Turkish Customs Co-operation Committee must pass the necessary measures to implement these arrangements.

The economic reasoning behind these arrangements is to allow Turkish and EU textile producers to exploit cheaper labour costs in third countries without risking their products losing preferential origin. However, the apparent advantages are more apparent than real in cases where it is raw materials rather than semi-finished goods, which are exported for processing. This is because the EU tariff structure follows

4 For further information on the standard exchange system, see Council Reg 2473/86 on outward processing relief arrangements and the standard exchange system (OJ 1986 L212/1). Turkey has not yet adopted this Regulation.
5 EU-Turkey Association Council Dec 1/99 (OJ 1999 L35/45).

that of most industrialised countries, namely the more processing a product undergoes, the higher the tariff to which it is subject.

Returned goods

When goods are returned,[6] the custom authorities of the exporting state must issue an information sheet INF 3 capable of identifying the goods returned. Specimens of this sheet are contained in the Turkish and EU customs provisions. Once issued, it must be presented to the customs authorities of the state upon re-importation of the goods.

Drawback of customs duties

The contracting parties are prohibited from drawback of customs duties and charges having equivalent effect with respect to ECSC Treaty products.

15.4 **Customs valuation**

Rules of origin have no bearing on customs valuation. However, it is an integral counterpart of such rules because they operate in tandem: the level of customs on a good depends on the origin of good. Thus, a discussion on origin rules is not complete without a few words on customs valuation, which is governed by the GATT and WTO.

It is defined as a customs procedure applied to determine the customs value of imported goods. If the rate of duty is *ad valorem* (*i.e.* according to the value of a good), the customs value is essential to determine the duty to be paid on an imported good.

Article VII of GATT 1994 lays down the general principles for an international system of valuation. It stipulates that the value for customs purposes of imported merchandise should be based on the actual value of the imported merchandise on which duty is assessed, or of like merchandise, and should not be based on the value of merchandise of national origin or on arbitrary or fictitious values. Although Article VII contains a definition of "actual value", it permits the use widely differing methods. In addition, "grandfather clauses" permit the continuation of some old standards.

---

6 For a discussion on returned goods, see Chap 14, para 14.7.

The WTO Agreement on the Implementation of Article VII of the GATT (Customs Valuation Agreement) was a product of the Uruguay Round. This Agreement applies only to the valuation of imported goods for the purpose of levying *ad valorem* duties on such goods. It does not contain obligations concerning valuation for purposes of determining export duties or quota administration based on the value of goods, nor does it lay down conditions for the valuation of goods for internal taxation or foreign exchange control.

Customs duties can be designated in either specific or *ad valorem* terms or as a mix of the two. In the case of a specific duty, a concrete sum is charged for a quantitative description of the good, for example Euro 1 per item or per unit. The customs value of the good does not need to be determined, as the duty is not based on the value of the good but on other criteria. In this case, no rules on customs valuation are needed and the Customs Valuation Agreement does not apply. In contrast, an *ad valorem* duty depends on the value of the good. Under this system, the customs valuation is multiplied by *ad valorem* rate of duty (*e.g.* 5 per cent) in order to arrive at the amount of duty payable on an imported item.

The Agreement stipulates that customs valuation shall, except in specified circumstances, be based on the price of the goods to be valued, which is generally shown on the invoice. This price, plus adjustments for certain elements listed in the Agreement, equals the transaction value, which constitutes the first and most important method of valuation referred to in the Agreement.

For cases where there is no transaction, or where the transaction is not acceptable as the customs value because the price has been distorted as a result of certain conditions, the Customs Valuation Agreement provides five other methods of customs valuation, to be applied in prescribed hierarchical order.

It should be noted that Turkey has adopted the customs valuation rules under EU law. Moreover, neither the EU nor Turkey may consider the costs of transport and insurance, loading and handling charges associated with transport of third country goods into the territory of the EU-Turkish customs union area for customs valuation purposes. This is conditional upon these costs and charges being shown separately from the price actually paid or payable for the goods concerned.

Chapter 16

· Community Customs Code ·

16.1 Introduction

Turkey shares a customs union with the European Union and is therefore a composite member of the Community Customs Code (the Code), which is an enormous body of customs legislation developed and promulgated at the Community level. Hence, the Code determines the origin of products in connection with Turkey and the EU.

It is embodied in two pieces of legislation: Council Regulation 2913/93[1] establishing the Code and Commission Regulation 2454/93[2] laying down implementing provisions for the Code such as on certificates of origin (the implementing Regulation). It replaced and largely codified the provisions in Council Regulation 802/68[3] so that the substance and interpretation of the Regulation and related judgments of the Court of Justice were not affected.

The Code deals with origin rules in Chapter 2 of Title II comprising six Articles. Chapter 2 of the Code is divided into two sections, which deal with preferential and non-preferential rules of origin respectively.

16.2 Non-preferential origin rules

The non-preferential origin rules set out in the Code largely reflect the text of Regulation 902/68. However, the structure of these rules has been simplified such that only the basic provisions of Regulation 802/68 have been maintained. Most of the provisions of Regulation 902/68 which deal with secondary matters, such as the origin of accessories and the form of the certificates of origin, are covered in Commission Regulation 2454/93.

---

1 OJ 1993 L253/1.
2 OJ 1993 L335/1.
3 JO 1968 L148/1.

Scope

The Code first defines the scope of the application of the non-preferential origin rules. In particular, Article 22 of the Code provides that the non-preferential origin rules are established for the purposes of applying the customs tariff as well as other measures established by Community provisions which govern specific areas relating to trade in products such as, for example, quantitative restrictions. Article 22 specifically excludes from the scope of the non-preferential origin rules the application of preferential tariff measures contained in agreements which the EU has concluded with certain countries (like the MNCs) or adopted unilaterally by the EU in respect of certain countries, groups of countries or territories.

Basic origin rules

The basic origin rules are set out in Article 23 of the Code and are identically worded to those in Regulation 802/68. This Article makes a distinction between products, which are wholly obtained or produced in one country and products in the manufacture of which more than one country was involved. In the latter case, products will be deemed to originate in the country where they underwent their "last substantial" economically justified processing or working in an undertaking equipped for that purpose and resulting in the manufacture of a new product or representing an important stage of production. The Code has essentially preserved the definition of the "last substantial operation" set out in Article 5 of Regulation 802/68.

Article 24 of the Code contains a list of products, which are deemed to be products wholly or produced in one country. This list is virtually identical to the list set out in Article 4(2) of Regulation 802/68.[4] Further, the same Article states that the expressions "country" and "territory" cover the countries' or territories' territorial sea.

Last substantial operation rule

As a result of international trade and the greater international division of labour, the manufacture of any one product tends increasingly to be

---

4 The list in the Code is almost identical to the list in the EMAs, shown in Chap 14, para 14.4. With regard to item (f) of the list relating to products of sea-fishing and other products of the sea, the Code makes it clear that this applies to fishery products taken outside territorial waters of a country. Products taken from the territorial waters of a country are covered by item (e) (products of fishing carried on in a country).

carried out by undertakings located in different countries. It must, therefore, be determined which of those countries is to be considered as the country of origin of the product in question. Where two or more countries are involved in the manufacture of a product (which is the case in the vast majority of manufactured products) the Code includes the "last substantial process or operation" as the decisive factor for determining the origin of the product in question.

Thus, in accordance with the Code a product obtains the origin of the country where the last substantial process or operation leading to its manufacture was carried out provided that the said operation:

- was economically justified;
- was carried out in an undertaking equipped for such production; and
- resulted in the manufacture of a new product, or represented an important stage of manufacture.

The two primary requirements are both that the process or operation must be the "last" and must be "substantial". Both of these requirements must be met simultaneously so that a substantial operation, which is not the last operation to be performed, does not satisfy the rule. Similarly, the very last operation to be carried out on a product is not necessarily substantial in the terms of the Code.

Moreover, the additional conditions must all be fulfilled to obtain the origin of the country where the process or operation was carried out. The first two additional requirements do not raise any particular problems since in practice all manufacturing operations are economically justified (otherwise they would not take place) and carried out in properly equipped facilities (otherwise the operation could not have been carried out). In practice, therefore, it is the third additional requirement, which usually determines whether a process is substantial. That is, the process or operation must have resulted in the creation of a new product, which did not exist before that process or operation, or represented an important stage of manufacture.

In order to determine whether a new product is created, a clear and objective distinction must be made between, on the one hand, the raw materials used in the manufacture of the product and, on the other hand, the resulting product. This distinction is based on the specific material qualities of the raw material and the resulting product respectively. Thus, for the operation to be described as substantial the resulting product must have its own properties and a composition of its own which it did not possess before that process or operation.

Activities which do not bring about significant qualitative change in the properties of the raw material are not of such a nature to determine the origin of the resulting product.

The Court of Justice developed the principle of distinguishing between raw material and processed product on the basis of their respective material qualities in the landmark *Handelskammer*[5] case concerning the processing of untreated casein. In that case the Court was requested to determine whether the degrees of fineness were substantial to confer the origin of the country of processing to the casein in question. The Court ruled that the only effect of performing these operations was to change the consistency of the casein and its presentation for the purposes of its later use. Furthermore, the quality control to which the grounded casein was subjected and the packaging operation related only to the requirements for marketing the casein and did not affect its substantial properties.

In accordance with the Court each material has its own characteristics and qualities which individualise it with regard to other products. For example, the raw cotton, as a product, has different characteristics, uses and material qualities than cotton yarn which is the product resulting out of the working or processing of the raw cotton.

The distinguishing criterion is therefore whether the resulting product can claim to have acquired through the qualifying process or operation certain qualities which permit it to fulfil a role that the individual parts or material used in its manufacture could not have fulfilled before that process or operation. If it can be claimed that the parts or materials already had the properties which characterise the resulting product then the operation is not substantial. For example, dyeing a fabric does not result in the fabric acquiring any new properties since it can still be used for the manufacture if various textile products in the same way that the undyed fabric could in the first place. On the other hand, the dyeing of unbleached fabric accompanied by certain other preparatory or finishing operations, such as bleaching, is regarded as a substantial operation. The reason is that the fabric acquires new properties it did not possess before and can be put to uses the unbleached fabric could not be put to.

Similarly, the sterilisation of medical instruments and the breaking-up of stone to produce ballast have not been considered as substantial operations as they do not add new properties to the products obtained

---

5 Case 49/76 *Gesellschaft für Überseehandel mbH v Handelskammer Hamburg* [1977] ECR 41.

from such operations. On the other hand, the production of corned beef from non-originating fresh beef, the cutting and polishing of diamonds, or the production of decaffeinated coffee, have all been found to constitute substantial operations which confer on the products obtained the origin of the country where these operations took place. Furthermore, the assembly of non-originating parts may be considered as the last substantial operation if it reflects the stage where the use of the parts becomes definite through incorporation into the product so as to give it specific qualities.

The qualitative change in the properties of the material must be significant for the operation to confer origin. Thus, an operation that involves a change in the properties of the material (albeit an insignificant one) may not confer origin.

The Court has not further refined the notion of "significant" qualitative change. However, the European Commission seems to consider a qualitative change in the properties of the product as significant if it is important when compared with the manufacturing process of the product as a whole. This criterion, therefore, involves a comparison of the operation in question with the other operations performed on the product so as to determine its significance, not in isolation, but in view of the totality of the operations which take place for the manufacture of the product.

An operation, therefore, resulting in a product having its own properties and comparison of its own which it did not previously possess may still not confer origin on the product, if it can be regarded as significantly less important than the other operations involved.

The "comparative significance" test approach seems to presuppose that the last substantial operation must represent in all cases an important stage in the manufacture of a product. This, however, does not seem to take into account that the Code requires that the last substantial operation must result in the manufacture of a new product or represent an important stage of manufacture. Therefore, the wording of the Code suggests that the last substantial operation rule be satisfied if either of the two conditions is met and not if both conditions are simultaneously met, as the Commission methodology implies.

For this reason the Commission methodology may go beyond the scope of the Code if it results in the determination of origin being made on the basis of the most and not the last substantial operation. There is no convincing reason as to why an operation which is "significantly less important" than previous operations carried out on a product is not substantial in its own right in the terms of the

Regulation 802/68 (and by extension the Code) as interpreted by the Court of Justice. The Code does not require that the last substantial operation is equally or relatively important in comparison to the other operations involved in the manufacture of a product. It only requires that the product after the operation in question obtains new material qualities that it did not have before.

The fact that the Code refers to "the" last substantial operation does not imply that technically only a single operation can confer origin. In many occasions it may be difficult to isolate one particular manufacturing operation to apply the last substantial operation rule. The case may be that out of a series of distinct manufacturing operations no single operation on its own is substantial within the terms of the Code. In such cases, the combination of two or more processes or operations may collectively form the "last substantial" operation. For example, in the case of ball bearings neither the assembly of the ball bearing from its constituent parts nor the heat treatment to which the inner and outer rings in their unhardened state are subjected can be considered as the last substantial operation. The same is true for the grinding and polishing of the inner and outer rings.

In view of the above, for the purpose of determining which operation(s) constitute the last substantial operation in the manufacture of a product the following assessment needs to be undertaken. Products should:

(1) Distinguish all manufacturing operations involved in the production of a product.

(2) Determine the last operation(s) during which the product gets new material qualities and features different from those of the materials used in its production.

(3) Determine which of the operation(s) under (2) are significant with regard to the manufacturing process as a whole.

Circumvention of origin

Article 25 of the Code contains anti-circumvention provisions. Considering that origin is the criterion used by the EU for applying trade restrictive measures to imported products, one of the ways of avoiding such measures has traditionally been to change the origin of a product which is subject to the measures in question. This can be achieved by transferring some or all of the operations carried out on a product from the country subject to the measures to another country with the aim of obtaining origin of that country and thus escape the measures. To deal with such a circumvention of measures, Article 25 provides that products manufactured under such circumstances will not acquire the origin of the second country even if the last substantial operation is carried out there.

In particular, the Article provides that even if a manufacturing process carried out on a product meets the last substantial operation rule, it will not necessarily confer on the product in question origin of the country where it was carried out. This is especially the case if it was established that the sole object was to circumvent the provisions applicable in the EU or the Member State to products from specific countries.

For example, imagine a producer of radios established in country A, which is subject to an EU anti-dumping duty on radios, transfers production of the radios to country B in order to obtain the origin of that country. In those circumstances, the anti-dumping duty imposed on radios from country A, the radios in question will not obtain the origin of country B even if they meet the 45 per cent added value rule set out for radios.

For this provision to be activated, however, it must be either clearly established, or the facts must justify the presumption, that the relevant producer had as his sole object to circumvent the EU or Member States, provisions applicable with respect to products originating in a given country. As this provision is seldom invoked, its content has not yet been clarified.

In the *Brother*[6] case, the Court of Justice was concerned with the transfer of the assembly of electronic typewriters from Japan to Taiwan where the producer already had a manufacturing plant. It had to determine whether this justified the presumption that the move was made with the sole object of circumventing the anti-dumping measures applicable to electronic typewriters from Japan. The Court did not consider that the move of the assembly operation itself was good ground for a presumption as there could have been a number of other reasons justifying such a transfer

The Court, however, took into account the timing of the adoption of the allegedly circumvented measures. It ruled that the transfer of assembly from the country in which parts were manufactured to another country in which use was made of existing factories did not

---

6 Case C-26/88 *Brother International v Hauptzollant Giessen* [1989] ECR 4253.

itself justify the presumption that the sole object of such a transfer was to circumvent the applicable provisions. This was subject to the fact that the transfer of the assembly had not coincided with the entry into force of the relevant measures. The onus for proving that the sole object for transferring the assembly operations lies primarily with the competent authorities. In the situation where the transfer coincided with the entry into force of the measures in question, the burden of proof is reversed. It is then up to the producer to prove that there were reasonable grounds other than avoiding the consequences of the provisions in questions justifying such a transfer.

These anti-circumvention provisions seems to link the application of trade measures with the nationality or even the identity of the producer involved which may potentially have grave consequences with regard to legal certainty. Since origin has been established as the primary criterion for the imposition of trade measures it should for reasons of legal certainty remain as such. Therefore, the Commission in such circumstances prefers either to show that the conditions for the acquisition of origin have not been met in country A or to take protective measures against imports of the product in question from that country as well.

Certificates of origin

Article 26 of the Code concerns certificates of origin. In particular it provides that, if required by customs legislation or other EU legislation governing specific fields, a certificate of origin must be produced as proof of the origin of the products imported into the EU. Thus, it is acknowledged that the presentation of the certificates of origin is not mandatory unless this is specifically required by the EU legislation. However, even if a certificate of origin is produced customs authorities may, if they have serious doubts as to the accuracy of the particular certificate of origin, require additional proof of the origin of the product concerned. This is in order to ensure that the country of origin indicated in the certificate complies with the EU's origin rules.

16.3 **Implementing Regulation**

The Code does not cover all the subject matters of Regulation 802/68. An implementing Regulation therefore contains, among others, the remaining provisions of Regulation 802/68, such as provisions relating to the origin of accessories or spare parts and the certificates of origin. Furthermore, as a measure of further simplification of the application of the origin rules, the implementing Regulation also consolidates into one text all the product specific origin Regulations which have been previously enacted under Regulation 802/68. Thus, only two legal instruments effectively treat the origin issues under EU law: namely the Code and the implementing Regulation. In general, the implementing Regulation has not made any substantial amendments to the provisions, which were in force before its enactment.

16.4 **Customs Code Committee**

Articles 247 to 249 of the Code introduced a new forum called the Customs Code Committee which has been granted certain powers in relation to customs issues arising under the Code, including issues relating to questions of origin. Thus, the Customs Code Committee, according to the Code, replaced the Committee on Origin, which operated within the ambit of Regulation 802/68. The procedure of the Customs Code Committee is identical to the procedure followed by the Committee of Origin.

In summary, the Committee is composed of officials from the Member States, which may examine all questions relating to product specific origin rules which implements the last substantial operation rule – that is, rules which provide a clearer definition of what constitutes the last substantial operation for a given product. The initiative for submitting questions to the Committee lies exclusively with the Commission and Member States; natural or other legal persons may therefore not raise any issues directly with the Committee. From a procedural point of view its chairman refers all questions to the Committee. The Member State officials on the Committee vote using a voting procedure weighted according to the size of the population in each Member State.

16.5 **Preferential origin rules**

Article 27 of the Code for the adoption of preferential origin rules lays down the conditions that must be satisfied in order for products to obtain origin and therefore benefit from preferential agreements or unilateral schemes introduced by the Community.

In the former case, the origin rules will continue to be determined by reference to the preferential agreements themselves, whereas in the latter case, they will be determined in accordance with the Code and, in particular, by the Customs Code Committee.

Chapter 17

Relationship between Preferential and Non-Preferential Origin Rules

17.1 **Introduction**

The Community Customs Code and its implementing Regulation set out the origin rules for normal trade measures, such as the application of the Community Customs Tariff (*i.e.* the EU's tariff structure applicable to non-EU countries) or quantitative restrictions. It also provides for special origin rules to be adopted concerning trade between the EU and third countries on the basis of agreements which derogate from the most-favoured-nation principle[1] (that is, which grant preferential customs treatment), such as the Euro-Mediterranean Agreements. Therefore, there is a clear distinction between normal origin rules (non-preferential origin rules) and origin rules in the context of preferential trade (preferential origin rules).

Preferential origin rules are specifically drafted to complement certain bilateral and multilateral trade agreements, which aim to give a particular benefit to the country or countries involved (beneficiary countries). Usually this benefit (also referred to as "preferential treatment") consists of tariff preferences in the form of duty-free importation (that is, importation without payment of customs duties) of the products originating in the beneficiary countries or importation at reduced customs duties.

To ensure that the benefit is limited to products made by the beneficiary countries, the implementation of the preferential agreements is conditional on these products satisfying the preferential origin rules, which form part of these agreements. Hence, in contrast

---

1 The most-favoured-nation principle is perhaps the most important principle against discrimination enshrined in the WTO agreements. It provides that any benefits granted by a WTO member to products from a specific country (*e.g.* customs duty reduction) should apply indiscriminately with regard to products from all other WTO members. There are, however, provisions permitting exceptions to that principle, *e.g.* the establishment of a free trade area.

to the situation regarding the non-preferential origin rules, there is no single EU instrument laying down general preferential rules; each preferential agreement has its own specific origin rules. In essence, preferential origin rules are the final outcome of negotiations between the EU and non-EU countries.

The aim of this chapter is to show the differences between the origin rules in the Turkish EMA *vis-à-vis* the non-Turkish EMAs. Turkey has adopted the EU's non-preferential rules of origin as part of its effort to enter into a customs union with other MNCs. On the other hand, the other MNCs are merely engaged in a free trade area with the European Union so that there is no reason for the former to adopt the latter's non-preferential origin rules.

17.2 **Strict origin rules**

The fact that the preferential origin rules only apply in the context of the agreement under which they were developed indicates that the benefits arising out of the agreement are intended to be limited only to the products with a real and substantial economic link with the beneficiary country. Non-preferential origin rules cannot always guarantee such a link through the application of the last substantial operation rule. This suggests that beneficiary countries must make a special economic effort in order to benefit from preferential access to the other party's market.

In practice, therefore, the EU has opted to negotiate preferential rules that are stricter than the non-preferential rules. For example, under the non-preferential origin rules television, radios and tape recorders obtain origin if the added value in the country of processing is 45 per cent; under the EMA preferential origin rules the minimum value is 60 per cent. Similarly, with respect to textile products under the non-preferential rules the carrying out of one complete stage of production (such as weaving in the case of fabrics) usually suffices to confer origin on the resulting product. In contrast, under the preferential origin rules, to obtain origin textile products must pass through at least two stages of production (such as spinning and weaving).

The European Court of Justice has confirmed the establishment of stricter rules of origin for preferential purposes in the *S R Industries*[2]

---

2 Case 385/85 *S R Industries* [1986] ECR 2929.

case. A French importer of sails from Hong Kong (S R Industries) was asked by customs authorities to pay customs duties because the sails, although of Hong Kong origin under Regulation 802/68, did not have preferential origin under the GSP origin rules.[3] S R Industries challenged the decision of the customs authorities on the basis that the Commission had established stricter GSP origin rules for sails than those adopted under Regulation 802/68. In particular, S R Industries argued that under the non-preferential origin rules sails would originate in Hong Kong if they were made from non-originating fabric while, under the GSP origin rules, they would only get preferential origin if they were made from non-originating unbleached yarn.[4]

The Court dismissed S R Industries' argument, confirming that the concept of the origin of goods could be interpreted in a different and stricter manner under the GSP scheme than in the framework of the common rules drawn up by Regulation 802/68. The Court, in fact, went even further by stating that such a different and stricter application was necessary to achieve the main objective of the GSP scheme. This is to ensure that the preferences only benefit industries which are established in developing countries and which carry out the main manufacturing processes in those countries. Thus, the Court not only clearly drew a distinction between the application of the preferential and non-preferential rules of origin but also confirmed the Commission's reasoning for applying stricter origin rules in the latter case.

17.3 Major difference between preferential and non-preferential origin rules

To gain a better understanding of the different nature between preferential and non-preferential origin rules, three of the most important differences are examined. These relate to the field of application of each group of rules, the basic origin rules underlying each group, and the existence of the concept of cumulation of origin in the preferential rules.

---

3 The GSP is the Generalised System of Preferences, a unilateral scheme whereby the EU granted preferential treatment for the purposes of origin rules to a group of developing countries and territories.

4 Under the GSP rules, more manufacturing operations had to be performed in Hong Kong than under the non-preferential origin rules for sails to obtain the origin of Hong Kong. In other words, for preferential purposes, manufacture of sails in Hong Kong should start at an earlier stage in the manufacturing process (from yarn) than under Reg 802/68 (from fabric).

1. Field of application

The preferential origin rules form part of the agreement or schemes that have clear commercial and/or domestic policy objectives. Consequently, preferential rules differ among themselves along with the economic and trade interests of third countries. Non-preferential origin rules are, however, neutral and objective and apply not only to products originating in third countries without exception but also to products originating in the EU itself.

Moreover, preferential origin rules are to be used only in the context of the agreement or scheme under which they were developed. They are therefore limited for use in trade between the EU and the non-EU country or countries concerned. Preferential origin acquired by a product under the terms of a preferential agreement or scheme does not, however, accompany the product in all its useful life. Outside the framework of the agreement or scheme in question the acquisition of preferential origin does not imply any consequences. Thus, the origin of the product imported (for instance under the EMAs) also has to be determined under the non-preferential origin rules if this is required under EU law for other purposes. For example, the origin of products in a tender under the public procurement rules involving the telecommunications sector[5] has to be determined in accordance with the Community Customs Code. The EMA origin of a product under the EMA origin rules would not be applicable in that specific case.[6] On the other hand, the Code has no such limits in its application, as it is the instrument, which will normally be used by authorities to determine the origin of a product unless the interested parties make claim for preferential origin.

Thus, it can be argued that the preferential origin rules are not real "origin" rules but special local content rules applicable in trade with certain third countries.

2. Basic origin rule

The most important difference between preferential and non-preferential origin rules lies in their respective basic origin criteria. The basic non-preferential origin criterion was the "last substantial

---

5 Council Dir 90/531 (OJ 1990 L297/1).
6 The argument may be of limited practical importance since the preferential origin rules are usually stricter than the non-preferential origin rules, so a product which qualifies for preferential origin in one country would almost certainly also originate in that country under the Code.

origin rule". In other words, in order to establish the origin of a product one must examine the country in which the last substantial manufacturing operation was performed on the specific product. This may not be the last country where the product was manufactured: the product may, in certain circumstances, originate in the country where parts of the product concerned were manufactured or where the product was semi-finished.

As far as the preferential origin rules are concerned, even though they differ between themselves, they all adopt the same basic criterion that products must undergo "sufficient working or processing" in the beneficiary country. In other words, in order to establish whether a product has obtained preferential origin, one must examine whether the manufacturing process performed in the beneficiary country meets the requirements set out in the preferential origin rules. If the preferential origin rules are not satisfied in that country, then the product has no preferential origin. With the exception of cases where cumulation rules apply, it is irrelevant to examine whether another country, which was involved at an earlier stage of the manufacturing process of the product, has or has not satisfied the preferential origin rule.

The underlying principle of the non-preferential origin rules is, therefore, where the last substantial operation took place. This is because the function of those rules is to assign an origin to the product. On the other hand, the underlying principle of a preferential origin rule is simply whether sufficient working or processing has taken in the beneficiary country. This will determine whether the product may benefit from preferential treatment upon importation into the EU.

While, therefore, the emphasis under the non-preferential origin rules is placed on what is the origin of a product, the emphasis under the preferential origin rules is whether or not the beneficiary country fulfilled the criteria for its products to enjoy preferential treatment.

The importance of the above distinction has serious practical consequences. If a product cannot obtain preferential origin under the preferential origin rules, it will not mean that the product has no origin. For statistical and other trade purposes, origin in any case will have to be assigned to products under the non-preferential origin rules. As a general rule, therefore, the non-preferential origin rules will remain applicable in cases where products cannot satisfy the preferential origin rules. The practical effect of importing a product under the non-preferential origin rules is that, notwithstanding the fact that it may come from the beneficiary country, it will not benefit from preferential treatment and thus would have to pay normal customs duties at the EU frontier. If it had originated in the beneficiary country under the preferential origin rules the product would, of course, have escaped the payment of customs duties.

Three situations may, therefore, arise in the determination of the origin of a product:

(1) If a product satisfies the preferential origin rules in the beneficiary country, it may be imported into the EU and avoid payment of customs duties.

(2) If the product does not satisfy the preferential origin rules in the beneficiary country, but does satisfy the non-preferential origin rules there, the product will still have the origin of the beneficiary but would have to pay the normal customs duties.

(3) If the product cannot satisfy either the preferential or non-preferential origin rules in the beneficiary country, then as the product cannot remain without an origin it will have to be assigned an origin in accordance with the non-preferential origin rules. The product may then be found to originate in another country which was involved in the production at an earlier stage.

Example

A television is exported from Morocco to the European Union. The preferential rules under the Moroccan EMA require, *inter alia,* that a television set have at least 60 per cent value added in Morocco. On the other hand, the non-preferential rules require that the value added in Morocco is at least 45 per cent. If the television has value added in Morocco of 60 per cent or more it could be imported into the Community duty free as a preferential origin product. If the television has a value added between 45 and 60 per cent, it would still be imported into the Community as a television of Moroccan origin but the normal customs duties would be payable. If, however, the television has a value added of less than 45 per cent, it could, in fact, originate in another country such as the country of manufacture of the parts, say, Japan. In that case, the product will be treated as a Japanese product upon importation into the Community.

3. The concept of cumulation

Developing countries may often find it difficult to meet the conditions set out in the stricter preferential origin rules. These countries, such as the MNCs, may have to obtain materials from outside their territory to manufacture the product in question. By doing so, however, they risk losing preferential status for their product. The EU has therefore developed a system that enables products manufactured with (non-originating) imported material may maintain their preferential status in certain situations. This exception usually applies with regard to imported material sourced from the other party to the agreement.

Under this system, the cumulation of the value added or processes performed in two or more beneficiary countries is permitted so that a product may obtain preferential origin even though the preferential origin rules were not satisfied solely in the exporting beneficiary country.

Thus, cumulation rules provide that the operations required to confer origin do not necessarily have to be carried out within the territory of the exporting beneficiary country: working or processing carried out in another beneficiary country may, within certain limits, be taken into account and result in preferential origin being awarded.

In other words, the concept of cumulation permits the treatment of non-originating material as originating.[7]

For example, under the Tunisian EMA origin rules a television manufactured in Tunisia must achieve a minimum Tunisian added value of 60 per cent in order to obtain preferential origin. Under the cumulation rules, this may be achieved even if the value added in that country is only, say, 20 per cent as long as the remaining 40 per cent of the value added on the value added originates in the Community. The reason for this is that under the Tunisian EMA origin rules, materials and parts originating in the EU may be treated as originating in Tunisia.

The cumulation rules may be unilateral, bilateral, multilateral or total/diagonal, depending on which parties to the relevant agreement benefit from the rules.

Unilateral cumulation

Unilateral cumulation (also referred to as the donor country content) exists when the benefits of cumulation are granted to only one of the two parties to the agreement concerned. Thus, only one of the two parties may freely use materials originating in the other party's country, whereas the other party must still count materials coming from the first party as non-originating.

---

7 This does not mean that the origin of material changes. The material retains its origin and simply counts as originating in the beneficiary country.

Bilateral cumulation

Bilateral cumulation exists when in an agreement involving two parties, both parties to the agreement may freely use materials originating in the other party's country. Such rules apply to all the EMAs, so that each MNC may consider parts and materials originating in the EU as originating in the country concerned (provided such parts and materials have undergone working or processing beyond the simple operations referred to in Chap 14, para 14.4). For example, under the Moroccan EMA, a television made in Morocco with 40 per cent Moroccan value, 30 per cent EU value and 30 per cent from other third countries would originate in Morocco as the combined Moroccan and Community value satisfies the origin rules for television which requires a minimum local value of 60 per cent.

Similarly, the Community may consider materials originating in the relevant MNC as originating for the purposes of determining whether products obtain preferential origin under the terms of relevant EMA.

In addition, the EMAs provide that working or processing carried out in the MNC (so long as such working or processing goes beyond simple operations) is considered as carried out in the EU when the products undergo subsequent working or processing in the MNC. Obviously, the reverse is true: working or processing carried out in the EU is regarded as carried out in the MNC when the products undergo subsequent working or processing in the MNC.

Multilateral cumulation

Multilateral cumulation exists when in one or more agreements involving several parties each party may use to a greater or lesser degree materials originating in the other parties' countries. For example, the old origin rules in the Hungarian Association Agreement (known as the Europe Agreement) stated that a product manufactured in the EU which was then exported to Poland or the Czech Republic where it undergoes further working or processing might still have retained its EU origin. This is conditional upon the fact that the processing in the intermediate country was not sufficient to confer on the product the Polish or Czech origin. The same, of course, applied if the product underwent no working or processing in Poland or the Czech Republic. In both the above cases, the product may still have been exported to Hungary as an EU product. This meant that any processing done in Poland or the Czech Republic was regarded as neutral: the processing did not positively add anything to the origin of the product.

Total/diagonal cumulation

Finally, total/diagonal (or full) cumulation exists where the territories of the parties to an agreement are treated as a single territory. That is, when the beneficiary countries are treated as one country so that producers in any one of these countries have unlimited access to materials originating in the other countries. Diagonal cumulation rules apply only to the Maghreb EMAs (*i.e.* Tunisia, Morocco and Algeria). However, the Commission has expressed a strong desire to negotiate similar rules with other MNCs that enter into free trade agreements between themselves.[8] The Commission hopes that cumulation of origin rules will encourage the integration of the MNC economies so as to create a Euro-Mediterranean Economic Area, *i.e.* a single free trade zone encompassing the EU and the MNCs.

The economic effect of the cumulation rules is considerable as it allows parties to have access to materials originating in other countries without risking the loss of preferential treatment for their products. Thus, it is substantially easier to satisfy criteria set out in the preferential origin rules. Moreover, cumulation rules encourage industrial co-operation between the countries involved and as such may become an important development policy tool. Obviously, cumulation is not permitted under the non-preferential rules of origin, which must be wholly satisfied in one country.[9]

How do the Maghreb cumulation origin rules work?

Exceptionally for the EMAs, diagonal cumulation applies between the European Union, Algeria, Morocco and Tunisia. Take the rules in the Tunisian EMA. Materials originating in Algeria or Morocco are considered as originating in the EU (with reference to the imports of

---

8 The Commission has stated that the objective is to have uniform rules of origin throughout the Euro-Mediterranean region. This requires that the customs authorities in the different MNC countries enter into administrative co-operative agreements with one another. In fact, the Maghreb EMAs oblige the Maghreb countries to take the necessary measures for the conclusion of arrangements with each other to enable the application of the cumulation rules of origin. Several MNCs have concluded bilateral free trade agreements between one another (and with some non-Mediterranean countries): Turkey and Israel; Morocco and Tunisia; Egypt and Saudi Arabia; Egypt and Morocco; Egypt and Tunisia; Lebanon and Syria; Israel and the Palestinian Authority. Jordan is concluding similar free trade deals with Morocco and Tunisia. Moreover, the Arab countries are implementing an agreement to create a pan-Arab Free Trade Area that took effect in January 1998, providing for annual 10% reductions in customs tariffs over 10 years. Egypt is close to concluding a free trade accord with Turkey and Lebanon.

9 Unless, of course, a customs union has been created as is the case with the EU Member States and between the EU and Turkey.

EU goods into Tunisia) or as originating in Tunisia (regarding the imports of Tunisian goods into the EU). It shall not be necessary that such materials have undergone "sufficient working or processing". They must, however, have undergone working or processing beyond the simple operations referred in Chapter 14, paragraph 14.4.

Moreover, the Tunisian EMA provides that working or processing carried out in Algeria or Morocco (so long as such working or processing goes beyond simple operations) are considered as carried out in either the EU or Tunisia when the products obtained subsequent working or processing in the territory of either of the two parties. Thus, working or processing carried out in the EU or in any of these three countries is regarded as having been carried out in the country where the last working or processing took place.

Hence, a television made in Tunisia with 20 per cent Algerian value, EU value, 10 per cent Tunisian value and the rest from other third countries would originate in Tunisia, since the this was the country of last manufacture of the television and since the 60 per cent minimum value added rule for the television is satisfied collectively.

It should be noted that the Tunisian rules provide an important qualification to any cumulation with Algeria or Morocco: the materials originating in Algeria or Morocco and exchanged with the EU for cumulation purposes must be governed by identical rules of origin in both the EU and Algeria/Morocco. The same is true for Algerian/Moroccan exchange effected with Tunisia.

Similarly, any product undergoing working or processing in Algeria or Morocco for cumulation purposes must be governed by identical rules of origin in any exchange effected between Algeria/Morocco and Tunisia or between Algeria/Morocco and the EU.

The Maghreb cumulation rules of origin in practice

If we take the Tunisian EMA as an example, the cumulation rules means that a Tunisian manufacturer will be able to source materials for his final products in Tunisia itself, Algeria, Morocco and all 15 EU Member States. Working or processing can also be partially carried out in one or more of these 18 countries without the preferential access to the EU being lost. The working or processing which is carried out must of course be "significant" and cannot simply consist of operations relating to the preservation of the product in good condition during transport or storage, nor simple operations such as dusting and classifying, packaging, re-packaging, affixing marks or labels or simply assembly.[10]

Therefore, for example, a Tunisian clothes manufacturer may have a factory in Morocco, which makes yarn out of Tunisian cotton. This cotton would then be woven into cloth and cut in Algeria while the actual garments would then be sewn in Tunisia. The final product would still be able to benefit from duty free access into the EU even if the actual origin rule relating to the manufacture of clothing was not satisfied by the amount of working or processing carried out in Tunisia. Operations which did not in themselves amount to the satisfaction of the origin criteria in the Tunisian EMA and which were carried out at each stage cumulatively satisfy such origin criteria.

Pan-European cumulation of origin

Turkey has been included in the common system of pan-European rules of origin[11] for industrial products. This means that Turkey forms part of a vast area including the European Union, the Central and Eastern European countries (CEECs), the Baltic States, European Free Trade Area (EFTA) and the EEA countries, all covered by pan-European cumulation of origin. Essentially, originating products can be moved around while still qualifying for preferential treatment.

Between 1 January and 1 July 1997 the protocols on rules of origin annexed to the EU Association Agreements with the CEECs (known as Europe Agreements), the Baltic States, EFTA, EEA countries and Slovenia were replaced by standardised text which also provided for the aggregation of materials and work or processing carried out in these countries. In other words, full/diagonal cumulation of origin rules was introduced between these countries. This pan-European cumulation of origin, means originating products from this vast area can move around at preferential tariff rates.

The inclusion of Turkey in the system for industrial products created an even larger, more effective free trade area. The restrictive limits set by the individual free trade agreements which Turkey has signed with the European countries referred to above have been merged and

---

10   The full list is available in Chap 14, para 14.4.
11   There are some good articles on this topic: Dan Horovitz, "'Made in Europe': new European rules of origin and world trade liberalisation", (1997) 3(1) *International Trade Law and Regulation*, 27-29; Hans-Joachim Priess and Ralph Pethke, "The pan-European rules of origin: the beginning of a new era in European free trade", (1997) 34(4) *Common Market Law Review*, 773-809.

Turkish originating products are accepted, as such, in all European countries covered by pan-European cumulation of origin.

17.4 **WTO Agreement on rules of origin**

The WTO Agreement on Rules of Origin (Origin Agreement) establishes common origin rules for all trade-related measures. Thus, a single body of origin rules applies to all countries that are members of the WTO and within each country for non-preferential trade purposes.

Hence, the Origin Agreement does not apply to preferential rules of origin, such as those contained in the EMAs. Several countries (including the EU) considered that these rules are usually negotiated bilaterally taking into account the particular objectives sought by the parties concerned; if problems arise under these rules, mechanisms are laid down within preferential agreements to deal with them. Notwithstanding the above, at the insistence of countries which had wished to see the Origin Agreement cover preferential rules of origin, a Common Declaration has been annexed to the Origin Agreement containing certain disciplines which will have to be respected when preferential origin rules are endorsed.

The Common Declaration defines preferential origin rules as those laws, regulations and administrative determinations of general application which determine whether products qualify for preferential treatment under contractual or autonomous trade regimes which lead to the granting of tariff preferences beyond the most-favoured-nation clause in the GATT.

In particular, the Common Declaration provides that countries, even though they may apply differential origin rules, will still have to respect certain disciplines. These relate to:

1. Origin tests and positive standards

If the tariff classification tests are used in preferential agreements, the headings and sub-headings within the tariff nomenclature which are addressed by the test must be clearly specified. Where an added value rule is used, the method for calculating the added value percentage must be indicated; moreover, costs not directly related to manufacturing or processing may be included for the purpose of the application of the added value test. Where a manufacturing or processing operation test is used, the operation conferring origin must be precisely specified in the rule.

Rules of origin should be based on a positive standard. Negative standards (that is, rules which state what is not enough to confer origin) are generally only permissible to the extent that they clarify a positive standard. Exceptionally, negative tests may be used in individual cases where a positive standard is not necessary.[12]

2. Publication

All laws and regulations relating to the preferential rules of origin must be published. This applies equally to judicial and administrative rulings. Publications must be made in accordance with the relevant provisions of the GATT so as to guarantee a certain amount of transparency in the adoption of origin rules.[13]

The publication requirement only applies to laws, regulations and rulings of general application. Thus, rulings, which relate to a particular situation of a specific producer do not have to be published. This is understandable, as most of the information in such cases could be confidential.

3. Application of assessment of origin

In the interests of legal certainty and security the Origin Agreement provides that a system under which exporters, importers or any person with a justifiable cause (such as producers) may ask the authorities to assess the origin of a product. Such assessments must be made as soon as possible but no later than 150 days from the time of the request. The applicant must provide all the necessary data to enable the authorities concerned to review the case.

Requests for such assessments must be accepted if made before trade in the product concerned began. On the other hand, if such requests were introduced at any later point in time they may still be accepted at the discretion of the authorities.

The assessment remain valid for a period of three years provided the facts and conditions, including the origin rules, on which the assessments had been made remain comparable. The use of this word "comparable" in the Origin Agreement rather than "the same" or

---

12 The circumstances under which a positive standard "is not necessary" are not discussed further in the Origin Code.

13 Article X:1 of GATT – this Article provides for prompt publication of rules so as to enable traders to familiarise themselves with them.

"identical" would appear to suggest that slight amendments to the preferential origin rules or of the facts or conditions without an essential bearing on the origin of the product does not invalidate the assessment. However, an assessment will no longer be valid if a decision, which is contrary to the assessment, has been made in a review of the origin rules or of the assessment itself.

Assessments of origin will be publicly available subject, of course, to provisions of confidentiality. The wording of the Origin Agreement suggests that assessments may not be published but only made available to interested parties, presumably following a request on the part of the latter.

4. Retroactivity

New preferential rules of origin that amend existing preferential origin rules will not apply retroactively.

5. Review

Any administrative action which authorities take in relation to the determination of origin must be open to prompt review by judicial, arbitral or administrative authorities which must, furthermore, be independent of the authorities which issued the origin determination in question. Such reviews must be able to result in the modification or reversal of the origin determination.

6. Confidentiality

All information which is by its nature confidential or which is provided on a confidential basis for the purpose of the application of the origin rules must be treated as strictly confidential by the authorities concerned. Thus, this information must not be disclosed to any third party without the specific permission of the person or government which has provided the information, except to the extent that it may be required to be disclosed in the context of judicial proceedings.

Chapter 18

· EMA and EU Institutions ·

18.1 Introduction

Institutional arrangements in the EMAs are not as elaborate or over-arching compared to those of the European Union. There is no equivalent to the European Commission, European Parliament, European Court of First Instance or Court of Justice, European Council or other institutional features of the EU. What does exist are flexible political arrangements designed to enable the parties to the EMAs to settle disputes, exchange ideas and co-operate in different political, social and economic fields. In addition, these institutions may enact new rules and procedures to further define some parts of the EMAs (such as rules of origin) and extend the scope of other parts (such as the free movement of services).

18.2 Association Council

Each EMA establishes an Association Council[1] consisting of the Council of the Union, members of the European Commission, and members of the relevant MNC government. Members of the Association Council may arrange to be represented, according to arrangements to be laid down in its Rules of Procedure.

The Association Council is to meet at ministerial level once a year and when circumstances require. The Presidency of the Association Council is to be held in turn by a member of the Council of European Union[2] and a member of the MNC government, according to the provisions to be laid down in its Rules of Procedure.[3] These Rules are

---

1 Due to the interim Association Agreement between the EU and Israel, the Co-operation Committee is preserved from the 1975 EU-Israel Co-operation Agreement and is imbued with the powers of the putative Association Council involving trade and trade-related measures (*e.g.* competition). Once the Israeli EMA enters into legal force, the Co-operation Council will be subsumed into the Association Council.

2 For a discussion on the Council of the European Union, see para 18.8, below.

3 The typical content of such rules can be found in the Rules of Procedure for the EU-Tunisian Association Council and Association Committee: Dec 1/80 of the EU-Tunisian Association Council (OJ 1998 L300/20).

to be drawn up by the Association Council itself, which will refer to a representative of the Council of the European Union and a representative of the EMA Government.

The Association Council is to supervise the implementation of the EMAs. Its powers, which may be delegated to the Association Committee, are to be exercised for the purposes of attaining the objectives of the relevant EMA. The Council is also to examine any major issues arising within the framework of the relevant EMA and any other bilateral or international issues of mutual interest. Its meetings are not open to the public, unless the parties agree otherwise.

In their performance of these functions such bodies are apparently entitled to assistance from the parties to the relevant EMA. Certainly, each party is required to take into account the legitimate interests of the other party to the EMA and a contractual obligation to refrain from jeopardising the achievement of the aims of the EMA. In particular, the parties promise to take any general or specific measures required to fulfil their obligations under the relevant EMA. They must see that the objectives set out in the EMA are attained.

Any decision taken by the Council is final and binding on the parties to the relevant EMA.

18.3 **Association Committee**

The Association Committee established by the EMA is composed of representatives of the Council of the European Union, members of the Commission (usually Commissioners), and representatives of the relevant EMA Government, normally at senior civil servant level. The Rules of Procedure also determine the duties of the Association Committee, which say that when circumstances require the Committee is to meet with the agreement of both parties to the relevant EMA. These duties include the preparation of meetings of the Association Council and deciding how the Committee will function. In particular, the Committee must consider any matter referred to it by the Association Council as well as any other matter, which may arise in day-to-day implementation of the relevant EMA. It also has powers to take binding decisions.

18.4 **Dispute settlement body**

In the event of prolonged disputes, the EMAs establish an *ad hoc* dispute settlement body designed to arbitrate such disputes between the parties of the relevant EMA. This body is further discussed in Chapter 20, paragraph 20.2.

18.5 Customs Co-operation Committee

Where a conflict arises between one or more of the customs authorities in the EU and the MNC regarding interpretation of the rules of origin or the verification of the origin of a product, such disputes must be submitted to the Customs Co-operation Committee. This is an entity where the EU and MNC customs officials meet to settle the dispute to the mutual satisfaction of each side.

Moreover, this Committee, as the name implies, enables customs officials to co-operate on issues relating to customs. With regard to the Turkish EMA, it is also endowed with legislative powers concerning such issues.

18.6 Customs Union Joint Committee in Turkish EMA

The Turkish EMA created a body called the Customs Union Joint Committee, consisting of officials from Turkey and the EU. It meets once a month with the chair alternating between both parties every six months and it may establish any subcommittees. It decides its own Rules of Procedure.

This Committee is entrusted with administering the EU-Turkey Customs Union. For example, if the EU amends the Community Customs Tariff, Turkey may refuse to align its customs tariffs to such amendments on a temporary (or more permanent) basis. However, Turkey must promptly notify the Committee of its decision and consultations must be jointly held in the Committee.

18.7 ECSC-Turkey Joint Committee

The ESCS-Turkey Joint Committee carries out the same functions as the EU-Turkey Association Council in relation to ECSC products. It therefore possesses legislative powers, such as the enactment of implementing rules for the Cartel, Monopoly and State Aid Provisions and provides a forum for settling disputes. In one minor respect, the

Committee differs from the Council. Turkey is granted the right to raise objections and "seize" the Committee (*i.e.* compel the Committee to make a determination) in respect of aid granted by a Member State which it deems unlawful under EU law. If the Committee fails to resolve the case in three months, then it may decide to refer the case to the European Court of Justice.

The Committee has adopted its Rules of Procedure.[4]

18.8 EU Institutions

Even though the EU institutions are not strictly part of the EMAs, they play a vital and pivotal role in the functioning of the EMAs. The following are the important EU institutions from the MNC point of view:

European Commission

The Commission is commonly described as the "guardian of the Treaty of Rome". It is the executive branch of the EU responsible for administering the single European market, ensuring that EU law is respected by the Member States and negotiating international trade agreements on behalf of the Member States. This body has the exclusive right to propose legislation in most areas within the EU's jurisdiction, except for foreign and security affairs. Most interesting for the MNCs, it administers EU competition law with the power to legislate in that area, authorises state aids and imposes provisional duties in anti-dumping investigations.

Twenty Commissioners (including the Commission President) head the Commission. Each Commissioner deals with a portfolio divided by subject rather than geographic location, ranging from competition to administrative reform. Overall leadership of the Commission is in the hands of the Commission President. Responsibility for the Middle East and North Africa is spread over the trade, external relations, development and humanitarian aid, competition and the foreign and security Directorates-General. The external affairs department administers the MEDA programme, a package of financial assistance for promoting economic reform in the MNCs and enhancing cultural co-operation between the EU and the Mediterranean countries.

Each Commissioner has a coterie of trusted advisers called a *cabinet*.

---

4   Dec 1/99 of the ECSC-Turkey Joint Committee (OJ 1999 L66/30).

Council of the European Union

The Council of the European Union (also known as the Council of Ministers) composed of the governments of the Member States passes legislation proposed by the Commission using a voting system weighted according to the size of the population of the relevant Member State, though in a few areas unanimity is still required. Ministers meet on a regular basis to discuss matters within their portfolios, so for example, Ministers of Agriculture meet to discuss agricultural issues. Each Member State holds its presidency for six months.

The Council is the principal actor developing the scope and content of the common foreign and security policy, such that it deals with the political and security aspect of the EMAs.

COREPER

This is a committee composed of senior officials drawn from the national administrations of the EU Member States, which generally prepare for meetings of the Council of the European Union. It is divided into two parts. The first part consists of deputy Permanent Representatives and deals with what are regarded as technical matters. The second part includes Permanent Representatives and deals with more controversial matters.

The detailed work of COREPER is devolved to working groups covering each field of EU activity as well as to *ad hoc* groups that may be created. Their detailed work is co-ordinated by COREPER. The working groups are composed of national officials as well as a Commission representative and the Member State holding the Council Presidency chairs them. Their work may be invaluable not only in a technical sense but also, more generally, in promoting mutual understanding between the Commission and the national governments.

European Courts

Both the European Court of First Instance and the European Court of Justice handle adjudication in the EU. EU law is supreme so that any conflicting national law in an EU Member State is void. The former Court's jurisdiction resides primarily in competition cases and EU staff cases and the latter has overall jurisdiction in all areas of EU law, except foreign policy and security affairs. Both Courts are assisted by an

Advocate-General who collates the facts of a case and submits an opinion before the court passes judgment.

Most appeals of a Commission's decision in a competition case may be appealed to the Court of First Instance. These may then be ultimately appealed to the European Court of Justice on points of law only.

European Parliament

This institution is the only EU body where the electorate throughout the European Union directly elects its members. Its powers have grown steadily with each Treaty amendment. The Parliament has powers to block the passage of much legislation, remove the entire Commission and veto its appointment. It can also approve international agreements to which the EU is a party and be consulted in important areas of EU affairs. Members of the European Parliament have the right to ask the Commission questions on a range of topics.

Although the European Parliament does not have the power to initiate legislation, its influence and prestige will surely continue to expand in the years to come.

European Central Bank

The Central Bank determines monetary policy for the Euroland countries, *i.e.* those EU Member States which have adopted the Euro as their national currency. It is a strongly independent institution, which guards its autonomy fiercely against any political encroachments. Its chief power is the ability to set interest rates so as to achieve price stability and therefore low inflation throughout the Eurozone.

European Council

Every six months, the EU heads of state meet to discuss a range of important issues and set the broad guidelines for EU policy. For example, the European Council in 1994 held in Corfu, Greece requested the European Commission to draw up a new policy towards the Mediterranean countries.

European Investment Bank

This institution provides loans and grants to the MNCs at concessional rates of interest for the promotion of economic and institutional reform.

Comitology

Most of the European Commission's legislative powers have been delegated to it by the Council of the European Union. The latter has not been keen to leave the former entirely free to pass legislation without the advice, or, often, supervision of a committee of representatives of the EU Member States. Hence, the Council passed a Decision[5] prescribing the procedures that must be adopted if the Council intends to restrict the powers it delegates to the Commission.

These committees, composed of officials from the EU Member States, European Commission, industry and other interested groups, wield enormous power, though it is quite difficult to obtain information on what the many committees are called as well as their membership. They, in effect, decide the content of much legislation without the scrutiny of the European Court of Justice. Agreements reached by such committees are governed by private law and act within the framework of the functions attributed to them by their statutes and the national legislation to which they are subject. The European Court of Justice cannot consider these agreements EU acts for the purposes of the review of their legality since no EU institutions take part in their conclusion. Moreover, even if the conclusion of such agreements may be a precondition for the entry into force of a Council enactment, this does not affect the nature of the agreements as measures of private bodies. This analysis also extends to the length of time for which the enactments apply may be determined by the duration of the agreement.

There is no doubt that the ability to influence these committees is fundamental for the MNCs. Many of the issues affecting them from technical standards and rules of origin issues to the imposition of anti-dumping duties is effectively determined by these committees. One example to show their importance is the promulgation of framework Directives, which aim to harmonise national law by laying down general objectives. The technical specifications needed to meet those objectives are, as, for instance, in the case of Council Directive 88/397[6] on toy safety, left for the relevant standards bodies.

Unfortunately, most MNCs are not entitled to participate in these

---

5 Council Dec 87/373 (OJ 1987 L197/33).
6 Council Dir 88/397 on the approximation of laws of the Member States concerning the safety of toys (OJ 1988 L187/1).

committees as active members or in a capacity as observers. One exception is Israel which has observer status in the committees responsible for Research and Development (R&D) and is permitted to participate in EU-funded R&D programmes called framework programmes. Such participation may potentially have beneficial spin-offs for the technological development of Israeli industry. It is the only non-European country, which is permitted to participate in all non-atomic EU-funded R&D programmes.

Another country with access is Turkey. Provision has been made under the EU-Turkey Customs Union for Turkish experts to express their country's position, though not to vote, in certain "technical committees".[7] These committees may include management committees (see below).[8] However, on the initiative of its chair, such a committee may meet with the Turkish experts being present. In other words, like non-EU countries generally, Turkey lacks the same right as EU Member States to participate in EU decision-making through the medium of management committees (see below).

A brief description of the different types of committee is warranted, given the mystery surrounding the operations of these committees. As explained above, there are several procedures governing such committees:

Advisory Committees

Procedure I places no limitation on the Committee's power to pass delegated legislation. It need only submit its draft to an advisory committee made up of the representatives of the Member States and chaired by a representative of the Commission. The chairman can insist on a vote by the committee within a given time-limit. Even if the vote is adverse, the Commission is not bound by it. The Commission is, however, required to take the utmost account of the opinion of the committee. The use of the advisory committees is, for obvious reasons preferred by the Commission to management or regulatory committees. However, the Commission has repeatedly observed that the Council has tended to confine the implementation powers conferred on the Commission within tight limits and there has been

---

7 Dec 5/95 of the EU-Turkey Association Council on the arrangements for involving Turkish experts in certain technical committees (OJ 1996 L35/49).

8 Annex to Dec 1/95 of the EC-Turkey Association Council implementing the final phase of the Customs Union (OJ 1996 L35/1). Dec 6/95 of the EU-Turkey Association Council (OJ 1996 L35/50) and Dec 2/99 of the EU-Turkey Association Council (OJ 1999 L72/36) extended the list of committees referred in the Annex of Dec 1/95.

recourse to advisory committees on far fewer occasions than the Commission had proposed them.

Management Committees

Procedure II enables the Council to become involved if the measures adopted by the Commission are not in accordance with the opinion of a committee made up of representatives of the EU Member States and chaired by a non-voting representative of the Commission. The Council can act only if the committee delivers an unfavourable opinion on the Commission's proposal by a qualified majority voting (*i.e.* voting system weighted according to the size of a Member State's population).

Under variant (a) of Procedure II, after an adverse opinion of the committee the Commission may defer application of the measures for not more than one month, during which the Council may take a different decision by a qualified majority. Under variant (b) of Procedure II, after an adverse opinion of the committee the Commission shall defer application of the measures for a period laid down in the Council legislation delegating the power to the Commission (the parent legislation) but not exceeding three months. During that period the Council can take a different decision from the Commission by qualified majority.

Thus, in Procedure II, under either variant, the Commission's legislative powers can be taken back by the Council but only if both the committee and the Council are able to obtain a qualified majority. The type of committee envisaged in Procedure II is often referred to as a management committee. In practice, these committees are used frequently and rarely give an adverse opinion. Thus, they present a very limited obstacle to the legislative power of the Commission.

Regulatory Committees

Procedure III imposes greater restrictions on the Commission's powers to pass delegated legislation. The composition of the committee is the same as Procedure II, but is commonly referred to as a regulatory committee. This is because the Commission can adopt the measures only if the committee gives a favourable opinion by a qualified majority. If the committee delivers no opinion or one that is not in accordance with the measures envisaged by the Commission, then the Commission shall without delay submit to the Council a proposal relating to the measures to be taken.

Under variant (a) the Council has a period of time laid down in the parent legislation, not exceeding three months, during which it can only act by qualified majority. If the Council does not act within that time, then the Commission adopts its proposed measures. Variant (b) is similar to variant (a) except that the Commission cannot adopt measures if the Council decides against them by a simple majority.

The effect of Procedure III is that unless the committee gives positive approval to the Commission's proposal by a qualified majority, the Commission must submit the proposal to the Council, a situation similar to the one where no delegation takes place. The difference remains, however, that even under variant (b) of Procedure III the Commission does not require a qualified majority from the Council, as it would in primary legislation – it has to avoid a negative vote by the Council. Thus, the delegator is giving the delegate a little more power than it would have if no delegation were made.

Choice of procedures

The question of which procedure and, indeed, which variant within a procedure, applies is determined by the parent legislation. The parent legislation may provide for the Commission to amend it by the delegated legislation within certain parameters and subject to an appropriate committee procedure.

Council safeguard measures

Where the Council delegates to the Commission the power to decide on safeguard measures (*i.e.* measures designed to protect the Council's interests) instead of prescribing them as above, the Commission is required to consult the Member States before taking a decision. The Commission must also notify the Council and the Member States of any decision. Any Member State can, within the time-limit laid down in the parent legislation, refer to the Commission's decision to the Council. Under variant (a) the Council may, within the time-limit laid down in the parent legislation, take a different decision by a qualified majority.

Under variant (b) the Council may confirm, amend or revoke the Commission's decision by a qualified majority; if it does not take any decision within the time-limit laid down by the parent legislation, then the decision of the Commission is deemed to be revoked. Thus, the

Council has delegated very little powers in the context of variant (b).

Council Decision 87/373 does not affect the procedures for the exercise of the powers conferred on the Commission in acts that predates its entry into force.

Reform of Comitology

The European Union is expected to enact a new measure laying down procedures for the exercise of implementing powers conferred on the Commission which will replace Council Decision 87/373.

The new Decision will simplify the committee procedures, grant the European Parliament a right of scrutiny over the implementation of acts adopted by "co-decision", *i.e.* in areas where the Parliament has a power of veto, and substantially increase transparency in comitology. It provides for criteria that will guide the legislator in the choice of committee procedures, while allowing for a certain degree of flexibility:

- the management procedure should be followed as regards management measures such as those relating to the application of the Common Agricultural Policy and common fisheries policy or to the implementation of programmes with substantial budgetary implications;
- the regulatory procedure should be followed as regards measures of general scope designed to apply essential provisions of basic instruments, including measures concerning the protection of health or safety of humans, animals or plants, as well as measures designed to update certain non-essential provisions of a basic instrument;
- the advisory procedure should be followed in any case in which it is considered to be the most appropriate and will continue to be used in those cases where it currently applies.

The simplification of committee procedures concerns especially the management and regulatory procedures, which will no longer each have two variants.

The most substantial change relates to the regulatory procedure. If the implementing measures of the Commission envisages adopting do not obtain the necessary majority in the committee, the Commission will present a proposal to the Council. The Council will no longer have the possibility of rejecting the proposal by simple majority (the so-called "double safety net" is therefore suppressed). If a qualified majority indicates its opposition to the text, the Commission will have to re-examine its proposal and negotiations will have to continue in order to reach a compromise. The effectiveness of the decision-making is guaranteed by the fact that after a time-limit to be fixed in each basic act, if the Council has neither adopted the implementing act nor indicated its opposition to it, the Commission can adopt the measures. However, the Commission has stated that in the review of proposals for implementing measures concerning particularly sensitive sectors, it will act in such a way as to avoid going against any predominant position which might emerge within the Council against the appropriateness of an implementing measure. It has made a statement of similar scope with regard to implementing measures under the management procedure.

Of significance, the proposed Decision provides for involvement of the European Parliament in the implementation of acts adopted by "co-decision." If the Parliament considers that the implementing measure the Commission intends to take exceeds the implementing powers provided for in the basic act, it can so indicate to the Commission, which will then have to re-examine the draft measure. In the framework of the regulatory procedure, the European Parliament is also granted a right of scrutiny in those cases where, due to the lack of agreement by the committee, the Commission refers to the Council a proposal on the implementing measures. The Parliament will receive extensive information on committee procedures, so it can fully exercise its right of scrutiny.

Information to the public on committee procedures will be substantially improved. The rules on public access applicable to the Commission will also apply to committee documents. A list of committees will also be published in the *Official Journal* and the Commission will publish an annual report on the working of the committees. A public register will also be set up containing the comitology documents and the Commission has indicated that it intends to make available to the public the documents communicated to the European Parliament on comitology proceedings.

Finally, it is foreseen that provisions relating to existing committees should be adjusted to align them to the new procedures.

Overall remarks on Comitology

Comitology will surely be more widely used in the future. Its more general use reflects the growing role of non-governmental agents in formulating economic policy and regulations and may operate in such a way as to avoid the problem that economic players may be reluctant to devote resources to developing standards which simply constrain them.

More fundamentally, such practice may reflect the tendency for the formal element of the validity of standards to come second to the informal strategic components of information, co-ordination and the mobilisation of values and aims. This tendency may result, in particular, from a capacity of economic players to develop new products and services, which is greater than the capacity of the European Union or national institutions to regulate them.

Non-EU countries (like the MNCs) whose interests are not represented in the bodies concerned may face an increased risk that their undertakings will see such bodies and policy norms "captured" by their competitors. In other words, undertakings from third states may become marginal to partnership strategies between public and private bodies designed to create comparative advantage in rapidly changing global markets.

The Commission wishes to limit the involvement of non-EU countries in the committees' operations. Recognition of this and the vital role played by the committees in connection with interests of non-EU countries means it is absolutely essential that the MNCs secure representation of their interest on the committees. This is important in terms of influencing the Commission's position on an outcome, such as ensuring the imposition of anti-dumping duties, which are more favourable to the MNC concerned than originally planned. Additionally, these committees would be a major source of information on the future policy directions and initiatives of the EU.

In short, the importance of these committees for the MNCs and the strategy for influencing them through lobbying cannot be exaggerated.[9]

---

9 For a discussion on lobbying, see Chap 21.

Chapter 19

· Judicial Enforcement ·

19.1 Introduction

Effective enforcement mechanisms lie at the heart of any preferential trade agreements, including the EMAs. Without efficacious enforcement, all these agreements are worthless documents. For those in business and trade, this is probably the most important issue impinging on the success of the EMAs.

These Agreements are enforceable in two main ways: judicially and politically/administratively. This chapter seeks only to discuss judicial enforcement mechanisms in the context of aggrieved traders attempting to enforce the EMAs within the courts and tribunals of the party in breach of such Agreements. The reason is that if a trader takes legal action in the courts of one party against the alleged breaches of the other party and obtains a judgment, the other party's judicial authorities are not obliged to recognise and enforce such foreign judgments. It is the prerogative of each country to determine to what extent to recognise and enforce judgments obtained in foreign courts. Under the Brussels Convention on Civil Jurisdiction and Enforcement of Foreign Judgments a judgment in one Member State is recognisable and enforceable by the courts of all Member States.

The parts of the EMAs incorporating provisions of the GATT and WTO agreements rely on WTO dispute settlement methods.

19.2 Judicial Enforcement within the EU

The EC Treaty contains several mechanisms enabling the EU judicial system to interpret uniformly the EC Treaty and legislation enacted thereunder throughout the EU. These mechanisms also encompass the agreements between EU and non-EU countries (like the MNCs). Within the EU, EMAs and related secondary legislation are guaranteed uniform interpretation and application to a large extent whilst providing a means for aggrieved parties to seek legal redress for inadequate implementation of these Agreements. There are six such mechanisms:

1. Article 226 infringement proceedings

If the European Commission considers that an EU Member State has failed to fulfil its legal obligations under the EMAs, then it may take infringement proceedings before the European Court of Justice.

For example, in the case of *European Commission* v *Greece*,[1] the European Court of Justice in Article 226 (old Art 169)[2] proceedings, decided that Greece had violated a trade provision – Article 3(1) of the second Lomé Convention[3] and hence had failed to fulfil its obligations under the EC Treaty. Surprisingly, however, the litigants or the Court did not discuss the issue of whether obligations under the Convention constitute obligations under the EC Treaty. In this context, it may be that a failure by an EU Member State to comply with an international agreement is in fact a breach of an EC Treaty obligation. That obligations states that EU Member States are to ensure fulfilment of the obligations arising out of this Treaty or resulting from actions taken by the institutions of the EU.

2. Article 227 actions

According to Article 227 EC (old Art 170), one EU Member State may take legal action before the European Court of Justice for failure to implement properly EU legal obligations. However, such action is very rare indeed due to the obvious diplomatic repercussions.

3. Article 234 preliminary proceedings

Article 234 EC (old Art 177) enables national courts and tribunals of the EU Member States to refer questions of EU law that require to be decided in a case pending before them to the European Court of Justice for a ruling. The Court's ruling on the points of EU law is then utilised by the national court or tribunal in reaching a decision on the case.

Article 234 EC rulings have constituted almost half of the European Court of Justice's workload in actions brought under the EC Treaty. The heavy volume of references from national courts and tribunals shows widespread penetration of Community law into the litigation

---

1 Case 241/85 *European Commission* v *Greece* [1988] ECR 1037. Another example would be Case 104/81 *Kupferberg* [1982] ECR 3641.

2 The Article number in brackets represents the old Article number prior to the modifications introduced by the Treaty of Amsterdam since it came into force on 1 May 1999.

3 This is a trade agreement between the EU and former European colonies.

before national bodies. It does mean, however, that the average period of time that a national court or tribunal has to wait for the Court's ruling is 18 months.

The Court of Justice can be asked questions of interpretation of the EC Treaty. It can be asked to interpret acts of the institutions of the Community or to rule on their validity. A substantial majority of the cases referred to the Court of Justice under Article 234 EC raise questions of interpretation rather than validity.

On several occasions the European Court of Justice has given preliminary rulings in proceedings involving Association Agreements. For example, in the *Sevince*[4] case, the Court of Justice claimed jurisdiction to give preliminary rulings on the interpretation of an Association Agreement in so far as it is an act adopted by one the institutions of the Community. Moreover, in *Eroglu*[5], the Court also claimed jurisdiction to deliver preliminary rulings on acts of bodies created by such Agreements, such as the Association Council.

The same reasoning implies that the European Court of Justice also has jurisdiction to deliver rulings on the validity of such acts under Article 234 EC.

4. Article 230 proceedings

Article 230 EC (old Art 173) allows the European Court of Justice to review the legality of measures adopted by EU institutions on the grounds of:

- lack of competence (*i.e.* acting beyond its powers);
- infringement of an essential procedural requirement (*i.e.* promulgating legislation without respecting the legislative process);
- infringement of the EC Treaty or any rule of law relating to its application (*i.e.* failure to respect fundamental legal principles like proportionality, legitimate expectations etc); and
- misuse of powers (*i.e.* enacting legislation for purposes other than those stated).

Private individuals have limited standing to bring cases before the European Court under this Article, so its impact on EMAs should be minimal.

---

4 Case C-192/89 *S Z Sevince v Staatssecrataris van Justitie* [1990] ECR I-3461.
5 Case C-355/93 *Hayriye Eroglu v Land Baden-Württemberg* [1994] ECR I-5113.

5. Article 232 proceedings

Article 232 EC (old Art 175) works in tandem with Article 230 EC to ensure that the EU institutions not only act within the powers given by the Treaty of Rome but also actually use those powers. The effectiveness of Article 230 would be reduced, in the absence of Article 232 EC if the institutions were able with impunity to fail to make legislation or to take decisions. In other words, this Article prohibits any failure on the part of the EU institutions from acting on their powers.

Like Article 230 EC private individuals have limited standing and so this Article should have minimal impact on the EMAs).

6. Direct effect

One of the tenets of EU law is that the EU constitutes a new legal order that confers rights and obligations on individuals. Certain provisions of EU law are directly effective in that they create individual rights which national courts of the EU Member States must protect without any need for implementing legislation in that Member State. The European Court of Justice has determined that a provision of EU law must be "unconditional and sufficiently precise" before it can produce direct effects.

The ability of individuals to rely on EU law before Member State national courts greatly enhances its enforceability. The alternative means of enforcement is, of course, an action against the Member State brought by the European Commission or another EU Member State under Articles 226 EC or 227 EC respectively for failure to fulfil its obligations under EU law. That process can be slow. Furthermore, individuals benefit from such action only when the EU Member State changes the internal law to comply with its EU law obligations, but that does not provide a remedy for the wrong done to them up to that time. On the other hand, national courts can quickly apply directly effective EU law, which takes precedence over national law and bring to bear the full force of their powers, including the award of damages to enforce their orders.

A provision of EU law will not be unconditional if the right it grants is dependent on the judgement or discretion of an independent body, such as an EU institution or a Member State. At the same time the relevant EU provision must be sufficiently precise, which means that the obligation the provision imposes is set out in unequivocal terms. In other words, if the Court of Justice needs to refer to more explicit secondary legislation to give the requisite provision sufficient precision and this legislation has not been enacted, then the relevant EC provision is not sufficiently precise.

The European Court of Justice has pronounced that EC Treaty provisions and EU Regulations[6] have direct effect before national courts. On the other hand, Directives[7] may only have direct effect against the defaulting EU Member State itself and "emanations" of that state (*i.e.* public or private bodies connected to that state) once the time-limit for its implementation has expired. That is, a Directive has vertical rather than horizontal direct effect (*i.e.* one private party may not enforce a Directive against another private party). Hence, a Directive may not be invoked before a national court against private or legal persons (*i.e.* against another private individual or private company unconnected to a Member State).

Unlike Directives it is not clear whether Decisions[8] have horizontal direct effect. In the case of *Bulk Oil*,[9] the European Court of Justice noted that certain EU Decisions obliged the Member States to inform the other Member States and the European Commission before making any changes in their rules on exports to non-EU countries. The Court said, however, that:

> "that obligation ... concerns only the institutional relationship between a Member State and the [European]Community and the other Member States. In proceedings before national courts between natural or legal persons such persons cannot attack a policy or measure adopted by a Member State on the basis that that Member State has failed to fulfil its obligations to inform the other Member States and the Commission beforehand. Such a failure therefore does not create individual rights which national courts must protect."

A different problem arises when an individual invokes a Decision against one of the individuals to whom the Decision is addressed. This

---

6 These are EU legislative instruments, which are "directly applicable" (*i.e.* they do not require EU Member States to pass national legislation to implement a Regulation).

7 These are EU legislative instruments, which give discretion to the EU Member States to decide in what manner to implement the Directive within a defined time period (*i.e.* by legislation, administrative decisions etc).

8 These are EU legislative instruments, which usually apply to the parties, addressed within it. They are mainly used in administrative decision-making, such as where the European Commission declares a commercial agreement between two companies as anti-competitive.

9 Case 174/84 *Bulk Oil v Sun International* [1986] ECR 559, para 62.

sort of horizontal direct effect may be appropriate if the provision is unconditional, sufficiently precise and any time-limit for its implementation has expired.

The European Court of Justice has on rare occasions found provisions of international agreements to which the EU is a party (such as the EMAs) directly effective. In *Bresciani*[10] the Court gave direct effect to Article 2(1) of the Yaoundé Convention of 1963 on the elimination of customs duties and charges having equivalent effect where a directly effective EC Treaty provision was incorporated into the Convention. In *Kupferberg*[11], the Court of Justice decided that Article 21(1) of the Free Trade Agreement between the EU and Portugal (before it became an EU Member State in 1986) was directly effective. The Court found the prohibition on discrimination in taxation to be unconditional and sufficiently precise to be relied on by traders in the courts in the EU. In the *Sevince*[12] case, the Court decided that certain Articles of decisions of the Association Council set up by the EU-Turkey Association Agreement were directly effective. In *ONEM*[13], the Court found Article 41(1) of the previous EU-Morocco Co-operation Agreement (*i.e.* a provision granting Moroccan workers in the EU equality of treatment to social security) to be directly effective. In *Anastasiou*[14], the Court concluded that provisions on the origin of products in the 1977 Protocol to the 1972 EU-Cyprus Association Agreement were directly effective. The Court stated that a provision in an agreement negotiated by the Community with non-Member countries must be regarded as having direct effect when the provision contains a clear and precise obligation which is not subject, in its implementation or effects, to the adoption of any subsequent measure. In *Chiquita*[15], the Court found a market access provision in the Atlantic-Caribbean-Pacific Convention[16] was directly effective because it was worded in clear, precise and unconditional terms.

On the other hand, the Court of Justice has decided several cases in which it has not found that an international agreement is directly

---

10 Case 87/75 *Bresciani v Amministrazione Italiana della Finanza* [1976] ECR 129.
11 Case 174/84 *Kupferberg* [1986] ECR 559.
12 Case C-192/89 *S Z Sevince v Staatssecrataris van Justitie* [1990] ECR I-3461.
13 Case C-18/90 *ONEM v Kziber* [1991] ECR I-199.
14 Case C-432/92 *Anastasiou and Others* [1994] ECR I-3087.
15 Case C-469/93 *Amministrazione delle Finanze dello Stato v Chiquita Italia SpA* [1995] I-4533.
16 Usually known as the ACP Convention between the EU and some of the developing countries of the Pacific and the Caribbean.

effective.[17] The Court has found that the European Union has been substituted for its Member States in the GATT, yet it has, to date, declined to give direct effect to any provision of GATT, as proven in the *Chiquita* case. However, in *Fediol*[18] the Court did find admissible a claim by the applicant relying on provisions of GATT referred to in Council Regulation 2641/84, although the applicant's claim was dismissed on its merits. Moreover, in *Hermès*[19], the Court of Justice declared that:

> "it should be stressed at the outset that, although the issue of the direct effect of Article 50 of the TRIPS Agreement [the WTO Agreement on Trade-Related Aspects of Intellectual Property Rights] has been argued, the Court is not required to give a ruling on that question, but only to answer the question of interpretation submitted to it by the national court [under Article 234 EC preliminary reference procedure] so as to enable the court to interpret Netherlands procedural rules in the light of that Article."

The Court of Justice approaches the direct effect of an international agreement on a case-by-case basis. A provision of such an agreement will be directly effective if it is unconditional and sufficiently precise. The EMA Competition Provisions will arguably be directly effective once the implementing rules are enacted.

7. Non-direct effect and Francovich liability

If an EU rule implementing the provisions of an EMA is not directly effective, an individual has recourse to two further methods of seeking redress against the defaulting Member State. First, the Court of Justice has established the principle that national courts should interpret national law in the light of the wording and purpose of a Directive (or Decision) that lacked direct effect. In effect, the national courts are required to give effect to the Directive in an indirect way so that national courts pretend that the Directive was directly effective. Secondly, an individual may claim damages against an EU Member State

---

17 An example is Case 12/86 *Demirel* v *Stadt Schwäbisch Gmünd* [1987] ECR 3719, where the Court did not find certain provisions in the EU-Turkish Association Agreement as directly effective. The Commission argued in that the Cartel Provision in the EU-Finnish Free Trade Agreement (before it joined the EU in 1995) did not have direct effect: Joined Cases 89, 104, 114, 116-117 & 125-129/85 *Åhlström Osakeyhtiö* v *European Commission* [1988] ECR 5193.
18 Case 70/87 *Fediol* v *European Commission* [1989] ECR 1781.
19 Case C-53/96 *Hermès* v *FHT Marketing Choice BV* [1998] ECR I-3603, para 35.

for failing to implement or improperly implementing an EU rule As a breach of the EMA also constitutes a breach of the EC Treaty, this will give rise to a liability first established by *Francovich*,[20] under these conditions:

(1) The result laid down by the EU rule involves the attribution of rights attached to an individual.

(2) The content of those rights must be capable of being identified from the provisions of the rule and there must be a sufficiently serious breach by the defaulting state.

(3) There must be a causal link between the failure by the Member State to fulfil its obligations and the damage suffered by the individual(s) (the level of damages falls under national jurisdiction).

Francovich liability is unlikely to have a significant impact on EU rules related to the EMAs since few of their provisions confer individual rights, except for the provisions guaranteeing equality of treatment in the area of social security for MNC citizens working in the European Union.

Overall comments on judicial enforcement mechanisms

Several enforcement mechanisms exist to ensure that the EU institutions and the Member States fully implement the EMAs and related secondary legislation and that no measures are promulgated which are contrary to them. However, the Court of Justice applies a more restrictive approach to the interpretation of Association Agreements (like the EMAs) than it does to the EC Treaty, even where the wording is identical. This is because the EU is aiming for an ever closer union among its peoples and has created the necessary institutional framework to establish a new legal order. Conversely, the Association Agreements (including the EMAs) merely aim to create a free trade area with flexible and uncomplicated institutional arrangements.

History seems to doubt the effectiveness of judicial mechanisms. Traders have been more inclined to take legal proceedings before national courts on the basis of the EC Treaty than on the basis of Association Agreements.[21] This outcome combined with the narrow

---

20 Cases C-6/90 & C-9/90 *Francovich v Italy and Others* [1991] ECR I-5357.
21 An example would be Case 238/87 *AB Volvo v Erik Veng (UK) Ltd* [1988] ECR 6211. In Case 125/88 *HFM Nijman* [1989] ECR 3533 the EU-Swedish Free Trade Agreement was invoked in conjunction with the EC Treaty.

judicial interpretation of EMA provisions, means that judicial enforcement may only be effective in a limited set of circumstances.

19.3 **Relationship between European Courts and non-EU countries**

Rules governing the European Courts seem primarily concerned with the uniform interpretation of EU law within the common market. Hence, the participation of non-EU countries in judicial proceedings are limited.

Locus standi (standing)

Non-EU countries have no standing to take proceedings before the European Courts under provisions such as Articles 230 and 232 EC. Their nationals may, however, have standing.[22]

Intervention rights

Non-EU countries are entitled to intervene in plenary proceedings before the Court of Justice, provided that the necessary interest in the result of the case can be established under Article 37 of the Statute of the Court of Justice. However, this provision stipulates that this entitlement does not apply to cases between EU Member States, between EU institutions, or between Member States and EU institutions. The rights of non-EU countries to intervene are limited to proceedings brought by private individuals against EU institutions. Hence, limitations to the possibilities of private individuals to take advantage of plenary jurisdiction of the European Courts indirectly limit the significance of the intervention rights of third states.

In the case of preliminary rulings under Article 234 EC, Member States and the European Commission are to be notified of references for such rulings under Article 20 of the Statute. Where the validity or interpretation of a Council act is involved, the Council is entitled to submit statements of case or written observations to the Court of

---

22 Case C-49/88 *Al-Jubail Fertilizer Co and Saudi Arabian Fertilizer Co v Council of Ministers* [1991] ECR I-3187.

Justice. However, no such entitlement is conferred on third states. As a result, non-EU countries may be excluded from Court of Justice proceedings leading to the delivery of preliminary rulings.

19.4 **Enforcement of EMAs within MNCs**

Enforcement of the EMAs within the MNCs depends on their internal legal orders and constitutional structures. For example, it is up to each individual country to decide whether and to what extent the EMA provisions should be made directly effective.

19.5 **WTO dispute settlement procedure**

Some provisions in the Euro-Mediterranean Agreements merely reaffirm WTO Agreements. These include the Subsidies Agreements, the Government Procurement Agreement, WTO Origin Agreement, GATS and the WTO anti-dumping rule. Since these fields come within the ambit of the WTO, any disputes must be settled under WTO rules.

The 1994 Dispute Settlement Understanding, one of the Uruguay Round trade agreements, created the WTO dispute settlement system. Its institutions function very much like a court of international trade. There is compulsory jurisdiction; disputes are settled largely by applying rules; decisions are binding upon the parties; and sanctions may be imposed if decisions are not observed.

Dispute settlement begins when a WTO member makes a request for consultations with another member or other members. This triggers a strict timetable of actions:

(1) A dispute settlement panel may be requested if the dispute is not resolved within 60 days.

(2) The dispute is considered and decided by an ad hoc dispute settlement panel.

(3) The panel's decision may be appealed and decided by a permanent appellate body.

A dispute settlement body, essentially the General Council of the WTO, oversees the process and exercises functions such as the establishment of panels, the formal adoption of the implementation of rulings and

Figure 1 *WTO dispute-settlement flowchart*

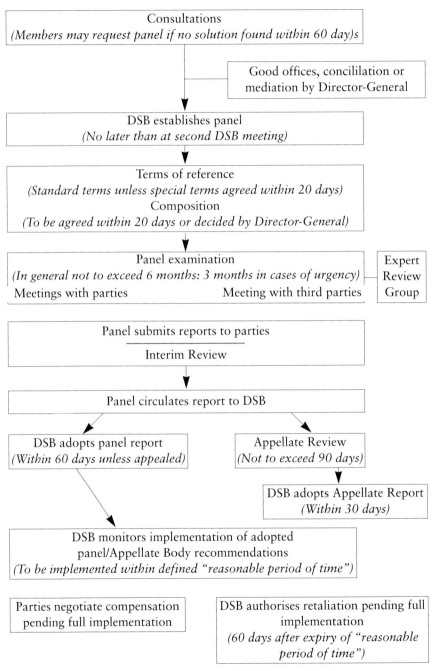

Consultations
(Members may request panel if no solution found within 60 day)s

Good offices, concililation or
mediation by Director-General

DSB establishes panel
(No later than at second DSB meeting)

Terms of reference
(Standard terms unless special terms agreed within 20 days)
Composition
(To be agreed within 20 days or decided by Director-General)

Panel examination
(In general not to exceed 6 months: 3 months in cases of urgency)
Meetings with parties   Meeting with third parties

Expert
Review
Group

Panel submits reports to parties
Interim Review

Panel circulates report to DSB

DSB adopts panel report
(Within 60 days unless appealed)

Appellate Review
(Not to exceed 90 days)

DSB adopts Appellate Report
(Within 30 days)

DSB monitors implementation of adopted
panel/Appellate Body recommendations
(To be implemented within defined "reasonable period of time")

Parties negotiate compensation
pending full implementation

DSB authorises retaliation pending full
implementation
*(60 days after expiry of "reasonable
period of time")*

Source: *GATT Focus Newsletter* (August 1994).

recommendations, and the authorisation of sanctions. A schematic summary of the process is shown in Figure 1 (above).

The WTO dispute settlement process replaced the negotiations-based system of the GATT with a more adjudicative and rule-orientated approach.

Government Procurement Agreement

Special rules exist in the GPA on consultation and the settlement of disputes in Articles XX and XXII. Under Article XXII, Signatories have adopted the WTO Understanding on Dispute Settlement as their own dispute settlement system, with a few adaptations to bring it more in line with the "plurilateral",[23] rather than multilateral, character of the GPA and the nature of the procurement disputes. In Article XX, signatories have introduced a novel concept of dispute resolution, the challenge mechanism. Each signatory must establish a challenge mechanism designed to allow private bidders to launch a complaint directly against a procuring entity of that Signatory, which has allegedly violated the rules of the GPA. To this effect, each Signatory country in its national legislation for a legal (or administrative) procedure is open to foreign private bidders. The (national) challenge procedure shall provide for rapid interim measures to correct breaches of the GPA and to preserve commercial opportunities. Such action may result in the suspension of the procurement process. Furthermore, they shall provide for a correction of the breach of the GPA or compensation for the loss or damages suffered, which may be limited to the costs relating to tender preparation or protest. This challenge procedure is meant to introduce a mechanism, which responds more closely to the specific nature of procurement disputes.

19.6 What if ?

Q: I am a Lebanese trader of ABC product and my main market is Spain. The Spanish authorities adopted measures, which according to the legal advice from my lawyers amount to quantitative restrictions contrary to the Lebanese EMA. How can I go about enforcing the EMA through the legal system to remove those restrictions?

---

23 In other words, the GPA encompasses some, though not all, of the WTO members.

A: You have mainly three practical options. First, the provisions of the EMA in question, namely, the prohibition on quantitative restrictions and equivalent measures have direct effect. This means that you can take legal action before Spanish courts which are then obliged to enforce those provisions and set aside the Spanish measures. EU law is supreme law and therefore takes precedence over conflicting Spanish domestic law.

Secondly, if you take legal action before the Spanish courts, they may make a request for a preliminary ruling out of their accord to the European Court of Justice. The Court will then provide guidance to the Spanish courts on how to adjudicate on the matter. Provided that the Spanish laws and regulations in question conflict with the Lebanese EMA, the European Court will direct the Spanish courts to set aside the contrary domestic measures.

Thirdly, you may make a complaint to the European Commission, which if convinced by the substance of your complaint may then request the Spanish authorities to annul the restrictions and ultimately may take Spain before the European Court of Justice. This option is quite cost-effective in that the Commission will handle the matter on your behalf. On the other hand, the Commission may refuse or delay handling your complaint due to its workload and/or political/diplomatic considerations.

Chapter 20

Political/Administrative Enforcement

20.1 Introduction

Judicial enforcement might be effective in only limited circumstances, due primarily to the narrow judicial interpretation of provisions in Association Agreements by the European Court of Justice. There are two other options for enforcing the EMAs and achieving a desired outcome: resorting to litigation on the basis of the EC Treaty and political/administrative enforcement.

20.2 Political enforcement mechanism in EMAs

There is basic dispute settlement mechanism in the EMAs designed to solve disputes on the basis of comity/political negotiations, unilateral measures and, ultimately, arbitration. First, the aggrieved party may refer to the Association Council any dispute relating to the application and interpretation of the relevant EMA. The officials from each party may then attempt to negotiate a settlement within the Association Council by means of a decision. If a decision is reached, both the EU and the MNC are obligated to implement the decision. In the event the dispute cannot be settled within the Association Council, either party may notify the other of an appointment of an arbitrator. The other party must then appoint an arbitrator within a strict time-limit (usually two months). The Association Council then appoints a third arbitrator, which must take decisions by majority vote. Each party to the dispute must take the steps required to implement the decision of the arbitrators. The arbitrators' decision is final and binding. The EMAs do not explicitly provide for the event when either party refuses to implement Association Council or arbitrators' decisions. In such event, the innocent party may adopt safeguard measures.

Dispute settlement body

The dispute settlement body is essentially an ad hoc arbitration-type institution with the aim of resolving disputes in a judicious and efficient way. It has no permanent secretariat, no permanent building or staff but is merely established when the need arises, *i.e.* when the political process for settling the dispute is deadlocked or has essentially broken down.

Such a body may be characterised as a judicial rather than a political institution, in that it adjudicates a case and pronounces a judgment, which the parties to the dispute are obliged to implement. In many respects, the whole of the dispute settlement process is similar to that in the WTO. However, there is one important difference. WTO members frequently use the WTO dispute settlement process with its emphasis on rule-orientated consultation and adjudication procedures. In particular, the members are subject to strict time-limits and procedures to settle a dispute. If the consultation process fails to produce a mutually acceptable solution, then the dispute must go before a dispute settlement panel and may ultimately end up with the appellate body.

In contrast, the dispute settlement process in the EMAs is subject to fewer procedures and time-limits: if the parties fail to reach a settlement in the Association Council, then one of parties "may" (rather than "must") refer the dispute to arbitration. In other words, there is strong emphasis on comity and political/diplomatic consultations instead of adjudication. As a result, the arbitration procedure is likely to be utilised sparingly, *i.e.* on occasions involving a big dispute in which fundamental national interests are at stake and where the political consultation process has completely broken down. Hence, the arbitration body is best characterised as a political, quasi-judicial body of last resort.

In the event of arbitration, each party appoints an arbitrator while the Association Council appoints a third.

Safeguard measures

Safeguard measures are a characteristic feature of "classic" free trade agreements and the EMAs are no exception. These clauses reflect GATT-based rules and indeed EU rules have been altered to comply with the GATT Agreement on Safeguard Measures. Article XIX of GATT has been strengthened by the new Agreement on Safeguard Measures, which requires serious injury or the threat of serious injury before measures are justified. The new Agreement sets out procedural conditions for the adoption of safeguard measures based on standards of transparency and due process, such as consultation in advance and publication of measures. Safeguard measures under GATT rules must be non-discriminatory, in that they apply to all imports irrespective of origin. Most importantly, the Agreement outlaws informal "grey area" safeguard measures which the EU used to use fairly heavily such as voluntary export restraints.

The Council Regulation on common rules for imports[1] establishes general procedures and conditions under which safeguard measures may be adopted. In particular, it envisages a staged process involving consultation and information exchange, investigation and surveillance. These, in conformity, with the GATT MFN obligations will be general measures applicable to all imports of the specified product whatever the origin. However, where the EU has a free trade agreement (like the EMAs) with an exporting state, a safeguard measure of this type – or a specific measure withdrawing preferences under an Association Agreement – is likely to breach the free trade provisions of the Agreement. However, there is no breach if the Association Agreement itself provides for such measures and the relevant provisions and procedures are observed. The EMAs provide for safeguard measures to be adopted by either side in the situations described in paragraph 20.4, below.

There are other safeguard measures contained in the EMAs. If either party to any EMA considers that the other party has failed to fulfil an obligation under the relevant EMA, it may take appropriate measures, *i.e.* safeguard measures. These usually take the form of withdrawal of preferences under the relevant EMA, *i.e.* the reintroduction of customs duties. Before doing so, the party must supply the Association Council with all the relevant information required for a thorough examination of the situation with a view to seeking a solution acceptable to both parties. In the selection of measures, priority must be given to those which least disturb the functioning of the EMA. Safeguard measures must be notified immediately to the Association Council and must be subject of consultation in the Council if the other party so requests.

Uniquely among the EMAs, the Turkish EMA states that if a party adopts trade protection (*i.e.* anti-dumping duties) or safeguard measures which creates an imbalance between the rights and obligations under the EMA, the other party may take re-balancing

---

1 Council Reg 3285/94 (OJ 1994 L349/53).

measures in respect of that party. In other words, if one party enacts trade protection or safeguard measures that are disproportionate to the nature and level of the unfulfilled obligation by the other party then the latter party may impose counter-measures to compensate for such disproportionate action. Priority must be given to counter-measures which will least disturb the functioning of the customs union.

In another respect, the Turkish EMA goes further. Either party may request the EU-Turkey Association Council to review the application of the principle of trade defence instruments other than safeguard measures by one party in its relations with the other. During any review, the Association Council may decide to suspend the application of these instruments provided that Turkey has implemented competition, state aid control and other relevant parts of EC legislation so as to provide a guarantee against "unfair competition" comparable to that existing in the EU.

20.3 **Administrative enforcement of EMA provisions**

The EMAs rely heavily on administrative co-operation between the officials and authorities of the EU and the MNC for enforcement of various provisions. Three primary areas demonstrate this point:

1 Cartel and monopoly provisions.
2 State aid provision.
3 Customs co-operation.

1. Cartel and Monopoly Provisions

Each EMA and related secondary legislation specify the framework for the co-operation of each party's competition authorities. Each authority is supposed to control anti-competitive conduct within its territory. Basically, the implementing rules of the Cartel and Monopoly Provisions envisage three situations:

(1) Cases where both Directorate-General IV (now the Competition DG) and the MNC national authority have jurisdiction.

(2) Cases where only one authority is competent but the measures it takes might affect the interests of the other party whose authority has no competence (*i.e.* jurisdiction) in the case.

(3) Cases which fall outside the jurisdiction of the national authority of DG IV (now Competition DG) and the national competition authority.

In the case of the first scenario – situations falling under the competence of both authorities – the rules allow both authorities to exercise their jurisdiction in such a case. However, these rules require them to co-operate closely in the process and they lay down in detail the way both authorities should co-operate with each other on the basis of comity principles. This means that either authority can request the other to exercise restraint in the application of its laws or even to take positive action with respect to certain practices affecting important interests of the European Union or the MNC concerned. If a conflict arises and the matter remains unresolved it will be brought before the Association Council.

As to the second scenario – where only one competition authority is competent although the measures it might take may adversely affect the major interests of the other party whose authority has no competence – the same procedure applies. However, the principles of comity are even more important in this scenario for they allow the authority with no jurisdiction to request the other authority to take action regarding practices which are harming the interests of that party but which are taking place within the jurisdiction of the other authority.

The third scenario – where neither authority has jurisdiction – will rarely arise since the Commission assumes extra-territorial application of EU competition law and most MNCs are adopting or have adopted EU-type competition laws based on the "effects" doctrine. In such an unlikely situation, both parties must consult one another in the Association Council to find a mutually acceptable solution.

Safeguard measures

If a party considers that a particular practice is contrary to the Cartel and Monopoly Provisions and that it is not adequately dealt with under the implementing rules then such a party may adopt safeguard measures after consultation within the Association Committee or 30 days within referral to that Committee. Such measures may also be taken during the interim period where the implementing rules have not been enacted and a particular practice causes or threatens serious injury to the interests of the aggrieved party or material injury to its domestic industry.

Practical considerations

The EMAs ensure that the principles of EU competition law provide the common criteria for determining whether a given practice is anti-competitive. However, EMAs (with the exception of the Turkish EMA) do not "harmonise" the sanctions or remedies when a given practice is anti-competitive. In other words, it is left to each party to decide the type of sanctions applicable in the event of a breach.[2] The European Commission and the other parties, which concluded Free Trade Agreements with the EU, share this thinking.

The case of *Adams*[3] adjudicated by the Swiss Supreme Court is a good example. This case concerned an ex-employee of Hoffman-La Roche who had informed the European Commission of the involvement of this company in restrictive practices. When he was convicted of infringing Swiss law concerning business secrets, he appealed to the Swiss Supreme Court. The court dismissed the appeal and ruled that the EU-Swiss Free Trade Agreement did not prohibit the prosecution or, indeed, anything else. It merely authorised the parties to take suitable measures against conduct specified therein.

It should be noted that the Turkish EMA incorporates the sanction applicable under EU competition law, namely the sanction of "nullity" (*i.e.* the offending clause in an anti-competitive agreement is void).

Application of EU competition law

From a practical perspective, the EMAs and the implementing rules allow each party to resort to their internal competition laws at any time to deal with anti-competition cases even if they come within the ambit of the Agreements. This means that the European Commission may resort to Council Regulation 17/62[4] and the EC Cartel and Monopoly Provisions to handle such cases. Hence, each party has a choice of whether to utilise the EMA Cartel and Monopoly Provisions or internal domestic laws for anti-competition issues affecting trade between the EU and the MNC.

In practice, the Commission has applied the EC Cartel and Monopoly Provisions rather than the provisions of Free Trade Agreements in the face of anti-competitive conduct by undertakings

---

2 The EU applies the sanction of "nullity" (*i.e.* the offending clause in an anti-competitive agreement is void) and civil fines for anti-competitive conduct.
3 *Adams v Public Prosecutor, Canton Basle* [1978] 3 CMLR 480.
4 Spec Ed 1962, OJ No 204/62, 87.

from non-EU countries which are party to such agreements. Reliance on the provision may partly reflect the Commission's view that the relevant EMA provisions lack direct effect.[5] It may also reflect concern to maintain the uniform application of EU competition law where competition therein is distorted by the conduct of undertakings from non-EU countries.

Thus, for example, in May 1979 the Commission took proceedings against three Swedish companies for breach of the EC Cartel Provision. The matter was not referred to the Joint EU-Swedish Committee, the Free Trade Agreement with Sweden was not invoked, and it was not shown that trade between Sweden and the European Union was affected. Instead, informal consultations took place.[6]

Wood Pulp case

In the well-known *Wood Pulp*[7] case, where wood pulp producers established in Canada, Finland and the United States had engaged in price-fixing arrangements which affected prices paid by purchasers residing in the EU, the Court of Justice did not object to Commission reliance on such practice. However, the point does not seem to have been put squarely to the Court that the Commission might have been interfering with the trade which the EU-Finnish Free Trade Agreement sought to liberalise without satisfying the procedural pre-conditions laid down in the Agreement for resort to safeguard measures.

There is another interesting point about the *Wood Pulp* case in terms of the jurisdictional scope of the EC Cartel Provision. The salient facts are as follows. The parties to the case were producers of bleached sulphate pulp, required for the manufacture of high-quality paper, based in Canada, the United States and Finland. For jurisdictional purposes, the Court was satisfied that the alleged price-fixing would have affected trade between the EU Member States if it were shown to have occurred. The Court observed that a restrictive practice has two elements: formation and implementation. It considered the latter element decisive to EU jurisdiction, though formed outside the EU. The alleged wood pulp cartel, though formed outside the EU, was implemented within it and accordingly fell within the EU's jurisdiction under the territoriality principle uncontroversial in international law.

---

5 The European Commission argued in Joined Cases 89, 104, 114, 116-117 & 125-129/85 *Åhlström Osakeyhtiö* v *European Commission* [1988] ECR 5193 that a breach of the Cartel Provision in the EU-Finnish Free Trade Agreement can only be invoked by a contracting party.
6 Utrikes-och handelsdepartementen, *Sverige-EG 1981*, Stockholm (1981) 22.
7 Joined Cases 89, 104, 114, 116-117 & 125-129/85 – see fn 5.

There was much confusion as to whether the judgment was materially different from the pure "effects" doctrine as espoused by the Commission (*i.e.* where an anti-competitive conduct affects conditions of competition and trade in the EU). It seems that the Commission interprets its jurisdiction widely enough to cover anti-competitive conduct located outside the EU but which affects trade and competition within it.

The *Wood Pulp* case suggests that the Commission will have no need to resort to Cartel and Monopoly Provisions in the EMAs due to the extra-territorial application of EU competition law. However, this is unlikely to be the outcome. At present, most MNC companies are not large enough or sufficiently engaged in international trade yet to have subsidiaries in the EU (with the probable exception of Israel and Turkey) so as to enable the Commission to enforce its anti-competitive findings. As a result, the EU will have little choice but to resort to the provisions of the EMAs. Of course, Finnish, Canadian and American companies are usually quite big with operations in the EU enabling the Commission to investigate and impose sanctions on such offenders as if they were residing in an EU Member State.

2. State aid provision

Like the Cartel and Monopoly Provisions, the EMAs and related secondary legislation provide a framework for the administrative co-operation of the state aid monitoring authorities of both parties. There are detailed provisions for the exchange of information on state aid and consultation between Directorate-General IV (now the Competition DG) and a national monitoring authority based on the principles of comity. If consultations do not reach a mutually acceptable solution, then further consultations must take place in a sub-committee.

Each monitoring authority is supposed to control the provision of state aid within its territory.

Safeguard measures

At any time during the whole consultation process and under circumstances identical to the Cartel and Monopoly Provisions, either party may impose safeguard measures – in this case countervailing duties. The only difference is that such measures may only be imposed in accordance with the procedures of the GATT 1994 and the WTO

Anti-Subsidies Agreement and the implementing rules make it clear that they must be measures of last resort. That is, all procedures prior to such imposition must first be fully exhausted before it can be done.

Before the Austrian accession to the EU, the State Aid Provision in the EU-Austrian Free Trade Agreement was invoked against Austrian aid to General Motors. Unlike the EMAs, the Austrian Agreement did not stipulate the type of measures which Austria or the EU could implement in the event of a breach of the Provision, but left it to solely to their discretion. The Commission stated that the aid breached EU "principles" regarding regional aid.[8] In the absence of the acceptance of the EU position, safeguard measures were adopted, which took the form of the reintroduction of the Common Customs Tariff in respect of the products concerned.[9] Following Austrian accession to the EU, the Commission authorised Austrian aid to General Motors for research and development, environmental protection and training.[10]

Another situation involving Austria was the *Opel Austria*[11] case. In this case, the Court of First Instance upheld a challenge by Opel Austria to a Commission Regulation imposing a customs duty on imports of car gearboxes from Austria (then not a Member State but a party to the European Economic Area Agreement) into the EU. The Commission justified this customs duty on the grounds that they were responding to failure on the part of the Austrian authorities to remedy an illegal state aid. The measures were in compliance with the EU-Austrian Free Trade Agreement and would in all probability have been judged valid in terms of that Agreement. However, the Court of First Instance accepted the applicants' contention that the Regulation should be judged in accordance with EEA. It reached that decision on the principles of public international law and EU law, even though at the time when the Regulation was adopted (20 December 1993) the EEA was not yet in force (it came into force on 1 January 1994).

This case illustrates the reality of the procedural requirements behind the adoption of safeguard measures and emphasises that they have to be seen as exceptions to the free movement of goods. Therefore, such

---

8   Guidelines on National Regional Aids (OJ 1998 C74/1). Its predecessor at the time of the Austrian state aid case was the Communication on the method of application of Art 88(2)(a) and (c) (old Art 93) to regional aid (OJ 1988 C212/2)

9   Commission Reg 3697/93 (OJ 1993 L343/1) withdrawing tariff concessions in accordance with Articles 23(2) and 27(3)(a) of the Free Trade Agreement with Austria (General Motors Austria).

10   H Morch, "Summary of the most important recent developments," (1995) 6 *Competition Policy Newsletter*, at 45.

11   Case T-115/94 *Opel Austria GmbH* v *European Comission* [1997] ECR II-39.

measures should be construed strictly, even in the context of the EMAs.

Anti-dumping measures

Under the Association Agreements anti-dumping procedures may be employed against recipients of aid granted by the third country concerned. In 1977, for example, the European Commission expressed concern about Swedish aid to the chipboard industry.[12] In the following year the Commission secured price undertakings from Swedish exporters of chipboard in the course of an anti-dumping investigation.[13]

Such practice means that the effects of aid may be assessed in isolation from consideration of the broader economic policy in which the aid is granted. Consequently, the grant of aid in non-EU countries, like the MNCs, may lead to the imposition of trade restrictions which cannot result within the EU from the grant of aid by a Member State. These restrictions may also be imposed on an undertaking in receipt of aid, which might be permissible within the EU. Certainly, aid may be authorised within the EU specifically because it enables a producer to sell at a price, which is below his real costs.[14]

Anti-dumping measures are intended to offset anti-competitive behaviour on the EU market of third country producers in selling their products at below their normal value. Unlike safeguard measures, they can therefore be targeted at specific products from specific exporters.

Practical considerations

Like the Cartel/Monopoly Provisions, the State Aid Provision "harmonises" the criteria for determining whether state aid has been provided, but leaves the consequences of such provision up to the discretion of each party.[15] This means both parties are entitled to use whatever remedy or sanction they wish in the event the provision of state aid is contrary to the Provision.

3. Customs co-operation

---

12 Utrikes-och handelsdepatementen, *Sverige – EG 1977* Stockholm, (1981), 20.
13 Notice of termination of the anti-dumping/anti-subsidies procedure concerning imports of reconstituted wood (wood chipboard) from Spain and Sweden (OJ 1978 C75/3).
14 For example Commission Dec 88/437 (OJ 1988 L211/24) concerning aid planned by the French government in favour of a shipbuilding contract for which there was competition between yards in several EU Member States.
15 The European Commission may prohibit unlawful state aid and impose fines if necessary.

According to the EMAs, each party's customs authority (including the Commission and authorities in individual EU Member States) must assist the other with a view to the prevention, investigation and detection of operations that contravene domestic customs legislation. There are detailed rules and procedures on how the request for assistance is to be made and the nature of that assistance, which could range from the provision of information to the authorisation of officials from the requested authority to appear before judicial proceedings as experts and witnesses. The EMAs ensure that the whole process is based on mutual co-operation so that generally no assistance need be provided if it contravenes any domestic laws and regulations.

Customs Co-operation Committee

Where a conflict arises between one or more of the customs authorities in the European Union and the MNC regarding interpretation of the rules of origin or the verification of the origin of a product, such disputes must be submitted to the Customs Co-operation Committee. This is an entity where the EU and MNC customs officials meet to settle the dispute to the mutual satisfaction of each side.

Moreover, this Committee, as the name implies, enables customs officials to co-operate on issues relating to customs. With regards to the Turkish EMA, it is also endowed with legislative powers concerning such issues.

20.4 Safeguard/trade protection measures involving trade and anti-dumping

All the EMAs include procedures, which civilise the process of imposing safeguard measures in the following circumstances:

1. Anti-dumping investigations (trade protection measure)

An exporting party must be informed of the dumping case as soon as the authorities of the importing party have initiated an investigation. When no end has been put to the dumping within the meaning of Article VI of the GATT or no other satisfactory solution has been reached within 30 days of the matter being referred, the importing party may adopt anti-dumping duties.

Before such measures can be taken, the party initiating the investigation must supply the Association Committee with all the relevant information with a view to seeking a solution acceptable to the two parties (the consultation process).

In the selection of measures, priority must be given to those which least disturb the functioning of the EMA (the selection process).

Such measures should be notified immediately to the Association Committee by the party concerned and shall be subject of periodic consultation within that body, particularly with a view to their abolition when circumstances permit (the notification process).

Similarly for the Turkish EMA, the European Commission will offer information to Turkey before the initiation of proceedings. Furthermore, the EU will give, on a case-by-case basis, where appropriate, a clear preference to price undertakings rather than duties in order to conclude anti-dumping cases where injuries are found.

2. Import surges (safeguard measure)

Where any imports are being imported in such quantities as to cause or threaten to cause:

- serious injury to domestic producers of like or directly competitive products in the territory of one of the contracting parties; or
- a serious disturbance in any sector of the economy or difficulties which could bring about serious deterioration in the economic situation of the region;

then either party may impose safeguard measures provided the consultation, selection and notification processes are complied with. Moreover, the difficulties arising from the situations referred to above must also be referred to the Association Committee, which may take any decision needed to put an end to such difficulties (the examination process). In addition, if the importing party subjects imports liable to produce such difficulties to an administrative procedure having as its purpose the supply of information on trade flows, it shall inform the exporting party.

Both the safeguard measures adopted by the importing party and any decisions taken by the Association Committee must be proportionate to the difficulties, which they seek to remedy. Also, they should least disturb the functioning of the EMA.

It can be seen that the main difference between the procedures for adopting safeguard measures under the EMAs, and those taken under autonomous EU rules in Council Regulation 3285/94 is the endeavour to find a mutually acceptable solution within the Association Committee. This culminates in a (joint) committee decision, with the unilateral measure seen as a last resort.

3. Anti-circumvention device and product shortages (safeguard measure)

Where the prohibition of customs duties and equivalent charges leads to:

- re-export to a third country against which the exporting party maintains, for the product concerned, quantitative export restrictions (*i.e.* quotas), export duties or measures of equivalent effect (*i.e.* measures which directly or indirectly, potentially or actually affect the movement of exports to the third country); or
- a serious shortage, or a threat of such shortage, of a product essential to the exporting party;

and where the situations referred to above give rise, or are likely to give rise to major difficulties for the exporting party, then safeguard measures may be taken provided the consultation, examination, selection and notification processes are complied with.

It should be noted that the first ground mentioned above is an anti-circumvention device so as to prevent the importing party from being used as a conduit to sell the product concerned to a third country and thereby circumvent the export restrictions maintained by the exporting party against the third country.

4. Infant industry clause (safeguard measure)

There is an "infant industry clause" found in all the EMAs, except in the Turkish and Israeli EMAs. This provision essentially allows the MNC to increase or reintroduce custom duties, which is in derogation from its obligations for the staged elimination of such duties. Since duty free access is the fundamental core of any free trade agreement, the increase or reintroduction is an "exceptional measure" and, therefore, a number of conditions must be fulfilled. Such measures must:

- only concern infant industries, or sectors undergoing restructuring or facing serious difficulties, particularly where these difficulties produce major social problems;

- consist of customs duties: not (less transparent) quotas or non-tariff barriers. For EU products the duty must not exceed 25 per cent *ad valorem* (*i.e.* the value of the product), and an element of preference for products of EU origin must be maintained;
- be temporary: for an initial maximum period of five years, extendable by decision of the Association Committee but in any event expiring at the end of the 12-year transitional period. (There is the possibility of yet further extension beyond the end of the 12-year transitional period in order to take account of difficulties of setting up a new industry); and
- not to be used for products if more than three years has elapsed since the elimination of all duties and quantitative restrictions for that product.

Procedurally, the MNC is under an obligation to:

(1) Inform and consult with the Association Committee of its intention to introduce the protective measures.

(2) Negotiate within the Committee a schedule for their removal.

The Committee cannot veto the initial introduction of the measures, but only when an extension beyond the five-year initial maximum period is sought.

The infant industry clause is an example of the asymmetric nature of the EMAS for those MNCs, which are seen as emerging into fully-fledged market economies, but still needing a greater degree of protection than the industrially developed trading partners. As such, it is a provision which conforms to Article XVIII of GATT which establishes a derogation for developing member countries from their obligations to reduce tariffs under GATT and the WTO. It also conforms with a GATT decision of 1979 permitting safeguard measures in the form of increased customs duties for developing new production facilities in tune with the economic priorities of the country concerned.

20.5 **Precautionary measures**

In the event exceptional circumstances make it impossible for the relevant party to comply with the consultation and examination processes in the situations described under paragraph 20.4, points 1-3 above, then certain things must happen. First, the relevant party must immediately apply the precautionary measures that are strictly necessary to deal with the situation and inform the other party of such measures. Secondly, it must comply with the consultation process.

20.6 **Commercial policies**

It is a fact that the parties to the EMAs may pursue commercial policies, which may conflict with the aims of the relevant EMA. Thus, the EMA institutions become involved to the extent necessary to avoid such conflict. The two main commercial fields where this is true are:

1. Agriculture.
2. Free trade/customs union agreements with third states.

1. Agriculture

Each party may modify the agricultural arrangements laid down in the relevant EMA, in the event that such a party introduces (or intends to introduce) specific rules as result of implementing its agricultural policies or modifying its existing rules for the products concerned. The party carrying out such modification must inform the Association Committee and at the request of the other party, this Committee will meet to take appropriate account of the other party's interests.

If the agricultural arrangements in an EMA are modified, the relevant party must accord the imports originating in the other party an advantage comparable to that provided in the EMA. Such modification may be subject to consultations in the Association Council, at the request of the other party.

Interestingly, the EU intends to maintain the integrity of the Common Agricultural Policy, even though the EMAs refer to agricultural matters. This concern is reflected in the case law. For example, *Haegeman*[16] concerned a countervailing charge imposed pursuant to the common organisation of the wine market on imports of Greek wine into Belgium. The Court of Justice characterised the imposition of the charge on Greek wines as a stabilisation measure under the Protocols of the Greek Association Agreement with the EU (similar provisions on stabilisation measures are not found in the EMAs). It did not have to be adopted as a safeguard measure pursuant to the Association Agreement itself. Thus, the Court accepted the legality of Commission action based on the needs of the Common Agricultural Policy.

16   Case 18/73 *R & V Haegeman* v *Belgium* [1974] ECR 449.

Therefore, it seems that the parties are free to pursue their own agricultural policies so long as they do not alter the trade advantages granted under the respective EMAs.

2. Free trade/customs union agreements with third states

Most EMAs provides that they will not preclude the maintenance or establishment of a customs union, free trade areas, or arrangements for frontier trade, unless such agreements alter the trade arrangements stipulated in the relevant EMA. However, consultations between the parties shall take place within the Association Council concerning agreements establishing customs union or free trade areas. Where requested, consultations shall also take place between the parties on other major issues related to their respective trade policies with third countries. In particular, if a third country accedes to the European Union, such consultations shall take place to ensure that account can be taken of the mutual interests of both parties.

The one exception is the Turkish EMA. Since Turkey and the EU are in a customs union with one another, their commercial policies (including tariff policy) towards third countries are substantially the same. Therefore, neither party may enter unilaterally into a preferential arrangement with non-EU countries. Both parties may only do so in tandem.

20.7 **Summary**

The administrative and institutional co-operative mechanisms place much emphasis on mutual understanding and collaboration between the parties' respective authorities. Moreover, either party may sometimes resort to their domestic laws to circumvent the procedures and rules in the EMAs, such as in the area of competition law. If the co-operative process breaks down, the parties have the option of adopting safeguard measures to bring about a desired outcome. The EU may be tempted to do so due to the asymmetrical nature of the relationship: approximately 50 per cent of Mediterranean countries' collective trade is with the EU, whilst it is only 5-10 per cent in the other direction.

Hence, the enforcement of the EMAs is an intensely political process, which means that political lobbying and persuasion will be a vital ingredient in the successful exploitation of the EMAs.

Chapter 21

Lobbying and the
Art of Influence

21.1 Introduction

Lobbying represents an indispensable means to take advantage of the opportunities offered by the Euro-Mediterranean Agreements. These Agreements are intensely political arrangements supported by a foundation of fundamental rules and procedures. Whatever the content of such rules, the most important factor in their effectiveness is the nature of their application by a multitude of officials and non-governmental actors. The art of lobbying, to be effective, involves influencing and ultimately moulding the discretion of officials and others to achieve a desired outcome. Traders and businessmen who seek to exploit these Agreements cannot neglect the cardinal rule: efficacious lobbying is the most potent weapon in their arsenal for exploiting the EMAs to advance their interests and limit any adverse policies and decisions.

This chapter seeks to outline a basic strategy for effective lobbying within the context of the Euro-Mediterranean Agreements. Before, doing so, however, the nature of the Agreements will be discussed to demonstrate institutional simplicity and fluidity as a marked feature of the EMAs, which will affect any lobbying efforts undertaken.

21.2 **The Nature of EMAs**

The nature of the EMAs was best exposed by the *Polydor*[1] case. According to the Court of Justice in that case, the interpretation of EU law must be determined in the light of the objectives and activities of the EC Treaty, which call for the creation of a unified single market having the characteristics of a domestic market. Whereas, the Association

---

1 Case 270/80 *Polydor v Harlequin Record Shops Ltd* [1982] ECR 329, para 20.

Agreements must be interpreted more narrowly since they merely aim to create a free trade area. More particularly, the Court observed:

> "the instruments which the [European] Community has at its disposal in order to achieve the uniform application of Community law and the progressive abolition of legislative disparities within the common market have no equivalent in the context of relations between the Community and Portugal."

Even if the relevant EMA provision closely resembles the corresponding provision in the EC Treaty, EU case law does not necessarily apply unless an EMA provision incorporates explicitly such case law (for example, the Cartel, Monopoly and State Aid Provisions). Or else, the EMA needs to include a general provision saying that the EMA provision(s) is/are identical "in substance" to the corresponding EC Treaty provision(s), the relevant decisions of the Court of Justice are applicable when interpreting the provision in question. Only the Turkish EMA includes such a provision.

Institutional arrangements are another important determinant of the EMAs' nature. Advocate General Rozès noted in the same case that apart from the joint committee no "common institution" was established [by the EU-Portuguese Free Trade Agreement].

Therefore, the Euro-Mediterranean Agreements are governed by *ad hoc*, simple institutions and limited objectives. This translates into the need for flexible lobbying campaigns, absent rigid formulations and making full use of political connections and coalition-building (*i.e.* networking).

21.3 A strategy for lobbying

Lobbying can be defined as the art or process of influencing people and/or organisation to achieve a desired outcome. It is a means to an end, though not an end itself. This process, to be successful, requires the right combination of style, strategy, approach, networking, leadership skills, adaptability, and people and organisation.

Lobbying in short is the art of influence. There is no formula for it, but if employed prudently and efficiently, the positive effects for traders and businessmen are incalculable.

What are the necessary steps for effective lobbying to take the greatest advantage of the EMAs? A basic strategy is outlined below for the type of lobbying to fit with the shape and circumstances of the

EMAs, especially institutional simplicity and limited objectives. It is not designed as a rigid formulation but rather as a flexible and adaptable series of steps that must be conditioned to the facts and objectives. In other words, lobbying on any issue has to be approached on a case-by-case basis, having regard to the particular circumstances. Experience and a "feel" for the issue are indispensable, but a few tips are always likely to be useful.

Identifying the issues

This is by far the most important exercise to go through before launching any lobbying campaign. You should establish at the earliest stage possible, what you wish to achieve. (*i.e.* new legislation, amendments to proposed legislation, etc) and the best forum in which to achieve it (*i.e.* national, European and/or international institutions).

Identifying issues is a long-term task and usually there is no alternative to continuous monitoring of developments through readily available publications and making and cultivating contacts within the EU institutions. This can be done in-house or by using external consultants, or by a combination of both.

Setting out objectives

One of the most essential ingredients is to set a realistic, precisely defined and attainable objective, around which a lobbying plan can be moulded. Without such an objective, the whole exercise might become unfocused and plagued by wasted efforts and fruitless results. In other words, once an issue has been identified, you need to evaluate both within your organisation and the industry in general the commercial importance (both direct and indirect) of the issue and the priority to be given to it.

For example, an Egyptian sugar company wants to pre-empt a European Commission finding that its dominance in the Egyptian market is abusive and therefore contrary to the Monopoly Provision in the Egyptian EMA. If the company wishes to reverse this finding, despite the fact some 90 per cent of the Egyptian sugar market is under its control, then its lobbying efforts are doomed to failure. The objective set is too ambitious: there is no way the European Commission is likely to view a 90 per cent market share as other than abusive dominance given the protected and monopolistic nature of the

Egyptian sugar market. This will certainly be the case even after taking into account the fact that the Monopoly Provision only applies to the abuse of dominance, not to mere dominance on its own. In such a scenario, the Commission may utilise the EC Monopoly Provision provided there is the requisite jurisdiction or it may request the Egyptian competition authorities to investigate and deal with the matter. Ultimately, the Commission may impose safeguard measures, such as the reintroduction of customs duties or commence an anti-dumping action against the Egyptian company.

Under these circumstances, the company should define the aim of any lobbying effort: to persuade the Commission that steps will be taken to eliminate the abusive behaviour complained of, such that EU competitors' ability to enter the Egyptian market is not jeopardised by its dominance. This objective is realistic so that all the energies can be channelled and chances for a more positive outcome maximised.

Allocation of resources

It is a cardinal rule that any means to achieve a defined end must always be adequately financed. There is nothing to be gained by drawing up an elaborate lobbying plan if the resources are unavailable. Therefore, resources are important to determine early on in terms of drawing up a plan and setting out the objectives.

Identification of allies

The European Union is not a monolithic entity but rather a diffuse community of interests. There is a multitude of personnel involving governments, business, industry, unions and non-governmental organisations. Each player has its own agendas and objectives. The trick is to identify the parties, which will mostly likely support your cause. There are no hard and fast rules on the choice of players.

There are a few basic ground rules, however.

(1) Always keep in mind that the European Commission is the main promoter of the Euro-Mediterranean project. As an institution, it has a lot of formal power (such as the Article 226 EC procedure) while at the same time it uses informal pressure on Member State governments to ensure that EU laws are followed or certain policies adopted.

(2) Undue concentration on the Commission might be wasteful. Sometimes, Member States may be more receptive to persuasion than the Commission. An example is where the Commission imposes provisional anti-dumping duties, but the Member States refuse to make such a duty permanent. Take Egyptian unbleached cotton and the United Kingdom. The United Kingdom is usually against duties on Egyptian cotton imports since its textile and apparel industries are highly dependent on it for their survival and profitability.

(3) Attempt to network and align with the appropriate non-governmental organisations, such as trade bodies, business associations etc. In Europe, there is a tendency for industrial and business lobbies to be more powerful, though not necessarily more vocal, than consumer and other socially-orientated lobbies. Therefore, greater emphasis should be placed on the potential loss of commercial opportunities and jobs if a particular action is taken or policy adopted. Decision-makers are far more likely to listen when jobs are at stake.

(4) The European Parliament should not be neglected. It has the power to delay and block legislation and the right to elicit answers from the European Commission on a range of topics.

(5) There should be an overriding desire to ascertain the individuals sitting on the committees (comitology), since they wield enormous power as explained in Chapter 18, paragraph 18.8. Many issues and disputes can be settled in these committees and many Commission policies may be influenced at that stage. Therefore, access to them is fundamental.

(6) Collaboration with pressure groups or the governments from the MNCs should be explored. Sometimes, a dispute or policy might affect the interests of several MNCs and hence there may be a lot of incentives to acting as a united front in relation to that dispute or policy. In such circumstances, the EU is more likely to be persuaded to change its policy than by acting alone.

To summarise, in order to assess what realistic chance there is of influencing the decision-makers it is necessary to appraise what others are doing on the same issue. This will involve analysing the attitude of, amongst others, companies in your sector or related sector, trade associations, trade unions, consumer associations, Member State governments, Commission Departments and Members of the European Parliament. It will also involve education of and co-operation with those with similar interests to yours.

Identification of opponents

The corollary for the identification of allies is the identification of opponents. This is very important so that their arguments can be anticipated and rebutted, or at least minimised.

An important point to note is that Mediterranean EU Members States like Spain and France may not always be the best allies. For instance, Mediterranean farmers have a reputation for being a vocal constituency willing to go to great lengths to protect their privileges, which partly explains why there is no free trade in agricultural products in the EMAs.

Organisation

Once the issues have been identified, objectives set and the allies/opponents pinpointed, the next task is to ensure that the lobbying team is organised in the best possible way. This requires a team properly led where everyone has a specific, well-defined role in a co-ordinated campaign to disseminate the agreed-upon message. In the absence of organisational efficiency, the entire lobbying effort will likely crumble.

Lobbying targets

Relevant targets will depend on what it is hoped to achieve. If new legislation is in contemplation or has been drafted (which is of significance to the MNCs), or if existing EU legislation is being amended, then the particular targets within the EU institutions or national governments will depend on the stage of the legislative process which has been achieved. If you are looking to influence or direct policy, you will have to identify the origin of the policy and those responsible for it or inputting to it – this will rarely be a single individual or department.

Co-ordination of effort

It is necessary to ensure that any lobbying does not conflict with the efforts of others with the same or similar aims. Consequently, a decision must be taken on who is best placed to lobby each target. Whilst trade associations fulfil a vital function it should never be assumed that they should be the sole channel through which influence can be exerted. Because of the sheer size of many trade associations they must, by definition, present the views of the majority of their members. Those in the minority will need to be represented separately if their voice is to be heard.

It may be advisable to form a coalition either through a trade association or on an *ad hoc* basis. The received advice has always been that a coalition representing Europe-wide interests is more likely to have influence. Where the interests of a particular group or company differ from others in the sector, however, a smaller coalition or even an individual company can be successful in achieving its aims through a well executed lobbying campaign.

Co-ordination of strategies

Legal and political strategies may sometimes need to be combined. For example, the issue may involve the actions of a particular Member State government, which infringe the Euro-Mediterranean Agreements (such as the Goods Provision) or implement a Directive improperly. The lobby is then likely to involve a complaint to the European Commission requesting it to bring infringement proceedings under Article 226 of the EC Treaty (old Art 169) and also complaints to national enforcement agencies, as well as proceedings before the national courts.

Lobbying tactics and style

Tactics and style are the most visible, and arguably the most essential, ingredients in the lobbying mixture. Such questions as how aggressive should the lobbying effort be, how to approach potential allies etc require definitive answers.

So what style should be adopted? In the EU and the rest of Europe, decision-makers adopt what is commonly termed as an "open" approach to various players regarding a proposed decision or policy. That is, they are easily accessible and any attempts at persuasion must be somewhere between subtlety and aggression. Hence, lobbyists cannot be too blatant in their efforts, otherwise the decision or policy-maker might recoil and refuse to listen to such lobbyists. One indicator of this is the fact that lobbyists refer to themselves euphemistically as "public affairs specialists" since the latter sounds more positive and innocuous than the former. A true understanding of the approach which is most likely to gain results in Brussels can only be obtained by long-term contacts and gaining an in-depth understanding of the EU's policies towards the Mediterranean region.

Besides style, there are questions of tactics. In other words, this necessitates the determination of the lobbying methods to use. Even though, each lobbying effort is probably unique and has its own determinants and requirements, the following is a safe course of action that could easily be amended when necessary.

(1) An informal approach to the relevant decision- or policy-makers to get a point of view across and thereby influence the outcome may be successful a lot of the time. It is both cheap and effective.

(2) There should be movement from informal to more formal actions. If powerful vested interests are arrayed against you and decision- or policy-makers are of little assistance, then alliances with potential allies should be forged. Alliances have a stronger resonance than individual actions. Moreover, more aggressive tactics may have to be adopted, such as lobbying campaigns involving not just sending letters and faxes, but also involving the media and prominent individuals or organisations.

(3) Once lobbying campaigns are initiated, tactical and selective use of litigation should be used, on the basis of EU law or the EMA provisions. This could be conceived as a stand-alone action or part of the campaign strategy to increase the pressure on the opponents. Here, the range of options for litigation should be explored, such as convincing the Commission to take legal action, or pursuing legal proceedings individually.

(4) The ultimate weapon may be to convince the relevant MNC government to invoke the dispute settlement procedures. If the dispute is not settled in the Association Council, then it goes to an *ad hoc* arbitration body whose decision is final and binding. An important point is that only disputes which materially affect the national interests of the MNCs will be likely to proceed to such a high level of dispute resolution.

To summarise: the precise tactics to be adopted depend on the aim and nature of the lobby. Bear in mind that, whatever means are used to present your arguments, effective lobbying relies heavily on communication. This means presenting clear and concise arguments:

- in a form tailor-made for the recipient, backed up by sound legal arguments and correct and unbiased evidence;
- in a form (whether in writing or orally) which is accessible to the recipient in terms of style, content and language;
- in a manner which is consistent with the policy and legal aims of the EU towards the Mediterranean region; by definition the EU has always operated through compromise; you are far more likely to achieve your aims if you can demonstrate that you are not seeking to create barriers to trade but to find a compromise solution which will solve your particular problem while still achieving the goal of the Euro-Mediterranean free trade zone;
- in conjunction with detailed and specialist knowledge in the area of Euro-Mediterranean law.

Information gathering

The most valuable commodity for lobbyists and businessmen in general is information: information dealing with competitors, decision- or policy-makers. It is the lifeblood of many businesses. This is especially true for lobbying, where information on opponents' arguments, a new policy-direction by the European Commission and so on can make or break the entire effort. In fact, deliberations of the Association Council/Committee are not open to the public.

Hence, if a trader or businessman knows that the European Commission is about to impose anti-dumping duties, or take other measures, then he can anticipate what needs to be done much quicker and act proactively rather than reactively.

At the same time, information is concomitant with flexibility. If, for instance, you find out that the something is going to happen, which is contrary to previous assessments, then the lobbying effort can be altered quickly to accommodate changing circumstances. To put it another way, hot information breeds rapid and targeted responses.

21.4 **Conclusion**

Lobbying is an important tool for modern day businessmen and commercial operators in the new global economy. There are now many agreements on the regional and multilateral levels with a view to opening markets and laying down common rules for trade and investment. The Euro-Mediterranean Agreements are of the regional kind designed to prise open for the first time the traditionally closed, oligopolistic and state-dominated nature of these economies. Hence, the commercial and investment opportunities being created, coupled with the deep domestic structural economic reforms sweeping the Middle East and North Africa, demonstrate the fundamental importance of taking maximum advantage of the EMAs through lobbying.

Whilst lobbying is no doubt the art of persuasion and a potent weapon and shield in the businessman's armour, it is not a panacea to all problems and disputes that may arise. Sometimes, lobbying efforts may fail in achieving their objectives for a variety of reasons. Success should not be assumed. But, ultimately, today's commercial climate puts a premium demand on all interested parties to avoid the ostrich mentality on lobbying. This is especially the case with the EMAs. The commercial prize is great and only those who adopt lobbying as their mantra will clinch the golden prize.

· Index ·